A EUROPEAN MOTORHOME ODYSSEY

A Change In The Aire

A EUROPEAN MOTORHOME ODYSSEY

A Change In The Aire

LESLEY PARR

CANDY JAR BOOKS • CARDIFF

2020

A Change in the Aire © Lesley Parr 2020

Edited by David Townsend Jones
Book cover design by Book Beaver
Design and production by
Adastra Consulting, Mumbles, SA3 4DD
Typeset in Perpetua

Printed and bound in the UK by
Severn, Bristol Road, Gloucester, GL2 5EU

ISBN: 978-1-913637-31-6

Published by
Candy Jar Books
Mackintosh House
136 Newport Road, Cardiff, CF24 1DJ
www.candyjarbooks.co.uk

For Jackson, without whom these memories and our story would not be here. You open my eyes to something new every day and for that I am eternally grateful. And for Geoff, for introducing me to this lifestyle in the first place and for your patience ever since in listening to my constant pleas to do it all again and again. Together you are my world.

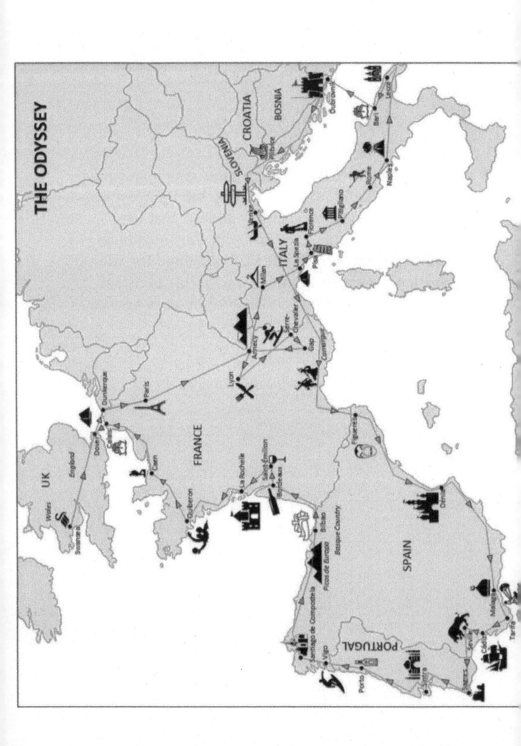

THE ODYSSEY

CONTENTS

PART 2. INWARD BOUND

FOREWORD

BELIEVE ME WHEN I say that as I embarked on my journey any thoughts of becoming an author could hardly have been further from my mind. It began with a few amusing texts, which brought laughter, usually at our expense, to friends and family, and which soon evolved into a blog. Only after the event did I discover that what I had documented was a story of personal change.

The very fact that it inspired me to write a book is part of that profound change. I hope it is the first of many new ventures in my life.

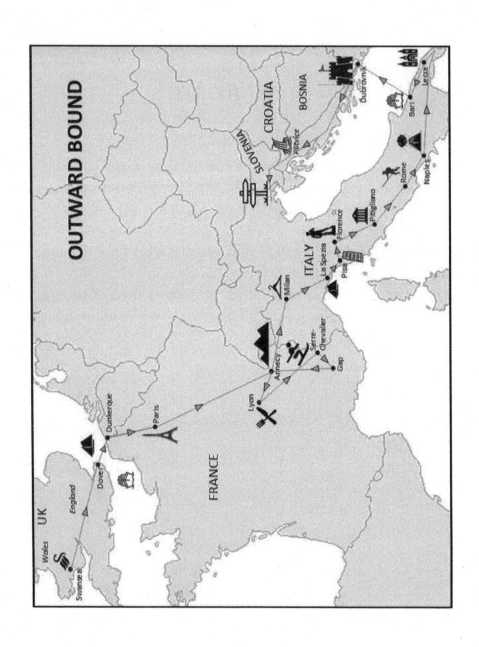

PART 1

OUTWARD BOUND

Wales

France

Italy

Croatia (with ten minutes in Bosnia)

Slovenia

1. HEADLESS CHICKENS

October to December

S OME SAID IT straight; others laughed it off. But as I remember it, the words 'out of your tiny minds' were written all over their faces when we broke the news to family and friends. We had decided to sell our very successful business and our much-loved family home, frequently referred to as our 'forever home', and, temporarily, leave behind the safe life that we knew, swap it all for a motorhome and embark on an adventure around Europe. This is what teenagers do, not middle-aged, responsible working parents.

Then there were the questions:

Where will you go?

Have you planned your route?

Living in such a small space, aren't you going to argue?

What will you do when you return?

We didn't have an answer to any of them. And, of course, I had concerns about our future. This carefree approach was utterly alien to me. I came from a rather old-fashioned family background where it had been drummed into me that my course through life would be GCSEs, A Levels, a university degree and then a well-paid career – no questions asked. My parents were inclined to be cautious in everything they touched, all the way from, say, their investments, which had to be as free of risk as conceivably possible while still standing some chance of achieving growth, through to what they ate, which was a staple diet of meat and two veg as opposed to anything of a vaguely foreign nature.

To me it never quite added up, considering my dad had been in the Merchant Navy and had travelled the world. Both my sister and I holidayed annually in Butlins until the ripe age of thirteen when we took our first flight and found there was a whole world out there. I will never forget hearing my dad expressing his disappointment in me to a neighbour a year or so after I left university. *We worked all our lives to pay for her to get a degree only for her to throw it back in our faces and go and work with dogs!* he said, standing right next to me.

By then I had a considerable amount of experience under my belt, having worked weekends and holidays in boarding kennels, where I not only gained knowledge of the job itself but also inadvertently acquired a business mind. A few years later I took the bull by the horns (dog by the collar?), quit my job, printed out some leaflets and hand-delivered them door to door to launch my own dog-walking business in Swansea. This was at a time when nobody outside London had ever heard of a dog-walker.

Fast forward fourteen years and I had grown that business from scratch to a thriving dog day crèche, at the time the only one of its kind in South Wales. I employed staff and controlled business decisions and finances, not to mention taking care of the wellbeing of the forty-odd dogs who spent their days romping around our fields while their owners went about their own daily lives. Best of all I never saw it as a job, such was my love for it. It was my biggest achievement in life until our son, Jackson, arrived. And while those achievements would no doubt have provided financially for his future, they would also have impacted greatly on his life.

I had met my husband, Geoff, when I was in my twenties. Although there were nineteen years between us in age, I aspired to the experiences his life had given him. When he was growing up, his father was attached to the armed forces, resulting in a somewhat unsettled lifestyle for the family. By mid childhood Geoff had lived and schooled in Singapore, Malta and Gibraltar before finally settling back in the UK. He had ticked the teenage traveller box when he took off with a back pack and hitched his way around Morocco, all thoughts of keeping in touch with his parents so far from his mind that he returned to discover that in his absence they had sold his motorbike and moved to Wales.

He was a free spirit, a surfer and a very accomplished snowboarder. It is no exaggeration to say he was one of the early pioneers of snowboarding in the UK, when he fashioned his own board from a plank of wood strapped to his shoes and set off to launch himself off the highest mountain in South Wales just because he had seen footage of an early snowboarder in a surf video from the United States. At this point little did he know the full impact that this moment of courage or madness (however you choose to look at it) would have on his life. He appeared quite by accident on a news channel and was catapulted into the world of competitive snow sports. This, combined with sports photography, took him around the world and on adventures that I held in awe. It was seeing some of his photographs published in magazines that first gave me the hunger to travel myself.

Later he had settled and become a dad and, as his daughter grew up, he had accepted the management roles his 9 to 5 job required, rushing home to teach on the dry ski slope or catch a few waves. By the time I appeared on his radar his daughter had grown up and flown the nest and he was single again. But the constant in his life was his snowboarding and surfing sports. When he became my instructor on the dry slope, we met and fell in love. And then once again his life took an unpredicted change of direction as he suddenly found himself immersed in my world of dogs.

Geoff had become a partner in my business in recent years and, like all businesses, it came with huge responsibilities and little free time. He had suffered a heart attack out of the blue, not long before we found out we were expecting a baby. That was really our turning point. When Jackson was born, from the moment I first looked at him I knew I could never again give myself to the business in the way I always had before. My life changed in front of my eyes and all I could think about was cherishing every second of family time. Geoff and I had always talked of future adventures together in our retirement, but if life had taught me one lesson it was that if you sit around waiting for the right time, you will wait forever. Sometimes life just throws something at you so hard that it shakes you awake and screams, *Make the most of me*, and for us this was Geoff's health scare followed by the gift of a baby as I fast approached forty. To hell with retirement! We needed to grab life and live it to its full, right now.

As we found out, selling a business and house in the current economic climate was no easy feat and so, as time marched quickly on, we opted to lease the business instead. By the October of Jackson's third year we had purchased a second house and were in the throes of living between the two and training our future commercial and residential tenants about the ins and outs of dogs and, more importantly, the handling of their owners, who equated their pets' importance to that of their children. Jackson was supposed to start full-time school the following September. We knew that from now on every day was one day less we would have to travel. We set a deadline to be in France by Christmas. Only one minor detail was missing: the motorhome.

Unwilling to look for one, and indeed financially unable until everything with the business was one-hundred-percent official, and with loose ends still being tied up, we hit December. Stress levels reached a peak and impatience got the better of us. We waved a tearful goodbye to our home and jobs, somewhat dangerously as the final lease agreement with our tenants hadn't even been signed. Christmas was fast approaching and, for our three-year-old, Father Christmas needed to be advised whether to deliver to our house in Wales or to a motorhome in France.

We put the time to good use, speed-reading every available book on the subject, and came up with a very basic but well-researched plan: choose the *smallest* motorhome that we could possibly live in for a year. I made the mistake of mentioning this to friends, so that when, on 22nd December, we were sawing off our gates in the pouring rain in order to park our 8.3-meter house on wheels in our drive, eyebrows shot up and jaws dropped. It seemed that we had been taking the wrong approach. Apparently what we needed was the very *largest* motorhome that we could possibly handle – if we wanted to come home still married, that was, so said our salesman, rolling his world-weary eyes. This was the salesman who had just witnessed the slamming on of our brakes as we had by sheer chance just driven past the hard-to-come-by German-made Knaus brand to which I had by now narrowed our search. There it just happened to be, sitting on the forecourt of a garage that we hadn't even planned on visiting. Twice the size and twice the price that we had budgeted for, we hastily reminded ourselves. We were simply going to look at the interior and check out the quality craftsmanship for which this make is renowned.

It was only after the event that I mentioned to Geoff that amidst my research I had read a piece of humorous advice that you should never let a woman look inside a motorhome before you are certain it is suitable from the outside. Oops, it was too late, and the super-king-size bed and spa shower meant I would not be swayed. We were reliably informed that after a certain age a motorhome will hold its value, particularly a well-sought-after brand like this. And that was that: we found ourselves the proud owners of a Knaus Sunliner.

Dotty, as she was named by Jackson, was essentially the fourth member of our team. She was a fine specimen, streamlined and classy and crucially sturdy enough to withstand all a three-year-old could throw at her. Unlike other makes you could feel the strength and quality in the closing of every cupboard door. The interior was beautifully designed, making use of smooth curves rather than straight boxlike features and giving you a sense of openness and space. We were spoilt with a choice of a king-size drop-down over-cab bed and a super-king-size bed at the rear with ample headroom for you to be able to sit up in bed and watch TV.

Seeking out flat surfaces is something you inadvertently find yourself doing when viewing a motorhome from the perspective of parents of a young child. Flat surfaces on which they can play, flat surfaces on which they can store inordinate amounts of junk. The concept of this extra bed seemed to serve all of these purposes. Treat it like a play room, we thought, shove him up there with a pile of toys while we are parked up and we'll get the rest of the space to ourselves. This wasn't Jackson's view on the matter, though. Who has a play room to which toys are actually confined? In his eyes the van was his play room, the table was his for drawing or Lego, and the aisle was for his train set or cars. The beds too were both his, one for toys, the other for watching his DVDs, rather than for sleeping or peace and quiet. There was a second TV in the seating area, behind which was the kitchen and then a dressing area with a huge mirror and sink. Opposite was the bathroom, a luxury all by itself. The shower was superior to the one we had at home, with a series of wall jets and neon lighting. Comfort was never going to be an issue, although driving might be challenging. From the front seats it was a little unnerving to look over your shoulder and realise the length of living space between you and the end of the vehicle. What's more, having never driven anything lacking a back window, it was only now I began to appreciate just how blind it can make you feel should you need to see behind you. Naturally we had ensured we had a reversing camera fitted and sat nav to keep us out of trouble. Here's a word of advice:

anyone who ever tells you that a gadget or two will keep you out of trouble is lying in your face.

Of all times to acquire your first ever motorhome, clearly 22nd December, the day of the showroom office party, is not the best. I think we were there for three hours and I'd be rich if I had a penny for each time the salesman looked at his watch and hinted that the boss was giving them the afternoon off to get ready to go out on the town. Could they have been faced with two more naive customers? Probably not. Lists of the vehicle's technicalities were rushed through and ticked off. We tried to write it all down but only stressed ourselves more. Then I fired the question that no doubt provided the humour for the drunken night ahead:

So, do you think we will be okay to go away within the next couple of weeks?

Well, yes, he said, *stay local the first few times you try her out, a couple of nights close to home, then over the coming months try a slightly longer trip and gradually build your confidence with the driving and the running of a motorhome. You should be fine to undertake a long trip on the continent by the summer.*

I can't remember who looked more embarrassed when I said that actually we were planning to leave for France just as soon as she was packed, in the middle of winter for eight months: me for admitting it or him for laughing out loud.

Christmas was quiet, since nobody expected us to be around. By Boxing Day we were doing relay runs to every available outdoor camping shop with lists to fully equip our van, from satellite navigation systems to cookware, from water carriers to mandatory breathalysers. We decided at midday on New Year's Eve that it would be a great opportunity to test the various aspects of the van. A quick phone call saw us booked into a local campsite for the night.

One minute into our journey we found out why online forums often referred to non-slip matting in every cupboard when our minimalist belongings, which we had literally thrown into any available space, all instantly relocated themselves. About an hour later we discovered that forward thinking is required when deciding what should be packed. We thought we were ready to party with a corkscrew and several bottles of the red stuff. But sitting at the campsite bar in the filthy joggers we had been labouring in all morning simply didn't cut the cake for a James

Bond theme night, and as the first guests arrived in dinner dress we retreated to our van to hide. I took the opportunity to read my Christmas present from Geoff, *Europe in a Motorhome* by H. D. Jackson. From the first page I saw it as a sign that we were making the right decision: there was a Jackson in the name and a Jackson in our van, so it was clearly meant to be. We laughed out loud at the mistakes described in the book and joked about what we would do when faced with the 'twelve-point turn' oblivious to the fact that we would soon find ourselves in the same if not worse predicaments. Well, if they can do it, so can we, right?

In the morning we learnt just how sensitive the smoke alarm was when we failed to make a slice of toast without awakening all last night's party-goers. We had no clue whatsoever about campsite etiquette, how to empty the toilet or hook up the electrics. The importance of being selective when choosing a pitch only really became apparent when we were being towed off the mud by a tractor. We sat at the table and formulated a step-by-step guide to follow immediately when we arrived at or before leaving a site and stuck it above the door for fear of driving off without remembering to unplug ourselves, or showering without shutting the cap on the dirty water tank, or a million other frightful scenarios that were now flooding our minds.

Back home we began packing in earnest. Every item was weighed before finding its home in the van. When you are novices like us, packing a motorhome requires a lot of patience. Nothing must bang, slide, scratch or fall. Everything must be accessible but secure for driving. I lost count of how many times it was all rearranged. The garage was Geoff's domain. He only needed to find space for four bikes, a kayak, life jackets, a table and chairs, two snowboards, skis, boots, a surfboard, a stand-up paddleboard, an array of tools and equipment for the van, Jackson's chosen selection of beach toys, oh, and the kitchen sink.

While we loaded the van, we yet again unloaded our house. In a stroke of luck, we found tenants four days before we left. With final items taking their place in the van, and me madly cleaning the now mostly empty house, the tenants were already bringing their belongings in through the front door. Then, after a brief stop at the solicitors to hand over the freshly signed tenancy agreement, exhausted, excited and a little apprehensively, because it was all suddenly real, we hit the road. The turnaround from bringing the van home to leaving for Europe had been four weeks, during which we had squeezed in one night's camping practice. Now we finally realised the truth of all those suspicions that we were totally mad.

2. OFF TO A GOODISH START

JANUARY

EARLIER BY A day than planned and quite by accident, we made it to France after some woeful sign-reading at Dover port deposited us in the wrong queue. Our plan was to buy a ticket for a crossing to Calais the next day but, before we could do much about it, we found ourselves queuing to board an 8 p.m. ferry to Dunkirk. Bring it on, we said to ourselves, this is the fashion in which we aim to continue. Truth be told, it was more attractive than the alternative option of reversing this huge thing out of there. In hindsight we should have used every opportunity to practise, because reversing in a tight spot is a manoeuvre that is regularly required and usually in stressful circumstances.

After our impromptu departure, we were lucky enough to meet another couple on board who pointed us in the direction of our first Aire de Service. I say we were lucky, but it was more a case of sheer terror at the prospect of driving off this ferry onto foreign turf, in the dark, with no overnight stop planned. With Geoff hastily instructing me to bring the Aires book on board and work out fast how to use it, I instead scanned the queues, homed in on another motorhome, followed its occupants and sought advice from, as it turned out, seasoned travellers who were only too happy to help. They steered us in the direction of an Aire that they regularly frequented on this crossing due to its convenient location just twenty minutes or so from the ferry.

I can't refer to an Aire now without elaborating on what one is because in truth I'd had absolutely no idea what Geoff was talking about when he read aloud from a book a few weeks back. They are an ingenious concept, lacking in our country, but which thankfully are plentiful on the continent and are comprehensively listed in a 'must not leave home without' guide called *All The Aires*. I have to say that this was easily our most referred to book on our journey.

Put simply, an Aire is a designated area where motorhomes are permitted to park overnight. Many of them are completely free of charge, particularly out of season, but even those that do charge are considerably cheaper than campsites. They cannot be pre-booked and usually 48 hours is the maximum length of time you can stay. Facilities range from absolutely nothing to very high-standard campsite-style services. Usually you will find an area for emptying grey water – your dish and shower water – a chemical toilet disposal facility and a tap for refilling with fresh water. These often come at a nominal charge of a couple of euros, and after several months on the road you may even become familiar with the seemingly endless array of different systems that operate. There are regulations in relation to your usage of these areas, but we learned from a very early stage that they all differ. The best rule is: if you are in any doubt, do as the French do.

In this case our first Aire turned out to be of the simplest nature: a gravel car park down a long, unlit track. Our only company was the lovely couple from the ferry. I still wonder whether we would actually have stayed here had we been alone and without their recommendation, because it was isolated to say the least. But, exhausted by the past few months, we slept like logs and awoke to find the sun shining and our neighbours gone. It was the weirdest feeling opening our blinds to the realisation that we were in another country, all alone, on the cusp of a new life. In that moment it all felt a little daunting and lonely, yet at the same time indescribably exciting.

It was almost as if we were dreaming. I found myself somewhere in an in-between state of mind. Despite being in a random, quite unattractive car park it was as if we were compelled to explore, for suddenly we no longer had anywhere else specific to be and there were no time constraints to work around. It was a challenge to our very natures to find ourselves in this new rule-less state. It felt nothing at all like being on a two-week vacation where every day counts because you'll be home before you know it. Now it was a case of to hell with it, if we really wanted to we could go back to bed and stay there till tomorrow. (Not that we did want to!)

Instead we wandered. We crossed a little stream, stopped to feed the ducks and admire nature. Every tiny detail seemed significant and exciting because suddenly we had time to pay proper attention. Aware that we were still drifting and not yet functioning properly, we strolled into town via a short cut from our car park and sought out a local French café in Béruges. The smell and then the first hit of the typically caffeine-loaded French coffee followed by the sweet taste of flaky croissant for breakfast are memories that will stay with me for life. It triggered an inner sense that released a flood of emotions with an overwhelming feeling of freedom, like I had never experienced before. It surpassed any expectation I ever had for this moment. I took a deep breath and literally felt lighter, as if the stress of the past six months had suddenly evaporated.

My elation was to be short-lived. We returned by the same route we had entered in the dark the previous night. But now the track had been transformed into a building site, with a hole and trench deep enough to sink a car. Its contents of earth and copious amounts of gravel for refilling were completely blocking us in. Had all this really been achieved in the time it took us to consume breakfast? Although the gravel car park had served us well, we were not excited at the prospect of spending another night there.

Fair play to them, though, because as our house on wheels approached, cigarettes were stubbed out and coffee cups set aside, and they immediately and without faze set about moving all the piles of earth and gravel to clear a path wide enough for us to pass. We still laugh about this experience and recall one another's facial expression at our first sight of those diggers, wondering how many people, experiencing this on day one, might have read it as a sign from the gods that they were not cut out for this lifestyle. Not us. We were eager to see more, and Champagne Country was calling us.

Our first proper drive on the continent was a joy. The sky was blue, the roads were quiet and the scenery was magnificent as we ambled through the countryside just trying to take it all in and process all these new sensations. It is funny how your first coffee, your first night, your first drive are so intoxicating. I can easily recall every smell, sound and colour, even though I still struggle to express precisely how it all felt. Perhaps it is down to the fact that a life-changing first time is such a unique feeling, one that cannot be compared or captured in words.

The one crucial criterion on which we had insisted when faced with seemingly endless options of motorhome layouts was that Jackson needed to be forward facing and directly behind us when we were on the road. When we started our research I had assumed that we would find a vehicle with three front seats and travel alongside each other, and had that been possible it would have been amazing. However, I quickly realised it was pretty much out of the question, because all the designs invariably allow for the front seats to swivel to become part of the lounge, making for a much larger living space. No matter, having Jackson just behind us enabled us to chat freely with him, albeit with a stiff neck, and he was as mesmerised as we were by his surroundings. It took him no longer than five minutes to realise that, in effect, he was travelling with the kitchen on board, and he kept me fit with his constant demands for a drink, a biscuit, a toy. There were times when I felt a little bit like an air hostess.

We found another Aire in a very quaint little village, surrounded by vineyards on the champagne route. Our guide book gave a brief description of each Aire. About this one it said: *Champagne tasting adjacent, bar 2 minutes*. Well, what more information do you need? This time we were on the roadside opposite a row of extremely luxurious houses and a château producing and selling local champagne, which was obviously closed at this time of year. In fact the whole street seemed deserted. We had an uninterrupted view, though, across vineyards and up into the green hills in the distance.

After the mayor had been summoned by the local landlady to person-ally deliver us some electric tokens and provide water from his half-constructed mansion opposite, we felt compelled to show some appreci-ation by sampling the local fizz. Very nice it was too, so much so that we decided to stay another night. We spent the next day enjoying a long frosty walk through the vineyards, skimming stones on a frozen lake and pinching ourselves at the realisation that this was our third free night with views for which the houses opposite had no doubt paid millions. I was suddenly overwhelmed by the realisation that we were here, in the moment, living our dream. This singular moment is the one that will stay with me forever and that I will go on to crave and long to repeat.

The dark hours were whiled away watching DVDs and writing my blog, which was my chosen form of communication with friends and family back home if they had the patience to follow. Naturally not a day went by without one or the other of us thinking about those we had left behind. Often it would be in jest at what mundane chore each of them would be undertaking at this particular time of day while we were living the life of Riley. But we would come to understand that communication with loved ones is crucial to the outcome of a trip like this. Geoff's daughter and granddaughter were particularly close to Jackson. My parents had passed before Jackson's birth but we had still brought him up with two sets of grandparents: Geoff's parents, who lived a long way away, and my auntie to whom I was very close. My sister was expecting her first child in a couple of months and I felt guilty about not being there to share her joy. We knew that Jackson was too young to fully engage in a telephone call, but also that he needed to be included if he was to slip smoothly back into these relationships in a year's time. He was always encouraged to personally select the postcards for relatives and friends, and we made a conscious effort to talk about everybody's news with him.

As for our news, there must have been times, like when we banged on about 'our moment', when our loved ones must have longed for an opportunity to shut us up instead of having to hear all about our perfect day. Still, they would definitely be getting their laughs at our expense over the coming months.

All did not go according to plan when we left Reims because we headed off in completely the wrong direction for twenty minutes. This was our first of many tests of tolerance and patience, not to say self-control, when in a confined space alongside our three-year-old. Let's just say that on this occasion some improvements were needed, with Geoff blaming me, me blaming the sat nav and Jackson learning some new words, which, no doubt, he would store in his memory for a particularly inappropriate time. But once we had turned around, returned to where we started from and set off in the right direction, the route to Paris along the A roads was really beautiful and all tension was quickly forgotten.

In our usual style we had not actually planned anywhere to stay around Paris. Our idea was to spend a few days here and leave the van unattended all day. In all cities this is a big risk. Research had led us to decide for peace of mind that all our belongings were not being ransacked while we were off enjoying ourselves, wherever possible we would use proper campsites outside major cities and make use of public transport. Naively we'd assumed that this would be easy. But as we began to study the ACSI campsite book en route we learned that most campsites do not open until March and that in January you only have a limited choice. On the plus side, ACSI sites are usually of a very good standard and offer fantastic discounts in off-peak periods, saving us a fortune on this trip. This fast became our other book that we would never travel without.

A few phone calls led us to Camping Champigny-sur-Marne, just on the outskirts of Paris, with a bus directly to the railway station and, from there, easy links to Paris and Disneyland, all at a lower nightly cost than we would pay for two hours parking in the city. Mind you, as the guidebook warned, the approaching streets are narrow. Our twenty-eight-point turn to get round a tight corner, with me standing in the middle of the road directing Geoff backwards and forwards like a yo-yo, trying not to take out a parked car, a railing or a bin, confirmed this. We were not by any means the largest motorhome in there, and it still remains a mystery as to how they got there, although they didn't appear to have moved in a while. We noticed a number of people living in palaces on wheels, commuting to work from the campsite and, no doubt, paying a much-discounted monthly fee, which if you ask me is a very sensible option.

On the first night we arranged to meet an old school friend of mine, Clare and her husband Arnaud, who live in Paris. This is when I actually discovered that my watch was still on UK time and that we had all spent the last four days in France on the wrong time. We were booked into a very posh curry house, and suddenly I only had five minutes rather than an hour and five minutes to get ready. At first sight of the restaurant I hatched a plan to tell Jackson that Arnaud was a policeman, resulting in flawless behaviour throughout the evening. In fact he was too nervous to engage in conversation and when we planned to see them again the next day I had to downgrade Arnaud to security guard.

Geoff and I had visited most of the sights in Paris previously, so our challenge was to devise a way to tour the city while accommodating a three-year-old and maintaining some level of sanity by the end of the day. The river bus ticked all the boxes, allowing us to hop on and off at various points of interest along the Seine while taking in the sights. Throughout all this the said three-year-old ran circuits around the boat, only to use up all his energy and need carrying as soon as we got off.

Our first stop was the Eiffel Tower. I had forgotten how wonderful it is, particularly when you stand underneath it. I remember seeing it for the first time when I was twelve and being blown away by it. But now we began to realise the differences we would encounter through travelling with a young child. I don't think he even so much as looked up until we prompted him, being much too interested in the police vehicles and guns. On this occasion there was heightened security following the November 2015 attacks in Paris and as a result the queues were vast. We decided that this time we would not go up and instead headed back to the boat.

Back on the river we took in various other famous landmarks and eventually opted for either the zoo or the dinosaur museum as our last port of call. But embarrassing reality took over and McDonald's outscored both of them. Starving and tired, we decided to eat and then walk to my friends' apartment. What a very bad idea. On the plus side we did gain a real sense of Parisian life by walking through the maze of streets from one district to the next. But by the end our legs felt like we had spent a day on the ski slopes, which wouldn't have been so bad had we not had two days in Disneyland ahead of us.

The next day we caught a bus from our campsite to the train station and then a train directly to the theme park, a straightforward journey taking just over half an hour due to both modes of transport running very regularly. Once we arrived we soon realised we would have to spend the next hour in a queue to buy tickets. To anyone planning to visit Disneyland I strongly advise purchasing tickets in advance so you can enjoy the luxury of walking straight in, as we were able to do the next day. At any rate, the security at the entrance was superb and we felt very safe despite the recent events.

One of the highlights of our trip was to witness the expression on Jackson's face as he set eyes on the Disney Castle and Main Street when we walked inside the gate. He was struck dumb for a moment before his face lit up like Christmas all over again. Even to grownups the colours, the sounds and the sheer scale of it make for a truly magical spectacle, and it was a visit we will never forget. Luckily this was probably the quietest time of year for the queues, which were only around fifteen minutes per ride. Anything longer would have been interesting with a three-year-old, so we were lucky, because I could see that in peak season they could easily be an hour or more. Even so, it is so cleverly designed that with most attractions you actually feel the ride has begun while you are still queuing. You are immediately drawn into the story and are in one way or another interacting with the experience while slowly moving ever closer to the entrance, and this ingenious sorcery makes the ride feel much longer than it actually is.

We opted for two days and purchased a ticket that allowed entry into both the main park and the Walt Disney Studios next door. It would be difficult to pick a favourite, since both offer completely different experiences, and in the studios we sat through some spectacular stunt shows. As for Disneyland itself, I don't want to spoil the surprises for anyone who hasn't been there, but just for a giggle I am going to tell you about the most frightening ride by a mile, which is the Tower of Terror.

Our bad parenting skills were laid bare, for neither of us had checked beforehand what this ride was. We simply queued up and thought ourselves lucky when Jackson turned out to be exactly the minimum height required to ride. In hindsight the only worse possible outcome from the next twenty minutes would have been if he hadn't been and I had opted to go it alone. I might have been charged with actual bodily harm to whoever had the misfortune of sitting next to me. Given the name of the ride, obviously we expected some frights, but we were thinking ghost train. Oh, how mistaken and unprepared is it possible for one to be?

It was designed like a tall tower block, which we entered at ground level to be introduced to the derelict hotel by a very spooky man who clearly kept seeing ghosts that no one else could see. I'm a tough nut to crack when it comes to comedy and wasn't much impressed by his attempts at humour, although Jackson was laughing hysterically. We were led into the library and instructed not to step off the carpet. Fully expecting the carpet to move, we were momentarily disappointed when nothing happened and we were again led off down a creepy corridor to an old-fashioned goods lift, the type you see in all good horror films. Again Jackson was measured for height and, at this point, Geoff got a little shirty, if I might put it that way, partly about the stupid idea that Jackson could have shrunk in the last fifteen minutes and partly at the dreadful thought that, if he actually had, we had all wasted the last fifteen minutes and would have to leave.

Anyway, our suspicion that our son was still the same height was confirmed and we were ushered into the lift along with about twenty other adults and strapped into our seats. Very clearly we were now on a ghost train and our senses were fully alert and ready for a hand on the shoulder. I say OUR senses, but I have no idea what was going through Jackson's mind and whether he was in the least bit prepared for any of this, although as it turned out it was pretty irrelevant.

What you need to appreciate is that the next bit all happened in the space of about two seconds. Bang, all the lights failed as we were left in total darkness, holding hands three in a row. Then whoosh, we were swept up in the lift in a flash to the top floor. I swear I experienced g-force and that Geoff's cap rose up off the floor to meet him. There was just enough time for the wall of the building to slide open to reveal daylight and to confirm that we were swinging out nine storeys above the tiny people down below before, yes, you guessed it, we were immediately plunged into free fall in total darkness, leaving our stomachs on the roof, all the way to ground level, accompanied by a chorus of screams and presumably some choice French words. I very nearly taught them a new English one beginning with F, but the g-force held it in. I am petrified of heights and had such a tight grip of Jackson's hand and my seatbelt for fear of MY life that I could do absolutely nothing to help my poor child, who was screaming: *Help me, I want to get off!* as we were again shooting swiftly to the top, this time knowing the worst was about to come again and again and AGAIN. Suffice to say that we survived and that from then on we paid a little more attention to the brochure description of each ride.

Each evening there is a fireworks and laser show for which it is advisable to cut short your time on the rides in order to get a good viewing position, because it really draws the crowds and is so spectacular that it made me cry. The whole Disneyland experience easily exceeded all our expectations and when, after the train and bus journey, we eventually returned to our motorhome each night, we were barely able to climb the step to bed. We realised this was something we would need to bear in mind when planning visits to cities along this trip, as there is no point in overdoing it if it means returning with an over-tired, crotchety toddler. In this instance we had had the option of parking and sleeping in the Disneyland car park itself, but had found that the general consensus of the reviews was that it was a very noisy environment with road sweepers that started work at 5 a.m. All in all, even allowing for the travelling, I think we made the right choice.

It probably caused great amusement among our friends and family, back home in the Welsh rain, who had already endured several blogs of sheer happiness, when I enlightened them about our reunion with reality a few days later when we were dished out a small helping of bad luck. Having the total freedom to make spur-of-the-moment decisions is what motorhoming is all about. You are not tied to one spot, so if the weather turns bad you just get a weather report and move to where the sun is shining, if you happen to feel like it. Likewise, if you decide over breakfast that you fancy an extra day here then that too is fine, and that's exactly what we did. We thought we needed to relax after Disneyland and, besides, we wanted to take advantage of the laundry facilities at this campsite and give the van a much-needed tidy. So I cleaned while Geoff spent three hours in the laundrette, my excuse being that I wouldn't have understood the instructions in French, although it did seem to work out in my favour.

We made the mistake of planning our departure from Paris too well, aiming to have an easy day, an early start and a pleasant scenic drive avoiding motorways, which are fearsomely expensive in France for a large vehicle, and to head for Dijon, which would be our midway overnight stop en route to Annecy. Simple! Well, here's how the day actually went...

First, we woke up late, drove over to the cleaning area at the campsite to empty the water and waste and refill and, unfortunately, arrived at exactly the same time as 'gold suit man'. Yes, head-to-toe gold suit and smart shoes, literally tiptoeing about in filthy water sorting his van out while announcing to us that he would be a good half-hour as he was giving it a thorough clean. How wonderful for him. If nothing else, it was entertaining and an inspiration to Geoff, who with no words spoken between us had obviously been nominated sole toilet emptier for the duration of our travels and who, fair play, stoically accepted his role. Thanks to the golden gentleman he had a free demonstration of how it was actually possible to remove, carry and empty a toilet cassette without turning your head 180 degrees and attempting to stretch your arm an extra foot while jumping back for fear of splash-back. Gold suit man carried out the procedure like a pro and was still fit for the catwalk when he had finished.

Finally we found ourselves on the road on the outskirts of Paris in absolutely mental traffic. Now we had spent a considerable amount of time researching various models of navigation system and opted for the 'Trucking Sat Nav', which enables you to enter your weight, length, width and, funnily enough, HEIGHT. As it turned out, our trucking sat nav was a complete waste of money and has now earned itself a new name, which I have to mutter under my breath.

Keep left! we heard it say and then *BANG* we also heard as we hit the bright orange swinging pieces of stupidly hard plastic suspended above the road, whose function was to warn of the low bridge that we were about to hit and, luckily, narrowly avoid. Two questions sprang to mind. First, what the hell was the point of warning you of a hazard by whacking you with something that caused equal damage? And second, what on earth was our sat nav even thinking? Now we had to reverse into four lanes of oncoming Paris traffic with our GB sticker in full view, holding up the whole road while bringing shame upon our country.

Looking on the bright side, after a quick walk the length of the van at the next traffic lights, when I could finally hold my head up again, I announced to Geoff that at least the skylights weren't cracked, which meant the top of the van could not really be damaged. So off we headed, in a somewhat stressed manner, on the flipping motorway, as I refused to use the sat nav and could not navigate us to the A road. All seemed well again.

NOT!!! Tired and hungry, we decided to pull over halfway through our journey. It was at this moment that I realised it was raining inside our van. No, the skylight above our bed was not cracked: it simply wasn't there. Where it was was somewhere on a road in Paris, and it had rained for four hours onto our bed. That was how Geoff spent his lunch break, sitting on the roof in the rain, with a saw and a plastic lid, cutting it to size and taping it on, while I stuck bin bags onto the bedroom ceiling and stuffed the bed with towels to soak up the wet. It could have been worse, bearing in mind our satellite dish and solar panel were on the roof too, but, that said, a working sky light is also kind of a necessity. Then, with one hour of light and over one hour of driving left, a map and a book with a picture of the Aire we had chosen, and a very stroppy three-year-old, we were on the road again.

In comparison the rest of the journey was uneventful. However, we arrived in total darkness, parked up, moaned for half an hour that the parking area was crap and not even flat, the bed was wet and the roof was leaking again. All this before I decided to look at the picture of the campsite again, made a comparison, took a brief walk in the rain and discovered that we were in the wrong place. One minute down the road was the flat area we were expecting and, after further repairs and a perfectly nice meal, we went to bed praying that we didn't drown in the night and that tomorrow could only get better.

3. FRIENDS TO THE RESCUE

FEBRUARY

BY A MIRACLE our repairs held out and we made it through a rainy night without any further leaks. After an uneventful motorway drive we arrived in the early afternoon in Annecy, in the Auvergne-Rhône-Alpes region of southeastern France. We took the scenic route around two different industrial areas to buy some snow chains, which in certain areas of mainland Europe are a mandatory part of your kit for much of the year. At all times, unlike at home, you are also required to carry reflective vests for the driver and all passengers, a warning triangle and a breathalyser. Now, ready to head up into the mountains, it was time for '#@?#ing sat nav' to have the last laugh again.

Due to the fact that apparently we had a very unusual size of tyre (wait for it, we were therefore bound to have a flat at some point), we had driven in circles from shop to shop looking for chains, which ended up costing the earth and which Geoff vowed we would never use as he had driven to the Alps countless times in the snow and never needed them. As a result, when we tried to pick up our route again the screen was a maze of purple lines where we had deviated from the original route. We set off in one direction and the purple line was overwritten with a blue line, indicating that we had already been on that road. Then, when we came to a roundabout, instead of a purple line leading us to the correct exit, the whole flipping thing was purple, saying: *You idiots have already been round this thing once looking for a shop.*

So I had Geoff frantically asking which way and, after driving right round it all again and turning everything blue and purple, the only answer I could give was: *How the hell do I know, just go left.* This entire sentence was repeated back to me by Jackson.

It was soon all forgotten as we started to climb an ever more winding road with Jackson designating himself chief of safety by shouting *Lights on!* at each tunnel we came to. We had breathtaking views of snow-capped mountains and tiny little towns down below, with chocolate-box wooden chalets dotted around the green hillsides. Just as the sun set we arrived at the home of Geoff's friends Carl and Véronique. Their house was as pretty as any of them although, I have to admit, the first thing that grabbed our attention was the driveway coated in snow, steeply rising and rounding a sharp corner directly underneath the overhang of the very beautiful house, leading on to the perfectly flat area on which we were aiming to park.

It turned out to be an impossible manoeuvre with at least half an hour of wheel-spinning, rubber-burning and edging up and around inch by inch, desperately trying not to take out either of our homes in the process. Eventually, after another half-hour of chatting and negotiating with the neighbours, we commandeered someone's parking bay two minutes' walk up the road.

After a lovely evening spent eating, drinking and catching up with our friends, whose two daughters spoke fluent English and, even more importantly, produced box after box of toys for Jackson to play with, we returned tired and tipsy to the van for the night. After the uphill hike from the front of the van to the back we climbed into bed and immediately ended up in a heap, faces squashed against the window as we discovered just how badly we were sloping left to right as well as head to toe. Solution: sleep diagonally and hope the alcoholic coma sets in fast. Result: it must have, as it was daylight when we awoke to discover that, from our diagonal position, Jackson and I had slid back to the window-hugging position while Geoff could only be described as a heap, clinging on to the foot of the bed and lying horizontally looking down over the three-foot drop to the floor. Later that day we fixed everything with levellers and blocks.

So the next four days were spent here in Annecy where there was no shortage of things to do. Annecy goes by many beautiful descriptions: the land between mountains and lake, the Venice of the Alps, a town where romance is the lifeblood. It deserves all of them. We had a wonderful walk alongside the beautiful lake, which seemed void of activity at this time of year, took in two swing parks and a wander around Old Annecy as well as some window-shopping in the new shopping centre. Old Annecy is filled with picturesque historic buildings overhanging the fast-flowing stream and canals winding their way throughout the town. It's a maze of narrow streets, cafés and shops selling local cheeses and meats, and the light ever changing on the water makes it a photographer's paradise.

Then there was the dog walk. Not just your average dog walk, mind you. Having been a dog walker for the past twenty years I consider myself reasonably fit, well at least I did until I came across Carl's interpretation of a dog walk. This was a vertical hike, at speed, up a mountain for two hours and then back down at even greater speed, as it was now pitch black. I have to say I was amazed at Jackson's stamina, but small patches of snow kept his interest and somehow he managed to find the energy to continuously bend and throw snowballs at us. I, on the other hand, had lung burn, not to mention leg burn, and I kept hold of Jackson's hand by way of an excuse that I was walking at his pace, as any good mum should, but really to disguise the fact that I thought I was dying. My legs took three days before I could actually get to my feet without wincing in pain. So that's it, I am well and truly OVER dog walking!! Add to that the fact that none of us actually remembered to take a phone or a camera to capture the stunning views above the clouds. At least their dog Aslan, all 75 kilos of Leonberger loveliness, took it all in his stride.

We could have happily stayed there for weeks. But we were aware that we were taking the neighbours' parking space and that we had been five days without hooking up our electrics and that, parked in a shady area, the solar charger wasn't doing much. So we needed to move on.

After a morning spent at a local motorhome garage we got the missing skylight replaced and parted company with over 400 euros. Carl made a huge difference to this situation. Having someone to translate mechanics' terminology into English saved a lot of confusion. Especially so when I had a last-minute panic and remembered that we hadn't specified that as well as a new skylight we also needed a mosquito screen to protect us whenever we opened it. If we had only bothered to look properly we'd have realised that this apparently goes without saying.

As a farewell, Carl took us to a restaurant on a plateau nestled deep in the mountains. This was our first sight of proper deep snow and emotions were mixed as we faced the half-hour hike surrounded by cross-country skiers to get to lunch. Jackson and I were in our element, enjoying the scenery and all the excitement, whereas Geoff, bless him, was now paying the price of a little too much to drink the previous night at Carl's, which had resulted in a twisted ankle when he forgot there was a step between the lounge and the bathroom. Of course he got no sympathy from any of us at the time, nor indeed now, but unfortunately it went on to plague him for much of the month to come.

We parted company with Carl and Véronique later that day and headed off to our new campsite an hour away at a ski resort.

4. CONCERNING TOILETS

NOT YOUR USUAL subject, I grant you, but, believe it or not, one to which you will be devoting many a conversation as motorhomers, so I feel it warrants a chapter in its own right. In my case I first began noticing toilets in France a great deal more than I normally did, and some entertained me so much that for a while I really thought I was embarking on an endless list of new experiences. On further reflection it is a very French thing that subsequently escaped my mind for large parts of our journey in other countries, only to slap me around the face all over again as soon as I returned to France.

For your delectation, I have subdivided toilets into various categories and rated them from a personal point of view. Allow me to start with our own personal motorhome toilet, which is quite a luxury really, particularly if required during the night or if it is snowing outside. However, this luxury comes at a price. Unfortunately what goes in must come out and obviously I allocated this job to Geoff and his sidekick Jackson, who never tired of watching this procedure while giving a running commentary on the event. It was little wonder, I suppose, that when staying on a campsite with a toilet block, Geoff would request that we save him a job by using the facilities provided. There were, though, moments when I had to question his judgement when he would troop off to a spider-infested, disease-ridden and grubby building and return covered with mosquito bites, if nothing else. Jackson or I would usually seize this moment for a sneaky foray into our own toilet without being sent on a guilt trip. My personal view of the matter was that we had spent a substantial amount of money for the luxury and we needed to get our value from it.

Cleaning aside, the other downside to our toilet was its size. I don't know what I expected but, having to enter sideways in order to close the door without having to stand on the toilet first, and then not being able to use the toilet without rotating it so your feet are now in the shower, at which point you can't reach the toilet roll and, now the door is closed, you can't remove it from its holder as limited space means it is pressed against the door… wasn't really how I'd imagined it. For these reasons Geoff and I gave it a score of 6/10.

Next we come to campsite toilets. I have encountered quite a few different ones. The most striking change from back home is that all but a few public toilets are unisex, so that three weeks into the trip I was still beating a hasty retreat believing I had walked into the wrong one every time I entered and came face to face with a man. You could do even better in a few bars and cafés where you actually had to walk right past the urinals to reach the cubicle. I felt myself blushing each time and never got used to the correct protocol in this situation. Was I supposed to retreat at speed? Or pass by swiftly and barricade myself into the safety of the cubicle until the coast was clear, then make a dash for it? Or should I just wish the gentleman a good day on the way past?

Often the embarrassment did not end there. In a campsite, having entered a unisex toilet, you often discovered that it wasn't simply a toilet block. You also had a choice of a washroom, a shower or a toilet, and on the other wall there could be a row of sinks where someone might be washing their dishes or even cutting their hair. Either way, unless you were lucky enough to enter and leave while all the doors were shut, nobody was at the sink and you were able to use the facilities without being recognised, it made for a less than comfortable experience. And it could get even worse. You could have Jackson with you and, as I discovered to my horror, he could start a conversation about the differences between boys and girls or about the mysteries of birth. Or, if he was taking it easy on you, he could just ask out loud whether you were having a wee or a poo, to which the best answer was: *Neither*, as you beat a hasty retreat back to the motorhome to upset Geoff by using our personal cramped toilet. So we initially gave campsite toilets a score of just 2/10. The score was based only on our French experiences, but later in our trip we met with very different experiences in other countries where many toilets were of such a standard of luxury and cleanliness that it was tempting to go and eat your dinner in them. So with this in mind we subsequently upgraded the score. In fact, on the occasions Jackson permitted me to use a bathroom without his presence, hence negating the awkward conversation scenario, I would go as far as to award an average score of 5/10.

Then there were the overly guarded toilets (okay, maybe justifiable when it was at the Eiffel Tower) whereby you underwent a bag search and a body frisk on the way in, resulting in a queue almost as long as for a ride at Disneyland. It did amuse me to see men's faces when they were clearly not used to the act of queuing for a wee, which is second nature to us women. For making us feel safe and bringing equality to women, if nothing else, we gave these a score of 8/10.

Last but by no means least, we come to French street toilets. By these I mean the ugly shiny silver buildings which look so modern and spacious from outside but, to my dismay and Jackson's delight, when you enter you are just faced with a hole in the floor. I was completely baffled by my first experience with one of these. I could see absolutely no evidence of a flush. First I found myself shouting to Geoff on the outside: *Is the door saying 'Locked'?* for the fear of God someone would open it and reveal me to the whole street. Next I was shouting: *I can't find the flush*, as if he was going to be of any help from the street. Then it was the sink, one of those newfangled water-soap-dry-in-sequence jobbies. But, try as I might, do you think I could get any water or soap? Absolutely no way, so I gave up and left. Next in were Geoff and Jackson, so I held the door open for them to save paying twice. But now this was where the French street toilet really came into its own. First the sink chose that moment to squirt out soap, followed in quick succession by water and a blast of hot air, all meant for me but too premature for the boys. So now I was out on the street hearing screams followed by shrieks of laughter from inside. They had just found the flush – or rather, it had found them. While Geoff was using the toilet suddenly there was a loud noise followed instantly by a tidal wave from behind them at the back of the cubicle as the whole floor self-washed around their feet and over their shoes. All this, as we discovered, was the price we paid for holding the door open! So for sheer entertainment value we collectively gave French street toilets a score of 11/10!

As our travels went on we encountered such an array of funny, weird and downright impractical toilets that, if I ever travel again, I might well write a book on this subject alone. There were the ski resorts where some brainy interior designer had decided that the toilets needed to be on a completely different level to the restaurant or the snow, ensuring that the journey was as difficult as possible, particularly with a three-year-old in ski boots. There were the motorway services where a strategically placed picnic table and bench in the sun momentarily invited you to begin your lunch, only to discover that if you looked left you were sat directly next to the open-air men's urinal, needless to say with very little privacy-screening in evidence. Then there were the super-market car park blocks where some bright spark thought it would be funny to place a security light directly above the, once again unpro-tected, open-air urinal so that if it was dusk or later you could rest assured the entire car park would have a grandstand view. Oh, and one very smart upmarket beach café and bar went for the ultimate clear, see-through glass-door-on-the-cubicle experience. Ingenious, what?!

All these finer details are what makes a trip so memorable. So all I can say is: bring on more toilets.

5. DASHING THROUGH THE SNOW

AFTER PARTING COMPANY with our friends we headed just an hour away to Le Grand-Bornand ski resort, which, even more excitingly, was a real campsite with a swimming pool and hot showers. Better still, there were washing machines with driers, an essential at this time of year as there is no drying space in a motorhome. We must have spent a fortune on the laundry, stripping the bedding and all the towels and altogether freshening up our wardrobes. Again ACSI membership came in very useful, granting us much reduced rates, although unsurprisingly the campsite was nearly full.

Being on a campsite in the snow was a new experience to me and felt like Christmas all over again. Picture it, nestled in a little hollow surrounded by steep snow-covered mountains on all sides.

Just across the river to which this place owes its name, there was a stunning view of the town with its white snowy roofs, an array of brightly coloured fairy lights adorning the buildings and a beautiful warmly lit Roman Catholic church clock tower. And, as if not to be left out, it seemed the motorhoming community had partaken in the spirit, with strings of lights and decorations inside and outside their vans. Jackson actually asked me if Father Christmas was coming again. *No*, I said, *it's February now*, secretly feeling very Christmassy myself.

This was to be the first place where we really got to interact with and delve into the minds of a community of people with two things in common: the love of snow and the love of motorhoming – a community, it suddenly dawned on us, of which we were now a part. And, since we remained here for eleven nights, we gained a wealth of knowledge, from practical tips on everything under the sun to what brings such a variety of people to this spot, where they are heading, and where it all started for them. In the process, needless to say, we gained some new friends.

Obviously there were holiday makers, returning annually to a much-loved place to squeeze in a week's skiing before returning to work. The majority were French, but there were plenty of Brits too and a scattering of German and Spanish, to name just a few nationalities. There were the long-termers, easily spotted by the array of clutter and decoration adorning not only the vehicle but its surrounding plot. Pets were travelling too, dogs, cats and even a parrot who could be seen bobbing up and down nightly on the dashboard in one van. There were the glampers in their enormous coach-style homes with expanding sides and leather interiors, and, by way of contrast, the toughies, as I like to think of them, in their tiny convertible vans or even tents. Many were stationed here for the season, while others were moving around, some with time constraints and others indefinitely, whose motorhome had become their permanent home.

The lifestyle of this last group, which until now was something to which I had never given any consideration, suddenly seemed very appealing. In one brief conversation I remember among three Brits there was one who was leaving the following day to return home for work having enjoyed his holiday; another who over supper the previous night, having been here since before Christmas with no firm plans, had just decided he'd had enough cold for now, so he and his wife were heading for southern Spain for some sun, possibly to return to the snow later in the season; and then there was us taking in as many European sights as we could pack into six months.

One generation lacking here, though, was children. Sadly for Jackson this was the place where it really hit us that he had nobody his own age to play with, and hadn't really ever since we left Wales. It was not school holidays and, I suppose, the average family travelling long-term with young children would more likely be in sunnier climes. That being said, Jackson certainly wasn't short of attention and, after getting himself stuck in a snowdrift on the campsite, he returned to the van pleased as punch and carrying a chocolate lollipop given to him by the kind lady who pulled him out. I can't really explain it, but although we didn't know any of these people it was plain that there was a strong sense of trust among fellow travellers. It was as though everyone looked out for everyone else and it all felt very comforting.

We hit the slopes a day later and I should not have feared for the lack of kids. Suddenly we were surrounded by them, mostly careering down the mountain fearlessly with immense skill and precision, leaving me feeling old and inept at the side of the piste figuring out what move to do next to reach the bottom in one piece.

Talking about pistes, Jackson had his first ski lessons here. At short notice our only option was private one-to-one lessons with an English-speaking instructor. It turned out this was the best possible value for money, because our boy came on in leaps and bounds. After four 45-minute lessons he achieved more than we could ever have imagined.

We purchased a limited-access pass for me while Jackson was free. Because Geoff's ankle was still giving him grief he opted for a walking pass, which still allowed him to use certain lifts. In this way we cheaply took Jackson up in his first bubble car to the halfway station on the mountain. After a few practice runs and a big face-plant on the nursery slope, he twice skied all the way to the bottom of the mountain holding onto one of my poles, over a mile and laughing all the way. In a typical three-year-old fashion he liked to assert his authority on the slopes. When I told him he needed to snow plough in order to slow down, the answer flew back: *No, I'm trying to go faster than you!* As we followed a winding snow road with a very gentle gradient he spotted a steep, icy shortcut used by experts to cut out all the bends and immediately announced: *I'm going that way.* I was thinking: *God help me when he decides to let go of the pole!* He then threw a full-on tantrum because I wouldn't carry an icicle around all day for him after he found it. I can tell you that a toddler stamping his feet in a temper while wearing skis is something well worth seeing.

He soon took control of his lessons, instructing the instructors about what he was doing next. While Geoff and I looked on helplessly, Crystal was delegated the role of making a snowball with her bare hands at the bottom of each run and placing it on the conveyor belt in front of Jackson before he would get on, just so he could have the pleasure of watching it ride up the hill and fall off the end of the belt at the top, and also just because he told her to. Then there was Christian who had to stop each time they passed the chair lift to answer, in a foreign language to him, questions on the ins and outs of its components and workings.

To our relief Jackson loved every aspect of the snow and given the chance would stay out in it all day. He was equally in his element collecting icicles off the van or pushing his toy snowplough around in a snow drift. I did a short phone video of the piste-bashers taking to the slopes at the end of the day and a snowplough clearing the road in town, which he must have watched about a hundred times. Fireman Sam is a job for someone else now: Jackson wants to drive a piste-basher!

At the end of a tiring day on the mountain, Geoff and I may have dreamed of putting our feet up in the van. But our energetic three-year-old had eyes only for the pool where he impressed us yet again and swam his first width completely unaided. It served to reassure us that whatever he might be missing in nursery this year he was certainly making up for in life lessons.

We would endeavour to teach him a new French word every few days. He already had a nice list by now and used them confidently, although *Qui* had proved to be of great amusement to him, and we did have one near miss when I tried to teach him *Pardon*, to which he loudly enquired: *What does hard-on mean?* Bless him, he couldn't understand why that met with uncontrollable laughter.

It was very hard to drag ourselves away from this place, but school holidays in the region were almost upon us and the campsite was fully booked. We were also advised that by the weekend traffic would be very heavy on the routes to Annecy, so we spent our last day drying out all our clothing and equipment in the fantastic heated drying rooms on site and reorganising our van ready for our morning departure. Jackson and I were booked on a flight from Geneva back to the UK for a brief visit, as I was about to become an auntie for the first time.

Did we have the sense to check the weather forecast, or even to notice that it was snowing pretty heavily as we crawled into bed? Of course not, otherwise we might have opted to find and read the instructions on our brand-new set of chains. I distinctly remember the salesman strongly advising us to put the chains on a few times in good weather for practice because, he said: *The moment when you actually need them it will be cold and snowing and stressful and you could be stuck in the middle of the road.* To which Geoff had replied: *Yes, yes,* muttering under his breath about the price and the waste of money.

So naturally we awoke to deep snow and excitedly proceeded to sit in the warmth of our van admiring the beautiful winter scene all around us. We even laughed as we filmed a very busy tractor towing one vehicle after another out of the campsite with blizzard conditions all around. But did even that scene give us cause for concern? Apparently not, well at least not until late morning when we decided we should make a move.

First Geoff decided to dig two tracks out from our pitch to get us onto the tarmac road through the campsite, which had been partly cleared by the snowplough but was swiftly turning white again. No sooner had he got the shovel out of the garage than the chap parked opposite took pity on us ill-equipped Brits and came over to offer him a serious shovel. A snow shovel had been on my list of necessary equipment before we left Wales, but at that point when snow still seemed a million miles away, our bank balance was swiftly diminishing and the van was in danger of bursting at the seams, particularly since we were catering for both summer and winter, I took it into my head that a cheap plastic shovel would do. It won't!

Anyway, even the serious shovel failed to get through the ice layer beneath the snow, and simply laying our plastic grip tracks under the wheels wasn't going to be sufficient either. Out came the snow chains and we proved the salesman right from the word go. The instructions were not waterproof and it was pelting down with snow. All our careful drying of Geoff's clothing was in vain as he persevered for nearly an hour laying the chains on the snow, returning every few minutes to the door, allowing a mini-blizzard to enter the van and all the heat to escape while he checked the instructions while we tried to keep them dry. Gloves made it impossible and I don't even want to imagine what it was like handling freezing chains bare-handed. To top it all off, the office was now closed for an hour and a half for lunch and the tractor driver had stopped for the same reason, so the road was again indistinguishable from all the surrounding snow. We gave up and admitted defeat.

We were rescued after lunch by an experienced campsite worker who had our chains on in two minutes flat, advising Geoff to ignore the instructions and do something completely different. We left hitched to the back of the tractor until we reached the main road where we were on our own. Or not, actually. It was a scene of carnage as troops of holiday makers attempted to make their way up the mountain. There were abandoned cars in hedges or side roads, and general chaos ensued with more hold-ups as people had to stop in the middle of the road to put their chains on. One car had skidded and flipped on its side where it remained with no sign of any occupants but obviously a very bad start to someone's holiday. There was absolutely no evidence of a road and yet somehow the traffic was moving, albeit slowly. Cruising along at ease at all of about 5 MPH now, with our chains showing their worth and Geoff eating his words, we couldn't help but laugh at ourselves as Brits when we go into all-out panic mode back home as soon as we get more than a few flakes of snow. So it was that slowly but surely we made our descent, admiring the beautiful snow-laden scenery. Then, after a brief stop halfway down to remove our chains, we picked up speed and headed through sleet into heavy rain while losing altitude.

We parked up in a free lakeside Aire on Lake Annecy to await our chauffeur to the airport the following day in the form of our trusty friend Carl. Even the shortest journey across the Swiss border to enter the airport would have incurred costs by way of the compulsory purchase of a Swiss motorway *vignette*.

That night my emotions ran high with excitement at the prospect of catching up with family and friends tinged with some concern as to how I was going to handle my first flight alone with Jackson, then juggle hospital visits, social arrangements and be solely responsible for a three-year-old 24/7 for the next two weeks. And in fact I didn't even have a home to go back to as ours was rented out. As luck would have it, friends of ours, Carrie and David, were away on holiday at exactly the same time and we did a very convenient swap. Jackson and I got to stay at their house in Mumbles and look after their two cats for them. Having a place all to ourselves was a huge weight off my mind because I could relax knowing we weren't interrupting someone else's routines. Amazingly, for once, a brief bit of organisation as I was packing to leave back in January had seen me leave a fortnight's supply of clothes and toiletries in the boot of my car parked up at another friend's house, so we were able to travel with hand luggage only, which meant toys, basically. I confess I was a little sad and even jealous to be leaving Geoff alone to continue what still seemed like a holiday without me, and I wondered what I would miss out on.

Ironically these two weeks would separate us for both Valentine's Day and our wedding anniversary, giving Geoff the perfect excuse to save money on both. I could see the sadness written all over his face. No I couldn't! He was going to have a ball snowboarding and enjoying the peace and, most of all, waking up to something other than Wallace and flipping Gromit on DVD. And every evening he would be able to play the game of 'find the object', as he still had no clue or interest in my packing system, just as I had no idea how anything worked in the van.

6. REUNITED IN ALBERTVILLE

TWO WEEKS LATER Jackson and I returned to France – as it turned out, two very eventful weeks for all concerned. In our usual style we'd had a few dramas, including getting locked in a bedroom in Carrie and David's house and breaking the toilet lid while attempting to climb out of the bathroom window. I consider it a form of early-warning system, like the rock-hard dangly things that smashed our skylight to smithereens, thereby warning us not to hit the low bridge in case we damaged our van. In this instance the foot through the toilet lid said loudly and clearly: *If you are that heavy your arse ain't fitting through that window!*

Then, after three hours' sleep the previous night, for reasons to which I will come back in a minute, I demonstrated the ultimate in bad motherhood skills as I carried Jackson into the house half asleep from the car and stood him inside the front door, instructing him not to let the cats out while I removed the key from the front door. What I had failed to notice was that his eyes had shut. I turned around and to my horror witnessed him in slow motion rolling down all twelve wooden stairs. This was the moment when I discovered that I had driven home from my sister's house leaving my mobile phone there. No phone, no internet, no contact numbers. I had to ring from the house phone to get another friend to look up the out-of-hours doctor's number. Of course it wasn't that simple, because they needed a contact number to call me back on. I had to hang up and redial the other friend and ask her to do a last-number recall and ring me back to tell me the number I was dialling out on. Thankfully after at last talking with an out-of-hours GP and keeping Jackson and myself (with a lot of effort and singing of nursery rhymes) awake until 1 a.m., he was fine.

Last and by no means least we return to the reason for my three hours' sleep the night before. Thanks to my sister and her husband I was incredibly privileged to be present at the birth of their first child, Rhys, an experience I never in a million years expected to have and for which

I will never be able to thank them enough. Boy was it different seeing it from the dad's perspective. I actually dare to say I think it might be just as testing on them. You have to master the art of reading concerned looks on doctors' faces while simultaneously reassuring mum that all is great, controlling your own nerves and preferably trying not to faint. Due to a very stubborn baby who was determined to stay in mummy's tummy well after full term, coupled with some complications during birth that unfortunately saw him spending a few days in HDU, Jackson and I didn't have as many cuddles as we had hoped. But every moment was exceptionally special, particularly for Jackson who was actually stunned to silence when he first set eyes on Rhys after talking to my sister's tummy for so long. Thankfully both mum and baby made it home safely on the morning that Jackson and I left for the airport, which made for a much more relaxed journey.

And so, completely exhausted, we returned to France to be reunited with Geoff and Dotty. Jackson ran straight into daddy's arms at the airport and I was kindly informed that I had been missed: poor Geoff had had to do both the cooking and the washing up.

It turned out that it hadn't been all plain sailing for Geoff while we were away. His first drive alone in the van saw him swearing profusely at the sat nav while reversing out of a dead-end track in snow, attempting to self-navigate for fear of trusting it from there on, being hooted at by drivers at tolls when, being right-hand drive, he had to keep getting out and going round to the passenger side to pay, oh and the fridge door fell off, like they do. Of course that was my fault for not loading it correctly, nothing at all to do with the fact that he forgot to lock it before driving.

He finally settled in Saint-Gervais having abandoned the Aire in Chamonix as it wasn't well positioned for the lifts. The Aire in Saint-Gervais was beautifully situated above a steep ravine in a very picturesque walking area, within easy walking distance of the lovely town with a spa. There was adjacent access to ski lifts and even a rack-and-pinion railway all the way up to Mont Blanc should you fancy a day out on foot or with a board. They used the *flot bleu* system of motorhome service point here in which you purchase electric and/or water tokens from the local tourist information centre and take turns to park up near the machine where there are several sockets, enabling it to serve more than one vehicle at a time. Apart from this expense the Aire was free, a very good deal really when all around people are paying a fortune for package holidays.

Ski-wise Geoff ripped some powder for the first few days (this is a good thing!), and his ankle seemed to have made a full recovery. But then a dodgy meal laid him up in bed feeling very ill for two days with food poisoning. He swore blind he didn't poison himself but, given the list of disasters in my absence, I wasn't sure I believed him. Now, illness in a van is almost inevitable when travelling for any length of time. But it is one of those situations you probably hardly think about until it happens, and that's when you discover just how different it is to being ill in the familiar surroundings of your own home. Being on his own at this point, Geoff still had to take care of basic maintenance of the van in these cold conditions, ensuring that he had water on board, that the waste tank didn't freeze, and so on. Forgive me for sharing too much information here, but he might have benefitted from being better prepared.

Just as you rush to the bathroom overcome with sickness is not the best time to realise that your toilet is basically just an open hole into a cassette, which is likely to already contain other bodily fluids at which you do not want to look as you retch. Nor do you want to risk splash-back. Next time, maybe try the sink? Well, before you rush there, remember that anything that goes down the sink gets stored in your wastewater tank until the next time you empty it, so unless you put the plug into the plughole, certainly in hot weather you are likely to be reunited with the smell of vomit next time you set the van in motion. Basically you are faced with the humiliation of removing your own puke in a bowl and disposing of it in the *flot bleu*. Nice, eh?

Poor old Geoff only discovered all this after the event when he was scooping plastic bottles of the stuff out of our blocked sink and carrying them across the snowy car park, still grey in the face, to dispose of them. This was the moment when he bumped into a British couple with the online name of 'Our Tours' whose informative website and printable packing lists had provided us with so much inspiration and value. Had he only been in a less compromised position than with a bottle of sick in each hand, he might have been able to thank them.

What was next on his list of calamities? Ah yes, poor Dotty joined him in the sickness epidemic, packing in her heating and thrusting him into sub-zero temperatures for the best part of two weeks. His initial diagnosis was that the heating fluid simply needed topping up, but a day later when Dotty spat the bright green fluid back out from an unknown place all over our carpet it seemed like time to get worried.

I've mentioned before that Geoff didn't know where to find anything in the van, but he did manage to find something to mop up with, seemingly by opening a cupboard and using the first thing that came to hand and then throwing it away. When he pointed out the bedding and towel cupboard, I enquired about exactly what had been thrown away, to which he replied: *I've no idea, I can't remember.* To this day I don't understand how you just cannot remember the item, undoubtedly of mine, that you disposed of, and it still remains a mystery. Clearly a case of out of sight, out of mind.

I don't think I fully appreciated how stressful this had been for him while I was in the warmth of balmy Swansea. At these temperatures it was extremely serious, because with water trapped in the system the pipes could freeze and burst, not to mention the fact that in a metal van it was pretty detrimental to Geoff's health to have no heating. Luckily we carried an electric fan heater, sufficient if run on full to maintain high enough temperatures in the van to prevent the pipes from becoming damaged, in the short term anyway. It did, though, mean several trips to the tourist information office to purchase a lot of electric tokens, which only lasted four hours and could only be inserted one at a time, meaning that Geoff couldn't be away from the van for any length of time and had to set alarms to get up in the middle of the night to put a new token in.

Limited Wi-Fi and a language barrier, at least when it comes to discussing heating systems, made finding a suitable repair centre very taxing. He literally set about driving from pillar to post, with each garage recommending somewhere else, some four hours in one direction, others four hours in the other direction, with the darned fridge door falling off on two more occasions and eventually causing irreparable damage. Even then he had to find a campsite with electric points and sit it out until they could fit him in, only to be told that the part he needed would take eight weeks to arrive. Eventually he resorted to ringing Alde, who made the heating system and who provided him with a list of qualified Alde mechanics in France. One advised him that they expected to have to replace the whole system at a cost of £2,000. The garage from which we had our warranty in the UK refused to accept financial responsibility for this unless we drove back to the UK for the repair. None of these options were feasible for us and it seemed it might all take months. With nothing to lose, Geoff continued to look farther afield for a specialist and eventually found a very helpful English-speaking German mechanic a few hours' drive away in Lyon. He set up a booking for 9 a.m. the morning after my return.

So our first night back together was tinged with the realisation of having to get up at the crack of dawn to drive to a specialist whose diagnosis would be the decider between continuing the trip or, NO, not giving up and going home, but buggering off to the sun somewhere and spending the rest of the six months without the need for heating.

We spent the night at a lovely campsite in nearby Albertville, south of Lake Annecy. Geoff had visited this site in my absence, in desperate need of electricity. At first sight of his troubled expression the owner had taken him under her wing. She had plied him with cookies and tea and within moments she was making telephone calls to various garages in an attempt to help. This was over a week ago and she seemed a little surprised to learn that we were still awaiting repairs. But she was as accommodating as ever and gave us a secret code so we could exit the barrier before they opened in the morning.

We hatched a plan to get Jackson to bed early to minimise the tantrum when he got rudely awoken at 6 a.m. This involved a long walk, or scooter in his case, along the river in Albertville, followed by a steep climb up to and around a medieval town called Conflans, followed by a museum, followed by a half-hour uphill climb to what Geoff translated on a signpost as saying *vineyard*, which I decided was a must as we had definitely earned a glass of wine. You've probably guessed already that the vineyard didn't exist, and I had to settle for a beer in a bar when we got back to town. Come 10 p.m. and, despite all our efforts, Jackson was still wide-awake watching *The Incredible Journey* on DVD.

I questioned what they had put in my beer when I spotted an elderly gentleman sitting on a bar stool and there, on the same barstool right next to him, was a pigeon. No, I wasn't hallucinating. Geoff asked a question in French and the chap explained that the bird had injured its leg. He then went on to elaborate on the point in French, of which I only understood one word, *mange* (eat), at which point Geoff had to pick my jaw up off the floor and explain to me that, no, the man wasn't going home to eat the bird, what he had said was that despite its bad leg the bird ate well. Coincidentally, five minutes later, we all left the bar at the same time. The pigeon was scooped up and perched on the man's hand as they walked through town a little ahead of us. We happened to walk past the car park just as they were driving out and he pulled up alongside us to point out the bird sitting comfortably on a fur cushion on the dashboard. He hadn't just rescued him from a gutter: he had actually brought this pigeon from his house for a walk and a pint in the pub.

So, what would the week ahead hold in store for us? Hopefully a quick repair to Dotty and then back to the snow. Or it might turn out to be a big job, we might be homeless for a few days and we might have to spend a few nights in a nice hotel, or something. What a damn shame.

The bad news was I didn't get that luxury stay in a hotel with a hot tub, after all. The good news was that thanks to the fabulous German mechanic Marcus, whose knowledge of this particular heating system was second to none, we were up and running again and soon basking in the heat, all for less than £300. He even extended his service to driving around the village looking for us when we failed to find his garage. All the time he worked on Dotty he taught us more about our motorhome than we ever knew. There is actually a serious point here. When you purchase any motorhome, particularly if it is your first, no matter what you write down and think you have understood, you won't realise how much you don't know until you are on your own and faced with a particular problem. It's almost impossible to learn enough about a vehicle of this nature in a three-hour slot on purchase day, and I think there is a gap in the market in the UK for specialist motorhome courses for owners to learn everything there is to know about the essential day-to-day running of the vehicle before they set off on their travels. Essentially this is what Marcus did for us.

He had to order parts, which meant we had a two-day wait without any heating. Now, in the middle of nowhere, or so it felt, finding an essential campsite with electricity for our fan heater was no easy feat. Campsites are like gold dust in France in February, unless you are in a ski resort, which is exactly where you don't want to be without an efficient heating system. Most campsites don't open until April. We managed to find one about 40 km away in Lyon and spent a day exploring the city.

Lyon is an attractive city at the junction of the Rhône and Saône. It is centred around the river, and if I had a penny for every time we crossed from one side of the river to the other to take in all the sites, I'd be a rich woman. I'm surprised it didn't burst its banks with the number of stones, and the odd cigarette butt when no stones were available, that Jackson threw in from all the bridges.

The city centre reflects two thousand years of history from Roman amphitheatres through Renaissance architecture to modern times. Crowning the hill with stunning panoramas over the city is the Basilica of Notre-Dame de Fourvière. We took the funicular up to admire the views. Then it was on to the Roman amphitheatre and a wonderful museum with an astounding display of local finds. I hate to admit the reason Jackson loved it, which was not for its educational value. He just felt the need to point out, to all nationalities, the willy on every statue in the museum.

In search of nourishment we headed back down to the old town and wandered through a maze of narrow streets flanked with old six-storey buildings and pavement cafés. When the waiter asked Jackson: *How are you?* the answer was: *Sausages*. A laugh all round, to which Jackson joined in with absolutely no idea what he was laughing at. So then the waiter said: *Oh, you would like sausages?*, to which Jackson replied: *No thank you, a crêpe*. I gave up.

The afternoon activity was a trip to the zoo culminating in a candy floss twice the size of Jackson's head. It dawned on us that day how these unexpected turns of events can bring you to places on your travels that you might otherwise have missed, which for me became one of the best parts of the whole experience. And as you will see, there were more to come. It just goes to show that there is little point in forward planning too much because these things are beyond your control. And I suspect it is much more fun tackling these situations freely than worrying about what you are missing by deviating from your preplanned schedule.

The return to the garage on Wednesday was successful and the job was completed, all bar one piece of tubing that had not arrived and for which we would have to return a week later because, although it wasn't essential at this moment, should it fail at some point in the future it would make much more sense to have it with us than to have to go through this whole process all over again. Not really being prepared for this news and realising that it would be pointless going too far only to return in a week, and with heavy snow forecast, which apparently had Geoff's name on it, another snap decision was made. Mountains, here we come.

Bearing in mind it was now 3 p.m. I did question Geoff's judgement when he suggested a drive. I assumed that we would find an Aire nearby, cook some tea and make a plan for tomorrow. But no, the snow was calling him, so we set off for Serre-Chevalier.

What should have been a simple journey turned into one of the most stressful so far, and I was only the passenger. The road was closed due to a rock fall. The diversion doubled our journey time and took us via the town of Gap, through very dramatic and rugged terrain. This might have been pleasant had it not been for the fact that it was dark, pelting down with snow, blowing a gale, we had a misted windscreen, a green toddler with a bucket on his lap, a stressed and tired driver and a hundred hairpins. Oh, and I nearly forgot to mention the bit that really got my nerves going, namely the sat nav warning us of forthcoming height restrictions half the height of our van. It was like living a nightmare with the prospect of another low tunnel around every next bend. Yet the whole time I pleaded with Geoff to turn around, which admittedly was not an option on this road, he just kept saying: *I wish that thing would shut the **** up!* For once I was relieved he was right and yet again

'@#£$ing sat nav', as it was now affectionately known, was talking rubbish. At 8 p.m. we admitted defeat and parked up in a supermarket car park in Gap and went to bed. Serre-Chevalier would have to wait until the morning.

We were up early the next day in a bid to escape the car park ahead of the shoppers. This paid off because it was a lovely sunny morning and we found we had a truly scenic drive ahead with plenty of time to stop and enjoy the views and even to stop for a coffee by a large lake, Serre-Ponçon. Here Jackson befriended a local cat on the long trek down the pebble beach to throw yet more stones into the water. The thrill never appears to wear off.

Little did we know, at this point, the significance of this lake in our journey when we said goodbye to the cat, never expecting to cross paths again. Farther into the drive we passed a perfectly still lake set amid trees and with a backdrop of snowy mountains. The sheer beauty of the reflections on the mirror-like surface silenced all three of us momentarily before I began shouting: *Stop, get the camera out!* and Dotty was swung into reverse. In the three seconds before Jackson hurled a stone in and messed up all the reflections in a rather arty way, we got some stunning photographs.

Then, as we walked all around the lake listening to the birdsong, it was another 'pinch me, I must be dreaming' moment. Back home we would be busy working, in the rain judging from reports we'd had from relatives, trudging around a muddy field with dogs and with me no doubt forming another list of pending jobs in my head. But no, we were here, simply enjoying life in all its glory, and it was real.

Next stop, when we finally dragged ourselves away from this beautiful spot, was La Salle-les-Alpes in Serre-Chevalier.

7. WAKING IN A WINTER WONDERLAND

MARCH

SERRE-CHEVALIER IS a lovely ski resort spread out over several villages along a single main road, making it all easily accessible from one spot. We had a choice of two Aires, one for eight euros per night and the other at a thermal baths for four euros.

Our plan was to look at both and choose, but laziness took over and we found ourselves parked at the first along with three other motorhomes. It was basically a car park right next to the chairlift, across the road from the shops and down the road from the bars and cafés. Most importantly it was next to a river, so Jackson could throw stones in whenever he got the urge. There were no facilities at this Aire but luckily we had a full tank of water and empty waste tanks and we were in a nice spot to utilise our solar panel. So we were set up for the best part of a week.

There was still plenty of daylight left and we needed to wear a certain toddler out fast. We wasted no time in heading off to the nursery slope down the road where Geoff and I exhausted ourselves by walking up and down pulling Jackson up on his skis then running ahead to catch him should he fail to stop at the bottom. Jackson may have wanted to disown us because we must have looked like a pair of idiots, but who cared, nobody knew us. I couldn't stop myself from laughing when Geoff suggested that Jackson should have an hour of practice to find his ski legs again after two weeks off. Jackson, staring at him as if he had just come from another planet, replied: *But I don't need to find my legs, they are here, look!*

After an hour we could walk no more and persuaded him to stop. Although we complimented him on his brilliance, the general consensus was that he had absolutely no clue how to control his speed and not a cat in hell's chance of stopping. So the next day, in case anyone recognised us, we used the nursery slope on the other side of the van, again having to hike up and down as we hadn't purchased a lift pass. We were swiftly astounded by the progress Jackson made and in no time he was snow ploughing and stopping at will.

For the afternoon we headed down to the town of Briançon in search of ski trousers for Jackson. Somehow we had lost his, probably left hanging in the drying room in Le Grand-Bornand along with the expensive door mat used as a kneeler during the chain-fitting saga and promptly left behind on the snow. His previous pair were an all-time bargain from a secondhand snow shop in Annecy. People trade in and swap outgrown equipment there and in the summer it offers the same service for mountain biking equipment. For children, who only wear something for one season before it becomes too small, it was perfect. Geoff had bought Jackson his first snowboard there for when he was a bit older and had treated himself to a good-quality Shaun Palmer snowboard with Burton bindings for 31 euros, while I had fitted myself out with skis and boots: much cheaper than hiring them at each resort. With these bargains in mind we now traipsed in and out of shops refusing to pay the extortionate price for a toddler's pair of trousers. Then, as luck would have it, we stumbled upon a charity shop, something new on this trip, full of ski wear, where we found an all-in-one suit for £5, albeit bright yellow, but at least we wouldn't lose him.

As it happens it was one of those just-in-time purchases. Snow was forecast for that night. I was like a child, opening the blinds on the van every hour just to check. Eventually around midnight I gave up disappointed when the car park was still bare. The next morning I was the first to wake and sensed the snow through the silence, the absence of any vehicles, birdsong or footsteps. I peeked out of the blinds and in a split second I had everyone awake in my excitement.

Nothing could have prepared us for the shock of opening our door to a foot and a half of fresh powder. The wheels of the van next to us had practically disappeared and it wasn't until its occupant got out and literally waded through it to fetch his shovel that I really appreciated the amount that had fallen. Then, as the French do, as does now, sadly, my husband, he proceeded to spend the next hour clearing snow away. It soon became apparent that they needed to leave that day, so they had a valid reason. Geoff, on the other hand, shovelled all the snow from all four sides of our van right down to bare tarmac and then stood on the roof sweeping it off straight back down onto the already cleared bits ready to be cleared again, though we weren't going anywhere. According to him it was an essential rule of motorhoming never to allow your vehicle to become coated in ice for fear of damage to the solar panel, satellite dish or tyres. I didn't ask any questions, considering myself to be ignorant about motorhomes, and Jackson and I built a giant snowman instead. More accurately I should say that I had a vision for this snowman and every time Jackson threatened to hinder it I sent him off to do something else. Bless him, he had his favourite toy snowplough out and was happily shovelling snow. This toy had survived the return journey to Swansea from France so that he could show it off when we visited my sister, but now irony was about to come into play. I parked the precious snowplough safely on the snow in front of the motorhome where we would be able to find it and then Jackson and I set off in search of eyes and buttons for our snowman. That was the exact moment that our neighbour returned leading a massive snow plough to our car park to clear a path for him to drive his motorhome out. In an instant, while we watched on helplessly, Jackson's snowplough was scooped up and deposited under six feet of snow. This was followed by tears and then by a demand for a toy piste-basher to replace it.

The rest of the day was spent walking and playing in the snow. Both conditions and visibility would have been difficult on the mountain. I will never forget this experience and will probably never encounter this amount of fresh snow again. I cannot imagine what was going through Jackson's mind. In some places he was up to his waist trying to walk. He had snowball fights. He sledged. He looked for animal prints and drank hot chocolate. It must have impacted his memory forever. I had a strong sense that anything was possible in a motorhome in a way I would never have believed a few months earlier.

That said, we awoke the next morning absolutely freezing, so cold in fact that it was hard to get our words out and we were almost afraid to venture out of bed. The heating had gone off in the night, broken again, we presumed. We managed to see the funny side when Geoff cut up a banana and it was semi frozen. When he opened the fridge it was warmer in there than in the van. We later discovered that the heating wasn't broken but the gas had frozen, which apparently can happen at temperatures of -16 or lower. We decided that in case it happened again we should move up the road later that day to a small site with electricity so we could run the heating without gas if necessary. But before we left our position right next to the ski lift we headed to the slopes, this time with lift passes.

Geoff enjoyed a morning of powder and peace while I watched Jackson on a nursery slope. He did really well, helped by the fact that there was a private lesson taking place in English and he just tagged on the back in the way only a three-year-old could get away with. An hour later he and I took the plunge and attempted a green run all the way down the mountain. It took over half an hour but he did it all on his own. To top it off it was Mother's Day and it really made my day. I could not have been prouder, especially when he gave me my Mother's Day present of a freshly picked icicle – I bet nobody else got one of them. I will be a bit less excited if he replaces it with an ice cube next year, though. He even said to me: *If there wasn't snow I would pick you a daisy for Mother's Day*. My heart melted on the spot.

We had lunch with Geoff in a mountain restaurant and sat on deckchairs outside in the snow eating chocolate cookies in the sun. Up to this point I'd had what could only be described as a perfect day. Then it was my turn for a ski. After asking Geoff what the drag lift next to me was like and distinctly hearing him say it was fine, I queued up. Alarm bells should have rung when I found myself laughing out loud at each person as they took off, I mean set off, no I mean took off, but NO, I innocently placed the poma between my legs, relaxed, waited for the gentle pull, then launched into thin air. My skis left the ground for a second and by sheer luck landed straight. And so the journey to hell began. I had never encountered a drag like this before. It went round bends, up what felt like an almost vertical slope and over bumps and ruts to the point where my knuckles were white from fear of the consequences if I fell off. I was out of sight of the piste and had no clue where it was, so I would be completely lost. I was also aware that I could invent a new game of human skittles, because one slip up from me might result in the one-by-one wiping out of whoever else was on the lift behind me when they encountered a tangled mess of skis and body sliding uncontrollably towards them.

With this picture clearly implanted on my brain I should have been relieved to reach the top and release the poma from my grip. In fact I was, but only momentarily. Then I found myself alone in blizzard conditions with almost no visibility. Somehow I managed to pick my way down the piste, struggling to even see the piste markers, and by the time I got back to Geoff and Jackson I had been well and truly put off the entire skiing experience.

I said angrily and in public to Geoff that he had told me the drag lift was fine. This wasn't the best moment for him to admit that he hadn't actually tried it but, as he helpfully put it: *A drag lift is a drag lift.* This is far from being the case and a closer look at the piste map highlighted that this was in fact a 'difficult' drag. I made two mental notes to myself. Never attempt another drag lift, full stop. And anyone who wants reliable information shouldn't ask their husband.

We all decided to head back down another green run as the snow was again setting in. Once more Jackson exceeded all our expectations. In fact it wasn't until we asked tourist information how long these runs were that we realised we had taken him from a 50-meter nursery slope to 10 km of skiing in one straight leap. Whoops!

We successfully resettled into a tiny site with electricity just up the road, for some peace of mind. It was a little more expensive and a bit disappointing, particularly for Jackson, because the British couple parked next to us in the previous Aire had been expecting family with children to join them the following day. And they must have thought us lightweights when they explained to us that this was their first year in a new van and that for the past nineteen years they had wild camped in this resort in a vehicle without any heating, relying on hot water bottles, a kettle and a gas cooker to keep warm. When their kids were young, they said, even the wet wipes would freeze overnight and the first one up in the morning would boil the kettle and light all the rings on the stove to take the chill out of the air. This all sounded way too hard core for us.

The view from our bedroom window when we woke up on our new site was astounding. We lay in bed with a cup of tea and the blinds open staring at a picture of white mountains and snow-laden trees. Being back on electric when you have managed without it for a while is a good opportunity to recharge all those electrical devices that would otherwise, in this weather, drain the battery and rely too heavily on solar. But it also requires you to re-programme your brain. I, for example, got the electric kettle out of the cupboard to save gas and had to boil it about four times before we got a cup of tea because without a whistle I kept forgetting I was trying to make tea.

As it turned out our new neighbours were also British and had been parked up here since December. They told us they returned every year for the entire ski season and bought a full season's lift pass.

That day I made up for all those two-minute showers I got in the van by spending a day at the thermal baths. It felt like an other-worldly experience. Sitting in a steaming hot tub outdoors in spectacular snowy scenery watching two eagles circling above us, I again felt suddenly overwhelmed at how lucky we were and realised that I had already exceeded all my expectations of this trip. It was another pivotal moment for me. The years of dreaming and wishing to experience all this were over. I had answered my questions about what it would feel like. That by itself was a dream fulfilled. It is only as I write this, finding myself rather surprisingly moved to tears and wanting desperately to express these emotions in their entirety to my reader, that I truly appreciate what a fundamentally life-changing moment this was for me.

This hadn't happened TO us. We had MADE it happen. Now I felt unstoppable. My life took on a whole new perspective. From early childhood I had been swept along in an inescapable current through education, then into working life and parenthood, to the brink of submerging my own child in this same current. And then I had leapt away from its grip and entered a whole new world. I felt the physical, as well as mental, impact of the freedom I had experienced these past few months and wished right there in the bubbles that I could reach out to all my friends and somehow pluck them from its grasp too. I realised it had taken me two months to reach this state of mind but also that there had been hints of it emerging from day one. I had discovered a part of myself that I had never known existed. Now I was certain that I would never let it escape. I might, like everyone else, go on to dream, but from this moment on if the dream was important enough, I vowed to let nothing stand in my way of following it.

The impact of a life change on this scale must be different for every individual. For me personally it transformed my priorities. The contrast between our 8 by 2 meter travelling house with a different garden every day and the type of living space I had become accustomed to my whole life, which had never seemed big enough, was mind blowing. I had quickly realised that the more space you have the more clutter you collect and that somehow this only served to entrap you. We had learned to survive, no, to thrive on the most minimal of material things. Anything that didn't fit into our living space no longer had any purpose in our life. All the cutlery and cooking utensils we ever needed fitted with ease into one small drawer and yet I had hauled four drawers full of unnecessary junk from house to house my entire life. I promised myself that I would de-clutter on an epic scale when I returned home.

The three of us felt closer than ever. The external pressures that cause us to take our stresses and tensions out on one another were long gone and, although we still yelled at each other over directions and map-reading, we instantly laughed about it. Although we had made choices and taken risks to make this trip possible, and might never be as financially secure as we had been when we owned our dog business, we had already made memories together to last a lifetime. All of this hit home at that precise moment in the spa with the eagles soaring above us, and that is why I will never forget a single detail of this experience.

8. TALES OF THE UNEXPECTED

R ENDERED PRONE BY a dose of something nasty the next day and unable to lift my head off the pillow, I certainly paid for my perfect day at the spa. Geoff and Jackson stationed themselves at the opposite end of the van as far away from my germs as possible and watched back-to-back DVDs while I recovered. But we were running low on gas. Still feeling queasy I had no choice but to get out of bed after lunch and sit out the drive back to Briançon with the window wide open for fresh air and a bottle of water to sip, praying all the while I could keep it down. I did, and luckily the fresh air worked wonders, because we were about to take on a much longer drive than planned.

It is striking how many of our decisions on this trip were made for us by circumstances beyond our control. As I have said before, I think we coped much better because we did not have a concrete plan. A friend of ours had said: *Every journey has a secret destination, unknown to the traveller.* We were about to discover ours.

Knowing we needed to be back in the garage on Friday, we assumed we would stay in Briançon until then. But when we arrived at the gas station there the LPG pump was out of order and the nearest garage selling it was an hour's drive away back in Gap. So there we had it, a decision made for us in an instance. Suddenly we were leaving Serre-Chevalier and making plans en route for our next stopover, which is how we ended up back at Serre-Ponçon, the lake with the cat.

All I can say is thank goodness for the broken pump in the mountains because, had it not been for that, we would have missed the most beautiful scenery yet on our trip. It was nearly sunset when we arrived. We took Jackson down to the shore with his scooter in the hope of catching a nice photograph and, what do you know, up turned the cat. Jackson decided to name him Salty, a lovely name except that it lived next door to the second largest manmade freshwater lake in Europe. Never mind, Salty needed no encouragement in joining us for tea, fresh ham and milk, and then he played with Jackson for nearly an hour chasing snowballs in the car park. Unsurprisingly there were tears, protests and requests to catnap Salty from one little boy, when we said our final farewell the next day.

For once that night we laid down a proper plan. Next morning we were up bright and early, with the van packed up and all prepared to drive to a small ski resort marked on the map, about an hour away, for Geoff to have an afternoon of snowboarding. Plans? Why bother? As we indicated right to leave the car park, a quick glance left up the road somehow tempted us to just grab a photo around the next bend before turning back. And then there was the next bend and the next, each view better than the last. Six hours later we had driven full circle around Lake Serre-Ponçon and arrived back where we had started, all ski plans aborted.

I honestly cannot do justice in words to the views we encountered. Suffice to say that at one point the sheer beauty of the scenery had me reaching for the tissues again. I'm not normally as emotional as this but it indicates the impact these sites were having on me. I just felt humbled and privileged to witness them and not one moment would be taken for granted.

At one end of the lake there is the most spectacular dam. Europe's largest earth dam, it took some 3,000 men 25 years to complete and it now produces the equivalent of all of the electricity used by the whole of the Alps. This sparked a good hour of questions from Jackson, including: *If I throw a stone in will it turn into electricity?* Believe you me, he threw stones in north, south, east and west, from bridges, cliffs and beaches. Even to this day he cannot pass a puddle without throwing a tantrum if no stone is available.

There were numerous campsites around the lake, all closed for the winter, which in a way made it even more special because we had it all to ourselves, although I imagine it is a hive of activity in the summer. The road we followed snaked around the hairpins rising above the lake, which took on a milky emerald appearance set amid snow-covered mountains and banked lower down by green fields peppered with spring flowers just bursting into bloom. Then we'd drop to within touching distance again along the pebble shores of the lake. Sometimes the colour of the water had us believing we were on a Mediterranean beach. Every bend brought out a different perspective and squeals to stop for just one more photo.

We parked up and re-enacted *The Sound of Music*, unable to resist the impulse to run through a meadow full of flowers in the sunshine with the blue waters of the lake in the background. We then rustled up a picnic, and after, desperate to share our experience, we literally bombarded our poor friends and family with photographs of the day. Only at a later date when following someone else's blog did we appreciate how much less intoxicating than we'd imagined it is to sit at home in the rain after a hard day's work looking at somebody else's wonderful experience. We owe our apologies to so many!

Having finally completed the circuit we set off in the direction of Les Orres ski resort at about 3 p.m. It was a simple journey, just as well after the six hours' driving we'd already done, and at 4 p.m. we arrived at our next Aire, a huge car park with designated motorhome parking right next to the chair lift. The next day was Thursday and we had to be back at the garage with the van again by 9 a.m. on Friday. So Geoff headed for the slopes first thing while Jackson enjoyed a morning of scootering around the car park while I drew the short straw and cleaned the van so as to give the mechanic the impression that we did not live like pigs. When the work was all done and the van was respectable once again Jackson and I took a bus up to meet Geoff at a halfway point on the mountain for lunch in glorious sunshine.

I have to confess, not having made any use of the snow here, Les Orres is not a resort I would rate highly. For me the architecture is ugly, with tall buildings seemingly encircling you and making it feel dark, cold and claustrophobic. Geoff certainly saw the best side of the resort up on the slopes, but the contrast is worth bearing in mind if travelling with non-skiers.

Our original plan was to get the bus back down together ready for the drive back to the garage. But Geoff, of course, couldn't tear himself away without one last off-piste run. This turned out to be a mistake. He returned to us and Dotty completely exhausted with 'jelly legs', his muscles screaming for a break, only to be confronted by a very grumpy Jackson who had spent a couple of hours too long in a car park. It all made for a very stressful and long drive in the dark. But by 8.30 p.m. we made it to a village just ten minutes away from the garage where yet another supermarket car park became our home for the night. This one though had a recycling point at which locals seemingly recycled at all hours of the day and night, dropping glass bottles in one at a time, and we suffered constant noise. This also was the car park that housed right in its middle the security-lit unscreened urinals. One can only imagine some local council passing those architects' plans as a good idea. They'd have done better just to plant a tree with a sign saying *Toilet*.

Despite our lack of sleep it was all good news at the garage. Now, with the job complete and the heating back to full working order, following a little gentle persuasion that it might be in their own interest, we even had the promise of full reimbursement from the garage in the UK where we had purchased the van under warranty. We reflected that the past month had certainly been an ordeal at times but had made us stronger. We had been tested and come out the other end feeling able to handle most situations that life might throw at us.

A few practical words of advice might help others in similar situations. For most potential problems on your vehicle, if you make contact with a UK specialist first, as in our case with Alde UK, you can get comprehensive advice in English. They should be able to put you directly in touch with their head office – in Alde's case in Sweden – who again should have someone who can communicate well with you. They, in turn, will give you a list of specially trained mechanics in your area, wherever that may be. This is a much more effective approach than what we originally did, namely driving from one local garage to the next and picking up conflicting advice from each. A valuable lesson learned.

With all the driving of the past few days we decided to take it easy and head to Aix-les-Bains, a small thermal spa town on Bourget, another large lake about two hours away. We only intended staying for one night but the weather was beautiful, sunny and crisp, and the campsite perfect for relaxing. It just seemed a shame to rush, so we booked for three nights. This town seemed all geared up for sports, with Olympic-sized swimming pools indoors and outdoors, heated, on the shore of the lake. After ten lengths we both found muscles we hadn't known we owned. Jackson had his first experience of a diving block. Fearlessly he positioned himself in a wonderful diving stance at the deep end, impressing the lifeguards as much as us. Then he demonstrated the loudest belly flop you have ever heard. Unperturbed by the experience he repeated and repeated it until he resembled a lobster. Practice did nothing to improve his technique.

From swimming it was on to a long walk. The town had little to offer us aesthetically but there was no shortage of chocolate shops. Feeling we had earned a treat after all our exercise we opted for a tea shop-cum-chocolatier. We soon realised that the service and clientele were at a level of posh way above our station in life. As if to ram the point home, Jackson, halfway through stuffing his cheeks full of chocolate eggs, declared, at full volume: *I need a poo!* and then went on to spit out chocolate in a gale of laughter.

Next day our bikes got their first airing on the trip. Accessing them and all the other ever multiplying stuff in our garage turned out to be an ongoing ordeal, requiring much juggling through the changing seasons in order to both access things and drive safely without causing damage to the more delicate bits of equipment.

The route around the lake was fabulous but hard going in the wind. We swapped bikes halfway in order to share the load that was Lord Muck himself, sitting comfortably and weighing over two stones in his bike seat behind our saddle. In the end we had cycled about 18 km. It felt more like 180, though, and when I dismounted I invented a new walk. Triathlon completed and more cakes devoured, our impromptu stay was over. Now it was time to move.

9. IN THE SHADOW OF MONT BLANC

L EAVING THE LAKES behind we were heading in the general direction of Saint-Gervais. Our technique for planning a route had evolved into looking at the map for places of interest between A and B and then opting for the most interesting looking road to get us there. In this case our journey took us on the scenic route over the Massif des Bauges range of mountains and would lead us back down into Annecy again.

By now Annecy had become a second home to us and we had started to refer to it as 'base'. It dawned on us that it really is an ideal place to live, within easy reach of so many places. We even surprised ourselves at this point that we were still actually in France, not too far from where we had started two months previously. Since we aimed to cover a large part of Europe by July we knew that sooner rather than later we needed to drag ourselves away from the snow and mountains.

The drive was well worth the effort as the rolling green hills dotted with wooden chalets unfolded before us. We began climbing and winding our way back up towards the snow line again. We stopped for lunch at a tiny peaceful ski resort and ate outdoors in the blazing sun watching everyone skiing in jumpers due to the heat, while Jackson spent an hour digging in the snow with a café teaspoon. Then our route took us gradually down the other side of the mountains until the whole of Lake Annecy came into view.

We decided to stay the night at the lake but chose a different Aire as we were lucky enough to have arrived early. This one was set back a bit from the road, which reduced traffic noise significantly but also made it very popular. It was first come first served and you could stay for a maximum of 48 hours. Parking here totally free made us wonder why we are constantly subjected to such extortionate parking fees back home. Here we had a lakeside view within walking distance of the town, with even the option of a free bus. All this would boast quite a price tag in the UK even for a few hours, let alone two days. One rule we generally set ourselves is that whenever we enjoyed facilities as good as this we would try to spend money locally whether it be just a coffee or meal or a supermarket shop – though with the number of motorhomers attracted to these areas the local economies could hardly fail to benefit.

Once again we took an evening stroll along the lake and into the old town. It is never the same twice and that is why I like it so much. Seeing the sunset casting its warm colours across the watery town you can hardly help falling in love with the place. It holds special memories for Geoff and me as the first place we holidayed together when we met sixteen years before this trip, and it never lets us down.

The next morning we needed to change some currency before leaving. We repeated the walk along the lake. I made a point of dressing Jackson in his best jeans for photographs as the weather was glorious. I was thinking: *It's a straight path, how could he possibly get dirty?* I turned my back for a second and he'd tried to perform a trick by riding his scooter down and back up a slimy slipway and now he was lying in mud and green slimy water. We had no choice but to complete the walk to town with him looking like he had a bad case of dysentery.

Later that afternoon we arrived in Saint-Gervais, returning to the very same base camp where Geoff had endured both food poisoning and near hypothermia in our absence a month earlier, and just in time for afternoon tea. Returning to our van we noticed a few more British vans parked up. We got chatting and now discovered that we were not alone in being complete novices embarking on this sort of adventure. Trevor and Peta had bought their first motorhome in August and set off in January, learning from mistakes much like us. In fact their first mistake was pretty much instantaneous. Trevor had done his research into break-ins in motorhomes and decided to outsmart prospective thieves. The first meal they cooked in their brand new oven had them remarking on the fumes from the oven coating – until they found, served up with dinner, the charred remains of his new iPhone. All credit to Apple, who delivered a replacement to him within three days, all the way to a campsite in France.

Echoing our experience, Trevor and Peta had also encountered the diversion up the mountain hairpin road that had so petrified me previously. They, though, somehow actually reversed back down part of it out of sheer dread of what lay ahead. Now I feel we were heroes for having survived it. No doubt it helped that it was dark and snowing too hard for us to see through the windscreen, so I probably didn't see what they did.

Although it snowed heavily all night, we were at a fairly low altitude and it didn't settle. The fact that we couldn't actually see the mountain made us feel less guilty about deciding to visit the thermal baths for a bit of pampering. (Honestly, the things we put ourselves through for our children and all the inconvenience of relaxing in hot bubbles surrounded by mountains and woodland, all in pursuit of helping Jackson's eczema.) As I learned on this trip, every spa is different and the properties of its water differ and lend themselves to particular types of healing. In Saint-Gervais the mineral content is renowned for treating skin conditions, though to be honest they smelled of poo. You did get used to it because, after initially gagging when you opened the door into reception and asked yourself the inevitable question of how much these people must be paid to work in such a stench, it quickly faded. That aside, it was pure luxury, a maze of waterways sweeping you along in the current and leading you to dead-end pools, each with a different bubble experience working your muscles from head to toe, including one pool that either I was the wrong height for or was intended as some form of colonic irrigation. After this we sat there hatching a plan for how we could earn a living from this lifestyle – maybe travelling the world reviewing spas?

We were among numerous Brits enjoying the experience, or in the case of one poor chap, being marched through the process by his wife, from steam rooms straight to ice-cold showers. It was when I overheard him saying: *But you know I can't even cope with the steam when I open the oven door, so do I really have to spend ten minutes in here, darling?* that I really felt his pain. Mind you, it wasn't as relaxing as it could have been for me either, what with Jackson swimming under water, jumping off walls and climbing all over me.

The next morning we were up and on the road again before breakfast. Geoff had arranged to meet his friend Carl again for a day off-piste in Les Contamines, half an hour away, and we were following a recommendation from Peta that there was a lovely campsite there with plenty to entertain Jackson. A wonderful day was had by all, Trevor and Peta joining Geoff and Carl and confirming my fears that he gets up to some pretty insane stuff when I'm not looking. Meanwhile Jackson and I had a fun-packed day starting with a snowy adventure playground with a zip wire, followed by a long picturesque walk into town following the river.

This went without complaint from Jackson who had quickly learned that each ski resort seemed to have the same shops, and now he had a plan. When his orange snowplough had got swallowed up last month he had set his mind on a green replacement. He rightly assumed that somewhere here there would be a shop stocking one with his name on it. Our timing was bad, though. We arrived at 12.10 p.m. and the shops were shut between 12 and 3.30 p.m. On display in the window was a splendid green snowplough, so now there was no deterring him and three hours had to be killed until they reopened. We had lunch out in the sun, much to Jackson's disgust as the table opposite had a fondue about which he made a big song and dance, declaring loudly that it stank. We idled away another hour in a swing park until finally the shops opened. Then we returned to the campsite by bus with green snowplough and happy child in tow, just in time to put all the washing on and look busy before Geoff returned.

This was to be our first night of entertaining in our van as we had invited Trevor and Peta to join us for a few drinks. Having lost track of time running between washing machines, dryers, showers and so on, the result was four bottles of wine consumed in a tip of a van, full of washing waiting to be put away, accompanied by copious amounts of eggy bread cooked at around 11 p.m. by Geoff in an attempt to soak up the alcohol, because neither of us had eaten. Now I learned some valuable lessons.

1. Never allow Geoff to cook after alcohol consumption. We all smelled of eggy bread for a week despite a late attempt to rectify the situation by remembering to open the air vent.

2. Never open the air vent if you are too incapacitated to remember to close it again – unless you enjoy waking up in temperatures well below zero.

3. Never allow yourself to progress or regress, depending on how you look at it, to the spins when you have to sleep four feet off the ground and negotiate a small foldable stool to get in and out of bed.

4. Don't expect too much from your skiing the next day.

That aside, I did make it to the slopes by 11 a.m. for a day of guiding by Peta. She had the patience of a saint, waiting for me at every junction, downgrading her skills by avoiding all drag lifts, black runs and moguls for me, and side-stepping back uphill to pull me up off the floor after I had a slight mishap on dismounting the chairlift. What a great day, though, the most skiing I had done since we arrived, because on my own I lacked confidence. Meanwhile Jackson had had his own excitement learning how to use a drag lift and skiing down the nursery slope unaided. Saying that, he almost caused Geoff another heart attack after making the strategic error of putting him on the lift at the bottom and then attempting to run up the slope faster than the lift to help Jackson off at the top, a decision that might have been a result of the wine the night before. Thankfully the lift operator stepped in by offering to take control of the mount, which allowed Geoff time to get to the top and stand ready for the dismount.

We dined out that night in Trevor and Peta's van, and when we returned the gesture the following night we felt very ill equipped with our non-matching plastic plates and plastic tumblers. In contrast, in their brand-new, still-smelling-of-fresh-leather motorhome we felt like we were in a hotel as we enjoyed a fantastic prawn curry on china plates with proper glasses. For most motorhomers this entertaining scenario is a nightly occurrence, but in many ways we were glad to have Jackson as a very good reason for not partaking, as a general rule. It wasn't just about the expense and the probable health issues following month after month of consuming alcohol at this volume. We also thoroughly enjoyed our family time, pyjamas on, feet up, shut the cold dark nights outside and watch a DVD together. That way the times we did join in for an occasional evening of excess were all the more special and appreciated. And as the weather changed and the days grew longer we could envisage ahead of us many an evening sat out under the stars with fellow travellers. But it was different in the depths of winter.

After a second trip to the thermal baths the next day we took a quick ride on the vintage Mont Blanc rack-and-pinion mountain railway up to Saint-Gervais. Then we did the steep woodland walk back down to the van at the baths. In the evening we socialised in our van with our new friends over the rugby match on TV.

The next day we said goodbye and headed up the road to Les Carroz to catch up with some Swansea friends who were there on holiday. Although not a long drive it was a hazardous ascent to the resort around hairpins so severe that they showed up as a solid pink blob on the sat nav, giving the impression that we were turning 360 degrees on ourselves. What's more, the rock overhang was so wide and low that we had to take some of the bends on the wrong side of the road, which, what with the constant fear of the mountain coming down on our heads, made for a tiring journey and hardly inspired me to try my hand at driving any time soon.

After some three circuits of the town we managed to park up in a swimming pool car park along with a couple of other motorhomes, assured by locals that this was accepted and free. We then met Hugh and Ali for a pub meal. It was a strange feeling spending time with people from back home, knowing that this was their week off work and realising that their mindset was completely different from ours. They had experienced the build-up to their holiday and were now in all the excitement of being here, but then before they knew it they would be back to normality, whereas we didn't fit any longer into any of that. Our build-up was long gone, our excitement lay in every day being in a new place, and we had no thoughts about it all ending any time soon.

I think it was here, when Geoff and I compared our thoughts, that we realised this had become a way of life for us, our equivalent to getting up at home and carrying on with our daily routine. Now we had reached a point where we had established a different form of routine in our van. There was the usual tidying, food shopping and maintenance to be done, but none of it felt like a chore these days and somehow it was just different. It felt neither like a holiday nor like being at home, but somewhere in between and very appealing. I now wonder how we must have come across to Hugh and Ali. Did they pick up on these differences like we did? At any rate, we spent three wonderful days with them thoroughly enjoying their company and catching up on all the gossip.

Les Carroz has the best nursery slope I have ever seen, long and smooth. There is a magic carpet to transport you effortlessly to the top, covered by a plastic tunnel illuminated by changing light sequences in the dark, protecting you from bad weather or, in good weather like when we were there, slowly cooking you by the time you get to the top. And all of this was free.

We booked Jackson a one-to-one lesson on the mountain, two hours without us, with an instructor actually on the pistes. He went off happily with Loie and when we collected him he was gushing with excitement. It turned out they had twice done a green, easy run, he had mastered a long drag lift by himself, and then they quickly progressed to the blue runs and again did two, top to bottom, which he insisted on repeating a third time with us just to demonstrate. Now, no kidding, he was telling me what to do with my skis when I made a turn. I realised I would need lessons if I was to keep up with him next year. All skied out, Hugh and Ali spent a day with us in Chamonix, window shopping because we couldn't afford to buy anything there, but it was a lovely place with spectacular views of Mont Blanc and the immense glacier above the town.

This was to be our last night in France for a few months. Excited as we were about the next stage of our journey, France had given us so much more than we'd expected, we had loved every minute and could have happily spent another few months there. There were so many places we hadn't visited and alternative routes we could have taken that would have pointed us towards completely different adventures – and this was winter, so even travelling an identical route would be different in summer.

We suddenly realised that if we never went home and travelled for the rest of our lives we would never see everything and would no doubt miss something amazing. Six months was never going to be enough. I felt a great hunger for it now and couldn't bear to think of driving past an area to which we might never return without exploring it. Not a single bit of me could think of any reason to go back home to what we had previously known when we had a whole world out there waiting to be discovered. Now I wished and wished that we had done this sooner and not the year before our son was due to start school.

So with the first chapter of our journey closed, we already knew that the next time we entered France we would feel very differently. It would signal the final stage of our trip, and no doubt thoughts of reality and school and work would be on our minds. But for now it was *Au revoir, France!* and *Buon giorno, Italia!*

10. LOST IN AOSTA

OPTING FOR THE easiest route into Italy, we drove to the Mont Blanc Tunnel. We could have chosen a more scenic route, but there are some seriously large mountains in the way and we figured that going through would be faster than going up and over. We didn't fancy a long drive as we'd had a busy few days previously, so we got ourselves really organised and not only found a campsite in the Aosta Valley, not far from the end of the tunnel, but we even phoned ahead and booked our space: a first for us.

It was only a short drive to the tunnel but we soon approached a sign telling us that the expected travel time was one hour per kilometre. The next sign said we had two kilometres to go. It's at such times that you really appreciate the benefits of travelling in a motorhome. We were barely crawling in the queue but while we looked down smugly on cars crammed to the roof with luggage and bored kids we revelled in the luxury of making a snack, a cuppa, using the loo whenever we wanted and giving Jackson a pile of toys to keep him happy. In fact we could have made money out of this. We should have opened a pop-up café/play centre/public toilet and earned some ice-cream money to spend in Italy. Had it gone on any longer we planned to take turns to go to bed...

There seemed to be police and customs officials everywhere and countless flashing lights passed us. After the events in Brussels a few days earlier and the history of this tunnel, it was a little unnerving not knowing whether there was an incident taking place ahead of us or this was just normal procedure. But when we eventually reached the pay station it became apparent that five lanes of queuing traffic were being merged into just one lane. We have since been told that this is a standard security procedure here.

All in all this was not the best moment to aggravate a driver who had sat there for two hours. But the woman at the toll decided to take Geoff on. She asked him the height of the van and then told him she wasn't sure she believed his answer. The difference in price was 100 euros so our champion was not about to submit. She brought out her measuring poles and managed to drop one into the side of the van, denting it and chipping the paint. Out leapt Geoff, heedless of my reminders about the hundreds of police just down the road. There was a brief confrontation during which she denied everything but graciously agreed we were the height Geoff had said, without measuring us. We weighed up the prospect of an extra 100 euros and decided to leave it at that.

We have a large selection of music onboard for all occasions, including Jackson's personalised CD of Christmas songs, which little did we realise at this point we would hear playing throughout Spain in the height of summer through open windows. I generally have no problem with Geoff's choice, but on this occasion Jackson and I were subjected to torture chamber conditions and forced to listen to what I can only describe as white noise, courtesy of Tangerine Dream. The terrible experience was magnified by the endless straight, dark, uninteresting tunnel surrounded by neon strip lighting hypnotising you and giving the impression that you were parting company with this world and being sucked into a black hole. Wouldn't a sane person have chosen something a little more upbeat for a tunnel? The only positive was that I genuinely couldn't distinguish between one track and the next so had no concept of time when we spotted the daylight of Italy ahead.

But now it was payback time. I will share the blame here with our renamed *#@*ing sat nav, as it was only after this incident that I learned there are different formats of coordinates, which apparently make a BIG difference – as in 2,000 metres of height! Until now by sheer luck we had used two books of Aires and campsites, both of which listed the coordinates in the same format. It turned out they can be written in degrees, minutes and seconds, or in degree decimal minutes, or even in decimal degrees, and you will have to take my word for it that you don't simply take out the decimal point and guess, as I did. It is way more complicated than that. Depending on what format you have chosen and pre-set for your sat nav, there are all sorts of divisions and multiplications of sixty and removal of decimal points to figure into your maths.

Thankfully Geoff had read all this up, and we even had in our travelling library Vicarious Media's incredibly useful guide *Go Motorhoming and Campervanning* by Chris Doree and Meli George. Their book not only instructs how to convert coordinates but is crammed full of useful information and tips on every aspect of motorhoming. I don't think we would have survived without it.

I must add that it isn't easy to convert coordinates amid a shouting match with your husband, bearing in mind that none of this came to light until we had reached the point of no return. In my defence, prior to realising my mistake, it all seemed feasible when the sat nav told us we were twenty minutes from our campsite, so I was completely confident when I instructed Geoff, against his better judgement, to leave the main road and head up a mountain road. The next part wasn't entirely my fault either, for I now referred back to the very brief description of the campsite in the book and saw it had a picture of a skier. So obviously it had to be up a mountain, then.

It felt like we were going backwards, with every hairpin adding another minute to our arrival time. Jackson, bless him, was in a right tizz in the back, trying to argue the very valid point that if I told him five minutes ago that we only had five minutes to our destination, how could I be saying now that we had ten minutes? But we couldn't turn round even if we wanted to, and so we continued ever upwards. When we finally got the flag up on the screen to show our destination was close our hopes were instantly shattered when the voice came back with: *In a quarter-mile navigate OFF ROAD!!* I was thinking: *WTF, who even knew that statement existed in a sat nav's vocabulary?* Geoff dumped the van in a lay-by of sorts, hardly necessary as there was more chance of flying to the moon than meeting another car up there, and went off to explore. It was almost as if he still believed there might really be a campsite somewhere up here, but in reality had probably just gone off to swear loudly about his incompetent wife somewhere out of Jackson's range. Meanwhile, thinking I should try to rectify the situation, I started messing about with the sat nav, which is when I discovered that coordinates have to be entered in a different format according to which book you are using. I changed the setting, re-entered the coordinates and bingo, the campsite now appeared back down in the valley where we had started, where Geoff had instinctively felt it should be. Not only that but it also confirmed that the address matched the one in the book, a minor detail I had previously failed to notice. I kept quiet about this when Geoff eventually returned with photos of deserted wooden shacks with snow all the way up to the roof.

We did a twenty-point turn and made the journey back down the hairpins in silence except for the odd groan from Jackson: *I feel sick, are these hairy pins?* — as he called them. *No, darling, they are just bends so you can't really feel sick!* For reasons that at this point I thought best not to disagree with, Geoff decided not to go to our chosen campsite after all, despite the fact that we were booked in and it was now safely and accurately highlighted on our sat nav. Instead, and crucially on HIS instruction, we were to go to one that he had read about that morning, a bit farther along the valley towards Aosta. This time I entered the coordinates, double-checked the address and soon we arrived, bang on target. There was just one problem: neither of us had read the bit that said: *Opening in May*. I confess I felt a huge sense of reprieve and we both ended up laughing about it.

This was the last campsite in our book as we had left home on the assumption that we would simply buy guides to all countries outside France as and when we got to them: a mistake, in hindsight. We thought it sensible to drive into Aosta itself and try to find the tourist office, having read that wild camping is not allowed in Italy and knowing that we were fast running out of options.

By sheer accident we stumbled upon a sign on a roundabout to Pila, a ski resort about which our friend Carl had spoken fondly but which we hadn't been able to find on any map. The following words emanated direct from Geoff's mouth: *We'll just go a little way and see, but I don't want to drive up any more hairpins today.* OMG, it made my detour look like a walk in the park. It was pretty much vertical, with each hairpin affording us a magnificent but terrifying view of the tiny town below, and it went on and on and on, again with nowhere to turn around, until we found ourselves, completely unplanned, at the Pila ski resort.

Looking on the plus side, it was still daylight and we immediately fell in love with the place. We parked in a car park with signs everywhere saying *No motorhomes*, but somehow we felt allowed because alongside us was another motorhome, also British. A cup of tea later the owners turned up. It seemed that this resort was an old favourite of theirs and now they were on their honeymoon. Myself, I'd have annulled our marriage if Geoff had taken me skiing on honeymoon in a campervan, but each to their own. They had slept the previous night in this car park, but as the following day was Good Friday they suggested we follow them to another free car park hidden just off the road.

We turned a corner and entered the most spectacular Aire we had yet seen. It felt like we were on top of the world, at eye level with all the surrounding mountain tops, in a car park full of snow and immediately adjacent to a swing park. It was a photographer's paradise and I had visions of getting up at dawn to see the sun rise above the clouds. Sadly, after tea as the temperature dropped our blinking heating packed in again. We managed to relight it over and over but after a short time it would switch off again, and electricity was not on offer here. It was so frustrating to see all those other motorhomes coping perfectly well with these conditions. We couldn't really understand what they had that Dotty lacked.

We were enlightened by a phone call to our ever-helpful mechanic, Marcus, back in Albertville. It seemed that the LPG gas we buy direct from the pump for our heating in the UK is pretty much all propane, but elsewhere in Europe it can contain more butane, which can result in problems igniting at high altitude or at very low temperatures, both of which conditions applied right now. All the other vehicles were probably using propane cylinders, which had different properties and critically did not freeze. This was not a problem we could rectify as we were only equipped for LPG and could not accommodate cylinders, so we had to accept whatever mix was in the pump, which obviously contained too much butane for these conditions.

We have since learned that a conversion is possible to bypass this problem, though we haven't looked into the expense. I would say, though, that if you plan to use high-altitude sites in winter it is probably worth it. I have to say we found the whole gas subject a bit of a minefield and still do to this day. It seems to require much thought and research prior to planning any trip.

With no way of running the heating we could hardly risk the water tank freezing in the night. So unbelievably, given the comedy of errors we had already experienced that day, we had no choice but to drive back down the mountain at 10 p.m. in the dark, leaving the newlyweds to wonder where the hell we had vanished to by the morning – since we could hardly knock on their door late at night and disturb them...

Truth be told, we enjoyed every second of the descent as the view was astounding. In a black starlit sky it felt like we were circling in a plane above the twinkling lights of Aosta town below us. I have never seen anything like it and we could not stop remarking on it all the way down. I noted that the knee-height crash barrier was for show only and would not have prevented a tumbling motorhome from reaching the valley. Luckily Jackson slept throughout so there was no sickness, though he must have felt like he had dreamt about the swing park when he opened his eyes in the morning.

This drive and the Aire that we nearly got to stay in at the top of the mountain stand out as one of the best of our entire journey and we have every intention of returning there one day for those sunrise photographs. And despite all the tortured events of this day, its story has been told and retold and holds so many funny memories for us. Hopefully it will help our fellow motorhomers, all of whom experience days like this, feel they're in good company.

Back at the bottom we told ourselves: *To hell with the 'no wild camping in Italy' rule, we're going to the cable-car park at the base.* We pulled in there to find another dozen motorhomes doing the same thing and, during the four nights we went on to sleep there completely free of charge, we never encountered a single problem. So ended one epic day.

Shattered after such an eventful day we slept peacefully in the car park that night. Unsurprisingly, it being Good Friday, we were rudely awoken by the arrival of no less than 300 cars and the clattering of skis and plastic boots thudding around the van at the ungodly hour of 8 a.m. Knowing when we were beaten, we decided to explore the old town, which was just opposite.

We were surprised to find ourselves instantly immersed in Roman ruins, including an impressive amphitheatre, all cleverly mapped out on various trails should you wish to follow them. We opted for the casual 'wander through the winding narrow streets full of shops and cafés and accidentally stumble upon surprises' approach.

Within the old town walls there was something for everyone and definitely the largest selection of ice creams I had ever seen. We set ourselves a challenge, unwittingly at the time, of seeing how many different flavours we could sample during our stay in Italy. It is because of this place and that challenge that I have now joined a slimming club. Jackson, of course, went straight for the chocolate flavour, the one designed to be the most noticeable on his clothes. Given the immense size of the scoop he was served, before long he looked like he had rolled in chocolate, a spectacular mess. His teeth were the only clean bit of him when he beamed a smile of the purest satisfaction. We had to sit on a bench and go through half a packet of wet wipes before we dared to enter another shop.

I don't know how he pulls it off, but it quickly became apparent that wherever we went Jackson would leave with a gift from someone: a chocolate Easter egg in one shop, which no doubt cost more than the bread we bought from them, biscuits in a café, a free doughnut in a coffee shop, and the list goes on. I think it was his blonde hair and blue eyes that clinched it every time, and the Italians do love kids. Thankfully it was a great incentive to persuade him to try out some Italian and soon, *Grazie*, *Ciao ciao* and *Buon giorno* were added to his vocabulary.

We needed to start learning ourselves because Geoff ordered a *latte* and was so excited when he saw it, after struggling to get a cup of coffee larger than an egg cup anywhere in France, so you can imagine his disappointment when his first sip revealed that in Italy this is hot milk. If you want any caffeine in it you have to ask for a *cafe con latte*. It's the complete opposite of France where you get about four shots of caffeine but never any milk.

Next it was a drive farther down the valley in search of a castle for Jackson to visit. No disappointments here. Looking at the map it was like a valley of the castles. He wanted to see them all, but in fact Fénis Castle, the first one we reached, was so impressive we didn't need to look any further. We purchased tickets, unable to understand a single word the lady said, and two minutes later we were being escorted back out through the gate as it became apparent that you could only visit on a guided tour, for which we had to wait half an hour, and which was all in Italian. It was still great fun, though, and to be honest Jackson and I probably wouldn't have paid any more attention had it been in English.

A walk a little farther down the valley, partly for fear of arriving back in our car park before all the skiers had left and having to manoeuvre Dotty through the mayhem, we found the town of Saint-Vincent, home to a massive casino and thermal baths and with chocolate shops to die for. I photographed the Easter eggs in the windows, calling Geoff back each time to show him while passing blatant hints such as: *I think I will have to treat myself to an Easter egg this year as they are too special to miss!* All to no avail, and I ended up with a few mini bars of chocolate.

Next morning we joined the chaos in the car park, a bit later this time, more like 11 a.m., but it was still heaving. We took the longest cable car ride imaginable all the way to the top with spectacular views on the way up, especially the view of hairpin alley, which we had already twice experienced at ground level. I now wonder why anyone bothers to drive up at all when they can park in town for the same price. They don't know how lucky they are – we never found a single car park in France that you had to pay for, and likewise with Italy, at least so far.

We successfully attempted our first chair lift with Jackson in our company. I would never do it on my own and left it to Geoff to lift him on and off, having enough problems of my own dealing with my skis, never mind a toddler. I felt very uneasy about having him up so high as he could have easily fallen out if he slid off the seat. It was a fine balance between keeping him safe and not putting the fear of God into him. He coped perfectly well, as he did with the blue run back down, and immediately asked to do it all again.

Later in the morning we encountered a properly difficult blue, icy and far from easy by my standards and clearly too much for Jackson. Yet I was very impressed by his courage and determination. He fell and got up, fell and got up, listened to advice and tried ever so hard. He just didn't have the strength in his little legs to dig the edges of his skis in and it was steep and icy, yet he made it to the bottom unperturbed. His legs must have been killing him, although he wouldn't admit it, and we decided to call it a day for him, allowing him to have four hours solid in the swing park in the snow while Geoff and I each had a couple of hours on the slopes.

I had my own scare on a red run when, at the meeting of three pistes, everyone had to wait for a helicopter to land and take a casualty off the mountain. This gave me time to take in how steep the slope immediately in front of me was when the consequences of getting it wrong were being demonstrated before my eyes. By the time they let us go, I swear I'd forgotten how to ski. That night I had to be administered wine purely for medicinal purposes.

A combination of wine, fresh air and exhaustion led to a huge mess all over our van, as we literally threw everything off the bed into the front of the van and then everything off the table joined all the dirty dishes that we were too lazy to wash that night. Jackson was first to wake on Easter Sunday and remarks of: *Wake up, the Easter Bunny has left an egg in our bed* were immediately followed by: *Oh no, a disaster, the Easter Bunny has made a terrible mess all over our van, he's chucked stuff everywhere!* Geoff and I joined in blaming it all on the poor Easter Bunny and we both fed our hangovers with chocolate for breakfast before tackling last night's mess.

After our late start we hopped aboard our bikes, one of us with Jackson perched in his seat behind carrying a bag of laundry on his lap and attempting to peer over the top, the other with two bags of washing dangling from the handle bars, as we rode into town in search of a laundrette. Over a cake, a while-your-clothes-dry treat, we discussed a signpost we had passed for Cogne. Geoff seemed to think this must be the area he had been looking down on from a ridge on one of his off-piste expeditions from Pila when he had spotted ski lifts. So, with little else planned for today, we thought we would drive up and take a look.

It turned out to be a dead-end valley, a really tight but interesting drive following a snowy stream bordered on either side by very steep cliffs. We spotted two chamois deer standing high on a slope in the snow. Since the start of our trip we had kept a list of all the birds and animals we could identify and this was something to add to it. Already the list was incredibly long and varied and we were still only in winter.

We ended up in a village where the streets were barely wide enough for an ordinary car, never mind our behemoth. Luckily there was a sign for motorhome parking just left of the village. As we rounded the corner we were astonished to find no less than fifty motorhomes, all hooked up electrically with a full service area, in the last place on earth you'd expect. I still don't know what they knew that we didn't, as the piste map indicated that the ski area here was only tiny, although a lot of cross-country skiing was on offer.

The office was only open from 6 to 8 p.m., so we did the cheeky thing of emptying and refilling all the water and waste tanks and then helped ourselves to a pitch and hooked up, using every available socket in the van to charge everything we had on board from shavers to laptops while we went hunting for food in the village. We respectfully returned to settle the electricity bill with the office, well within the stated times. It was still locked, so we quietly unhooked and drove off all charged up and clean, for free. I'm embarrassed to admit it but this was actually the second time we had got away with it. In Les Carroz we drove to an emptying area where we had to buy a token for five euros to open the *flot bleu* and use the facility. But there was no instruction about where to purchase the token, and a brief walk across the road revealed a proper campsite with beautiful showers and toilets. We took turns to sneak in, wearing slippers to look like we were staying there, enjoyed hot showers, a hair dryer, and then, just to add insult to injury, Geoff walked over with our toilet cassette and emptied it in their chemical toilet facility, all free of charge. Our luck would soon run out, no doubt.

On the bank holiday Monday we made another early start to escape the car park and drove farther down the valley to Forte Di Bard, a castle perched high on a cliff, which, just then, was home to the National Wildlife Photographer of the Year exhibition. It was a major challenge trying to park since everyone seemed to have had the same idea, but it was well worth the effort. The castle and location were spectacular, with a series of funiculars taking you up to each level to make it all the more exciting. The photographs in the exhibition were stunning and we were lucky enough to meet the parents of the previous winner and see his work from all around the world. They lived in this area and he had grown up here, undoubtedly being inspired by the magnificent scenery and wildlife enveloping his childhood. It seemed unbelievable to think that someone could have been lucky enough to have witnessed all this and captured it so beautifully, let alone filled whole books with his images. Like me, he had a degree in Zoology – so where did I go wrong?

We also found an interesting sculpture trail. There was no available explanation in English, so we named it ourselves: 'A Penis For Every-one'. I'll leave the rest to your imagination and just say it was different, really very different, and the sculptor or sculptors had certainly paid particular attention to detailing specific body parts, much to Jackson's amusement.

Now it was time for one of the Spontaneous Parr Decisions (SPDs), yet again. We were about to pull out of a junction onto the main road back to Pila when Geoff said: *We could just move on somewhere else now instead of driving all the way back to the car park.* There were no problems with that except that we still didn't have a detailed Italian map and only one campsite book with no list of Aires. There is nothing quite like an SPD late in the day when you are already tired, when a completely unthought-through decision can raise stress levels, yet in a strange way they always added to the excitement. At any rate, that was goodbye to Aosta and time to head for the lakes.

A few hours later in the dark, on the verge of an argument, since not surprisingly we couldn't find an Aire anywhere, we pulled into a car park behind a hotel just off the motorway and full of lorries. The two golden rules of wild camping are: (1) never use motorway Aires and (2) lorry drivers (forgive me if I offend someone here, but it is a quote from our guidebook) are the most commonly convicted thieves. So of course we chose a combination of both. For some irrational reason it felt safe because every lorry was British.

Being too tired to cook, we ate at the hotel buffet and then had an attempt at an early night. What a joke! That was when the live band started and the van began to literally bounce, and I can assure you it wasn't us... It went on until 2 a.m. after which there was a noise, which I truly thought was a drum solo. After ten minutes, though, I realised it was a lorry refrigeration system or generator, which meant it would last all night. Then at 5 a.m. the engines began warming up for a good half-hour while the drivers clanked around tightening chains before they began to move, by which time those that had chosen to drive through the night were beginning to arrive for their sleep. Now to my book another rule of wild camping has been added: (3) never, ever, *ever* sleep in a lorry park unless you are comatosed first!

11.THE ITALIAN LAKES

FOLLOWING A TERRIBLE night we headed for the region of Northern Italy known as Ispra, home to Lake Como and Lake Orta, with Lake Maggiore farther to the east, as well as one or two very small ones. They are all within easy distance of one another, the first being Orta, one of the smaller, less developed lakes, which appealed to us. In fact it is surprising how few people speak of this lake. It seems that the Milanese are reluctant to tell visitors about its beauty for fear of threatening it with the money-blighted commercialism of its bigger sisters, Como and Maggiore.

After yesterday's camping error we phoned ahead and booked a pitch for two nights in a little campsite on the lake. The drive was very pleasant through ever-changing countryside and past small farming towns and expensive villas, really different to France though equally attractive. Most noticeably the wooden chalets in the rural areas we had seen in France were here replaced by colourful stone houses with large verandas and the very traditional tile roofing so characteristic of Northern Italy. Everything seemed somehow more cramped here too. Although beautifully kept, the gardens were much smaller, while the villages seemed cluttered unlike the open-plan style of alpine France.

Then there were the roads, many in a poor state of repair. It seemed common practice to dig up a piece of road, then remove all the road works and leave it unsurfaced with no warning of an uneven road surface. Presumably this indicated the poor economic state of the country whereby they could not afford to do one job and do it well but instead did lots of minor repairs, none of them well. The roads were like patchwork with some repairs looking like they had been done with a teaspoon full of tarmac every few centimetres rather than resurfacing the whole thing properly. It made for a very bumpy, noisy journey.

Every time we encountered a particularly bad patch, I had to dash up the length of the van retrieving items that had bounced out of cupboards and off shelves onto the floor, which became an everyday occurrence in Italy. Conversation was often impossible as we were deafened by the rattling, and as for Italian drivers we all agreed that it would be a miracle if we made it out of Italy in one piece.

We made it to the lake where we spotted our first stork nesting on top of a telegraph pole. Entering our campsite via a small underpass from the main road, we immediately found ourselves on the grass right at the edge of the lake. It was an idyllic spot.

We sat in the van with the door open eating lunch and admiring the astounding view. Over the next two days it would become a ritual to save some of each meal to feed the fish, ducks and swans who would queue up outside our door.

To work off our lunch we set out on foot around the seven-kilometre peninsula. With Jackson on his scooter it went without complaint and we were glad of the exercise, although we were not prepared for the heat. Two days ago we had been in the snow with thermals on. Now here we were in T-shirt weather. I loved the change. It was the end of March but it felt like a summer's day back home.

On top of the hill, across the water from our campsite, was an array of enticingly beautiful buildings. Sacro Monte di San Francesco, the 'sacred mountain of Orta', is a collection of twenty small chapels dedicated to St Francis of Assisi. The grounds, on steep slopes and leading down to the town itself, were designed with great thought and attention to detail and filled with ancient trees and paths that led to special meditation spots. From the top we had stunning views over the lake and across to the small island of San Giulio, which we later visited by boat. The island had a magical enchanted appeal with a circular path winding around the Benedictine monastery where visitors were requested to walk in silent meditation. Fat chance in the company of the ever-questioning Jackson.

After the five-minute boat ride back to the mainland we whiled away the time in the picturesque old town, explored its narrow streets and drank coffee in the plaza overlooking the port, before following the lake back to the campsite. We could not decide whether it felt more like Sri Lanka or Portmeirion in North Wales. In contrast to this sleepy haven as soon as we approached our campsite along the main road, with no pavements on either side, our stress levels immediately shot up. Cars flew past us at ridiculously high speeds, regardless of the fact they could see three pedestrians including a young child on the road. One solitary car kindly slowed and tried to take a wide berth, only to be blasted by the horn of the car behind them, and was then overtaken right alongside us, forcing both them and us into the gutter.

But back at our van the beauty of this place seemed if anything to grow. A ghostly fog descended, enshrouding the tiny island before enveloping the entire lake. I busied myself with the camera before we tucked ourselves into the comfort of the van for the evening. We already knew that this place was different and somehow special, and now we realised we had fallen in love with it.

We awoke to a very dull day in contrast to the previous one, but undeterred we packed waterproofs and set off in the other direction for another walk. This time, though, we returned like drowned rats some hours later. Unfortunately a spell of intermittent bad weather was forecast for the coming week, so we decided to move on the following day, having already been lucky enough to catch the lake at its best.

We set off in poor visibility and without much of a plan, taking a route via the bottom half of Lake Maggiore, having seen from the map that this was the less built-up route. We now realise this was a mistake having been told that we missed some lovely scenery on the opposite side of the lake, although in this weather we probably couldn't have done it justice no matter which way we went. We found it difficult to get any good views and there were no stopping places for photographs. We were disappointed, having been spoiled by the beauty of Lake Orta and particularly as Maggiore was on the list of places to visit we had drawn up before leaving home. But enough people have persuaded us that we should return one day in better weather.

Next on our route was Lake Lugano. While trying to look for an Aire close to Varese, where we planned to visit a friend the following day, I thought I had stumbled upon a printing error in the camping book. Some of the campsites were listed in the Italy section of the book and others in the Switzerland section. I had never realised before how close we were to the border, which actually runs right through the centre of the lake. We encountered at least three border crossings on the way to our campsite.

We had high hopes for this site as it was one of the Camping International chain, which we had found to be of very high standard in the Alps. Unfortunately, in sharp contrast to the previous one, this site was very run down. It seemed like everyone except us lived on site permanently and had become oblivious to the state of their surroundings. The reception was particularly dated with a computer so old I scarcely remembered them looking like that, and the receptionist in a moth-eaten jumper was exceptionally unhelpful. It did, though, have a playground and a trampoline – if you didn't mind the rusty toys left lying around – and it was two minutes' walk from the lake.

The evening developed into a boat-building exercise thanks to a handy little book I had on board full of outdoor activities for children to suit all weathers. It was crammed with ideas from snow ornaments to wind chimes and we had some good fun with it. Jackson helped us to gather building materials and we returned with a selection of leaves and twigs for three different boats. I pretty much built all three but my reward was last choice for the race the next morning.

We had a brief post-boat-building evening stroll along the lake to a stretch of water separating the two countries so narrow that you could almost throw a stone from Italy to Switzerland. The difference between the two was uncomfortably plain to see. The banks on the Italian side were a stretch of basic cafés and ice cream shops in stark contrast to the luxury villas in their handsome grounds opposite, with their expensive cars out front and water garages underneath housing speed boats. And now we found that a very weird phenomenon had occurred in the ten minutes we had stood here. As we turned back and started to retrace our steps we saw that someone had highlighted every piece of dog mess (and it was shocking to see how much there was) along the path with a vast array of national flags on cocktail sticks. We never caught up with the phantom poo-labeller and I can only imagine what type of person this might have been. But good on them if it drew attention to the problem.

While on the subject of poo it is worth mentioning that another thing we noticed in Italy is that, although campsites and Aires were generally more expensive than we had been accustomed to, most did not supply toilet paper and you had to carry your own. On this far from luxurious site we even had to pay extra for hot water to shower. In the toilet cubicles there was a hand-held shower next to each toilet for those emergencies when you forgot the toilet roll. Inevitably Jackson found this a source of great amusement and would insist on picking it up like a telephone and shouting into it: *Who you gonna call? Ghostbusters! Who you gonna call? Bum wash!* He literally rolled about laughing at his own joke every time. I blame daddy for giving him these ideas.

The great boat race took place early the next day. We each named our boats. I had *Sticky Pinecones* after it took me an hour to clean the sap off my hands and our table. Jackson called his *Sticky Sticks* (presumably because it was made of sticks) and tough-guy Geoff named his *Ferrari*, and, ha ha, jinxed himself from that moment. According to Jackson's rules mine was a coastguard boat, his was a police boat and daddy's was a water taxi. Amazingly they all sailed well, which ruined the prize for 'last boat to sink' because we would have been there for a very long time. *Sticky Pinecones* had been chucked together last as by then I was over the boat-building thrill, so it had no proper sail and just drifted along behind the other two. *Sticky Sticks* set off fast, but *Ferrari* caught up once it turned itself around and the wind caught its sail. Geoff would have won hands down except that it got stuck behind *Sticky Sticks* and when it eventually broke free it set off at speed straight into the reeds: bad luck *Ferrari*! Jackson won and immediately declared the prize to be a bar of chocolate.

By now it was time to say goodbye to the lakes and make the short journey to Varese to stay for a few days with our friends from Swansea. We caught a glimpse of Lake Varese as we passed it but again in a vehicle like ours it was impossible to stop for photographs. The World Rowing Championships were due to take place on this lake in the summer and there was much evidence of team practice underway. But we felt we had seen the best first with Lake Orta and none of the others could match it.

Naomi and her family had moved to Italy a couple of years ago. Her husband Tom was in the armed forces and we had always promised to visit but had never quite made it. Practically on their doorstep now, we had phoned to ask whether we could call only to learn that they were relocating back to the UK a week later. Tom worked for NATO and was given a new position every few years, and Naomi and their two small boys, Harry and Rupert, moved with him. In her ever-optimistic style she welcomed us regardless of all the mayhem they had going on around them, and they entertained us warmly and gave us one of the best weeks of our trip.

We conveniently arrived at teatime on Friday enabling us to leave the van in the school car park just around the corner, where it remained until Sunday night when their neighbour kindly allowed us to use their drive. I cannot describe how beautiful Tom and Naomi's house was set amid a large garden, perfectly safe for the kids to burn off all their energy. They were surrounded by fields and woods, the sun was shining and I found myself envying the Italian life they led. The house itself was enormous and probably seemed even bigger due to having to be emptied a few days later. It was everything a home should be, bursting at the seams with evidence of children all around. Outside a huge veranda surrounded the house where we sat in the sun sipping prosecco while the boys played. I remember thinking I could live right here. Of course, it was paradise for Jackson, having friends to play with and, icing on the cake for him, they had trains, dinosaurs and Lego.

Over a bottle of wine or two and a pizza the enormity of the task facing Naomi and Tom began to dawn on us. It was Friday and the packers were arriving on Monday morning, at which point they would have to move into a hotel. Tom would drive back to London taking the dogs and plants on Thursday and Naomi would fly back with the kids on Friday ready to coordinate the unpacking at the other end ahead of Tom's arrival. Simple, really – and now, adding to the equation, they also had a house full of visitors. Already the place had begun to look worse for the presence of Jackson and any toys that may have been previously packed were now all over the floor. A new plan was agreed: drink more wine!

The following day was jam-packed. The three boys played in the garden in the sun for the best part of eight continuous hours. They had bike races, built sandcastles, swung high enough to grab branches on the tree, you name it, they did it. Geoff helped Tom dismantle furniture and remove nails and fill in holes in the walls, and Naomi and I walked the dogs through the woods with three kids on balance bikes in tow and rewarded ourselves with an ice cream before returning for her to continue packing. Geoff prepared a curry for everyone and then we were all invited next door for a kids' tea party with the neighbours, who were also in the forces, and their three children, as a bit of a farewell to Naomi, Tom, Harry and Rupert. Again the kids let rip and first it was cricket, then water fights and tree climbing. I don't think Jackson knew what had hit him, he'd barely seen children for months and now he was playing from morning till night.

We partook of aperitifs, but not like I know them. They lasted until 9 p.m. or later, on empty stomachs, so shall we say none of us were especially sober when we got back for the curry. It was such a great and memorable evening though with the two families, both of them military families who generally have to relocate every two years. From the little I learned about military life during those couple of days, I cannot give enough credit to Naomi and Emma. With their husbands regularly away, they have to step up to the plate and look after the kids, the pets and the house, and through all this they have to constantly make, part with and remake new friends, learn new languages, new schooling systems and set up home again and again. I could sense the sadness and loss that Naomi and Emma would feel after Monday and I imagined it would be even harder for the children.

For once it wasn't me that woke up with a bad head the next day but Jackson. I think he had overdone it in the sun and maybe not drunk enough fluid to compensate for all the playing and he was sick several times in the morning. Geoff went back to continue helping with the packing and Jackson slept most of the morning in the van while I sat close by with a bucket. He recovered by lunchtime but had an easy day and, when Naomi and Tom went off for another farewell drink in the evening, we all declined the offer to join them as we couldn't keep up with the pace. We opted instead for the luxury of a bath, our first in three months; better than alcohol.

Monday brought Naomi and Tom a setback when the packers had

got the wrong day and didn't turn up. Jackson and I kept out of the way as Harry and Rupert were in nursery. Geoff went over to help dismantle kids' garden toys and then Naomi took us to a local farm for lunch, briefly allowing herself time to breathe and take stock of the situation again. How they kept track of what the other was doing I will never know. There were dogs to be taken to the vets for flea treatments, a necessity before travelling back to the UK and, as if they didn't have enough on their plates, they had planned a full-on party to celebrate Harry's fourth birthday. I think Jackson felt like it was his birthday, playing with a whole play centre full of kids, bouncy castles, balloons, cake and slides: his idea of heaven.

All partied out, and that was true for all of us, it was time to bid farewell the next morning and leave Naomi and Tom at the mercy of the packers (which we have since learned did not go well), a flooded basement and, later, a filthy hotel room. There was just time to accept a delicious home-cooked breakfast of egg butties courtesy of Emma, whose drive we had been sleeping on, before we hit the road.

We left a lot lighter than we arrived thanks to our perfect timing, as Naomi and Tom smuggled all our ski equipment and snow clothing into their removal van with a plan to be reunited with it in London sometime. So it was time to accept that our winter sports were over for this trip and, now that we had created some space, we could shop for a table and a barbecue. At last spring was in the air!

12. FIRST ONE TO SPOT THE SEA

APRIL

W E PAID A brief visit to a local garage recommended by Tom, this time to have our fridge repaired. Surprisingly it was free of charge as it was just some dirt blocking the gas pipe. Or in hindsight maybe it wasn't, as it broke again a day later.

That done, we took a route towards Milan. We had taken a decision to head south due to bad weather being forecast for the north and, as we eventually planned to cross to Croatia, which meant we would at some later point pass again through this area, we decided to shelve our northern sightseeing in the hope of catching better weather in a month or two. It was already apparent that there was far too much to see in Italy for the time we had, so we made the tough but also easy decision to bypass Milan, big cities not being easy when you have a three-year-old in tow. Lots and lots more lay ahead of us that we simply couldn't afford to miss.

I say we bypassed Milan. Not quite. We managed to get hopelessly lost in its suburbs for what seemed like forever but eventually made it back to the motorway and recovered some of the time we had squandered. Alas I then squandered some more by suggesting we exit the motorway and choose a scenic route for the last part of our journey. An hour gone, hardly any distance covered, a hundred hairpins behind us, two sickly passengers and a grumpy driver later, we rejoined the motorway and followed it without any more nonsense all the way to La Spezia. Mental note one to myself: if the map indicates rapid height gain over a short distance, what it's saying, in plain English, is hairpins. Mental note two: if I do that again to Geoff I may not be around to finish this tale.

Our plan was to stay in Sarzana. Arriving there was a very special moment because, believe it or not, it was our first sight of the sea since arriving in France in January. I later worked out that it was the longest time in my life I had ever been away from the sea. Before then, living as I did within walking distance of an array of beaches, I had tended to take the sea for granted. Being quite a country girl, I rated mountains and greenery over sand and sea. But now I realised how much I had missed it.

As we approached the campsite we spotted two hoopoes flying alongside the van, something new to add to our list. The site was on the river just by its mouth, with lovely shaded pitches. First on our agenda was to rummage through the garage to find the box labelled 'summer clothes', all vacuum-packed as a space-saving measure, and swap the contents of our wardrobes and shoe box. Now all the routines we had finally drilled into ourselves to maintain a comfortable temperature inside Dotty had to be reversed. Instead of leaving all the blinds open to allow the sun to warm the inside, we had to remember to close everything to keep the sun out so that we could return to a cool living space. Then, once inside, we had to open every door, window and skylight to cool the van down as much as possible for bedtime. At this stage the duvet seemed a strong candidate for the nearest bin. Whereas Jackson, poor thing, had become accustomed to hearing demands of: *Shut the door, quick, you're letting the heat out!*, now he was suddenly assailed by: *WHAT are you doing? DON'T shut the door!* And soon the fly screens would become a necessity and we would be drumming that into him too.

Awaking to another very hot day we drove to Lerici, about half an hour away, to catch a boat to Porto Venere, the start of the Cinque Terre, meaning 'Five Lands'. It was slowly dawning on us that nothing is straightforward for tourists in Italy. Navigation is a nightmare because Italians seem averse to signposting anything. No matter how popular an attraction may be, usually the only signpost is when you actually get there, rendering it more of a reminder in case you've forgotten what you've spent the last hour driving in circles looking for. Next up, should you actually be lucky enough to find your destination, forget all thoughts of driving anywhere near it in a motorhome. The streets will inevitably get narrower and narrower. Make one wrong turn and all hell will break loose as you are sucked in with an ever-diminishing chance of ever turning round while all the time being honked at, sworn at and gestured at. And lest you think this is just personal bad driving skills that got us into these messes, I can guarantee, from the many stories we heard, that you will have this experience at least once.

What it seemed to teach Geoff was to be more aggressive and drive the way the Italians do. Don't give way to anyone. Sit between lanes in a traffic jam or they will squeeze alongside in the tiniest of gaps and then, should you wish to turn left or right two minutes along the road, well just forget it, they won't let you. Watching them at it was simultaneously petrifying, hilarious and unforgettable.

Then, should you be lucky enough to find a car park anywhere that allows motorhomes, you'll find you have to pay by the hour in advance. You'll also be expected to know precisely how long your expedition will take and woe betide you if you are a minute late. In Lerici, in the time it took us to get to a snacks stall in the car park to ask for change for the meter, try to decipher the rush of Italian and gestures that were an answer to my request, presume the answer was *No* and purchase a one-euro snack to get the necessary change, get a ticket for eight hours' parking and return to the van, the traffic warden was upon us. Then, to top it all off, we rushed to the boat, fearing that we might miss it, only to find that the card machine was broken. We were sent off into the maze of busy streets to find a cash machine, getting back by the skin of our teeth in time to jump aboard. Fortunately all the stress was well worth the effort.

The Cinque Terre comprises five small coastal villages on the Italian Riviera listed on the UNESCO World Heritage List. Set amid some of the most dramatic coastal scenery you will ever see, these brightly coloured fishing villages literally cling for life to the edge of rugged cliffs above the sea. Collectively they are home to some 4,000 inhabitants but they attract well over two million tourists a year from every part of the globe including unbelievable numbers of loud-voiced Americans.

The first stop for a change of boat was Porto Venere, where we got a glimpse of what to expect from the rest of the day. It was a small port with brightly coloured houses all along the front, so tall that they naturally form part of the fortress that protects the castle above. From there the rest of the trip was as flexible as we liked. We could stay on the boat all day or get on and off at any or each of the five villages. Boats sailed regularly so we could spend as little as half an hour at one village or while away most of the day there if we preferred. Or, for the energetic or mad, we could walk in the searing heat between the villages, a long hike up and down the hills separating each village. We were tempted by the obviously stunning views from inland, but we valued our legs more than our taste for adventure and the view from the boat gave us a completely different yet equally pleasing perspective without any of the pain. You could even catch a train through a series of interconnecting mountain tunnels.

As ever in steep little places one wondered how anyone ever got the building materials in originally. Did they have unlimited access to a helicopter? How did parents of young children manage with all the the steep inclines and steps? How was the rubbish collected? And actually, how were the houses all still standing in those precarious positions? What couldn't escape our attention was the touristy feel, the clear signs that these peaceful havens of old had been overrun by mass tourism, bringing with it all the inevitable tacky souvenir shacks. And this was still out of season. In the middle of summer it must be a hell hole.

We had started the day with a plan, because I am not a boat person and have been known to get seasick on a Lilo. We aimed to go as far as we could by boat before I felt sick, then get off and walk back. Obviously this was before we realised the terrain and distance involved, which ruled out the walking option. To my surprise, although we were on a boat going all the way to the farthest village, I felt great, perhaps because I had an American lady in my ear the whole way distracting me.

We disembarked and spent a few hours in Monterosso al Mare, had lunch in a pavement café overlooking the beach, wandered round the shops and streets packed with artists and crafts workers, and Jackson even had a paddle. There were several people swimming in the sea but at this time of year they must have been mad. Having glimpsed each village as we dropped people off along the way, we had made a mental note that Riomaggiore looked the most interesting and worth a stop. Jackson, though, had spent so long looking down at the bubbles in the wake of the boat that he felt sick, and we got off at the stop before. Instead we caught the train to Riomaggiore where we spent an hour eating calamari in a samba bar. A small and very vintage-looking fire engine came down the single cobbled street with its bell ringing and two firemen, who also looked vintage, running ahead, hurling all the roadwork and shop signs off the street onto the pavement while a third fireman rode on the outside of the fire engine hanging onto the door. We couldn't resist following this spectacle and when we found it deserted at the railway station, Jackson re-enacted the whole scene for us. We completed the journey by boat and arrived at our van with minutes to spare and the traffic warden waiting to pounce.

Back at the campsite we sat and contemplated the prospect of moving on to Pisa in the morning. The idea was to get an early start to give us time to get lost, park the van and catch a bus in to see the city. The obvious solution was to do most of the van preparations before turning in for bed.

By now we had pretty much perfected our routine, although I always enjoyed purposely forgetting to close one cupboard door or drawer purely for the sake of hearing Geoff tut as it flew open on the first bend. My duties included getting Jackson ready, which equated to at least five normal chores, preparing the inside of the van, setting up the sat nav and organising the maps. I was also not averse to fetching fresh water and emptying grey (shower and dish) water.

Emptying the toilet, though, remained firmly delegated to Geoff. We laughed at the common practice of French and German men in particular, sporting brightly coloured rubber gloves, who happily stood and engaged in full-blown conversation while continuously swilling the last bits of poo round and round in their cassette for anything up to half an hour. I always scrutinised them because rumour had it that some of them tended to stick the end of the toilet cassette right over the end of the fresh drinking water tap during this vigorous cleaning ritual, which was why we only drank bottled water and never ever allowed our water containers to come into contact with any taps. Anyway, I convinced Geoff from an early stage that these good manly citizens wouldn't think much of him if he sent his wife to do the job, and thus it remained and always will remain his job. Every time I see a woman doing it I silently cringe and pray he hasn't noticed.

Anyway, despite this little sermon about our cleaning and organisation agenda and the 'obvious solution' to get all of it done the night before we left for Pisa, we did absolutely none of any of it. As a result we were late leaving the next morning.

13. THE LEANING-OVER TOWER

IT'S ODD HOW when you expect the worst it often surprises you. We drove an hour to Pisa and right from the outskirts of the city there were signposts at every junction directing you with ease to an overnight parking area designated for motorhomes, albeit a two-kilometre walk to the city centre, but hey, we needed some exercise after all the Italian treats we'd insisted on sampling. Getting parked there was another matter as there was a barrier system and a coin machine with separate prices for daytime and nighttime hours, electricity etc., with all the instructions in Italian so I might as well have been blind. It seemed we needed to purchase a day ticket until late evening, then there was no extra charge until 7.30 a.m. when we would have to purchase another ticket. We sat outside the closed office, ticket in hand and clueless for a while before realising that logically the sign next to the barrier must translate to 'lift it yourself and enter'.

No sooner had we parked than Jackson spotted kids by the van opposite. He got his scooter out and was immediately followed up and down by a three-year-old girl on her scooter and a five-year-old boy on his bike. They were a Belgian family who spoke excellent English and, while the kids burned off some energy and I packed the bag for Pisa sightseeing, Geoff got talking to the husband while his wife fed the six-month-old baby. It was great to meet people who encountered the same hurdles in getting out of the van at a reasonable hour as we did. It was already lunchtime and they too were trying to see Pisa, but shouts of: *Shoes on! Bikes away! Hurry up! Come and put sun cream on! Go to the toilet before we leave! Come on, I have asked you twice already!* were all to no avail and three times over in their case made us feel right at home. Eventually the flock was rounded up and we walked into Pisa together.

I'm not really sure what to make of Pisa. It's definitely not some-where I would like to live, it's not particularly pretty and it's very touristy and tacky, to the point of spoiling the experience. For some reason I expected the tower to dominate the skyline, so to find it tucked away behind loads of other buildings was a surprise. That said, I'm truly amazed that it is still standing. We couldn't climb it as they do not allow under-eights in, so we entertained ourselves by people-watching instead. I have to confess that after laughing at them all and passing some very rude remarks on their behaviour we joined in and did exactly the same as everyone else. And from that day on Jackson referred to it as 'The Leaning-over Tower', and we too adopted that name.

Selfie sticks are essential and fashionable tools here and if, like us, you don't own one, you're a nobody. No need to fret, though, you can choose from 300 different lookie lookie men trying to sell you one for anything from four to twenty euros, along with umbrellas, balloons, and of course genuine Ray-Bans.

But if you do possess a selfie stick it moves you on to another level. How interesting a pose can you strike up (instead of just asking one of the 10,000 people there to please take a photo of you)? We witnessed people balancing on top of fence posts on one leg, one arm stretched out, selfie stick in hand while the other arm tried to balance the body but also appear 'relaxed'. We watched a couple taking a selfie of themselves kissing in front of the tower. Eight attempts later all the signs of sincerity in their embrace had well and truly disappeared. Some old-fashioned souls rely on others to press the button, which does free up two hands to give the appearance of pushing the tower back up. But then you mustn't forget to turn around and push from the other side to see if it looks better pushing it over. Some smile, others look embarrassed, and some look as if they are having a poo because at no point are their hands actually in contact with any solid object: they're just stood in the middle of a crowd pushing thin air.

There were chains of people pushing, which could easily be confused for a conga dance. There were people standing in the middle of the pavement, both arms out embracing thin air with lips puckered, kissing what would be a miniature tower in the print because the photographer was lying on their back on the floor. Then, last but very far from least, there were the men who lay on the ground and photographed 'the leaning erection'. Oh, and the girl who perched on a stone pillar and opened her legs wide while rolling onto her back, legs in the air. I don't even want to try to understand that one. All the same, the more we saw, the more we laughed and then we started doing it ourselves, and that in the end is what we'll remember about Pisa in years to come.

We hung around until dusk expecting to see the tower lit up but discovered that this is one tourist gimmick they hadn't thought of, which was a bit disappointing. We weren't the only ones, for even in the dark people were still turning up for photos expecting a lit-up spectacle.

We ate out in a pavement café and had a brief walk around the rather nondescript city, trying to find an off-licence in anticipation of a sociable evening with the family opposite. We stumbled upon a corner shop with some very pricey wines on display. When we enquired if they had something local and cheap, the owner brought out an unlabelled bottle of red 'house wine' at four euros. Expecting vinegar, we purchased just the one bottle. Annoyingly it turned out to be the best bottle of wine we tasted anywhere on our eight-month trip and to this day we regret not going back for more the next morning.

Jackson went straight to sleep when we got back while we sat outside in the car park with our neighbours and a bottle or two or three and shared travel stories until the early hours. They had travelled far and wide in West Africa, Asia, India, Australia and New Zealand and hadn't changed their style since their kids had arrived. They went somewhere different every single school holiday and stayed anywhere, not just in campsites. One by one they ticked off new destinations they had explored. Hats off to them for leading a life to which I aspired. They didn't even return home to give birth and had one daughter with a Chinese passport and a son with an American one, enabling them to joke about the differing standards of maternity treatment in the two countries. Having had every intervention imaginable in America with her firstborn, she never even got an examination in China, where they don't believe in touching the mother or the unborn child and, like it or not, you just have to go it alone. In truth a few years down the line there seemed to be no difference in outcome.

We parted company at 2 a.m. with a piece of paper with some coordinates and a name, which we stuck on a map, as neither Geoff nor I could recall any part of the conversation that had involved coordinates. Needless to say we were not up by 7 a.m. to purchase a car park ticket but the attendant just lifted the barrier and asked no questions.

14. ART AND CHAOS

FROM PISA IT was straight on to another city, Florence. Feeling optimistic about finding an equally straightforward traffic system leading us to a motorhome-friendly car park ,we set off without having done too much research. This approach was a fast track to failure. While staying with our friends near Milan we had purchased a *Guida Camper Europa* guidebook to the Aires and campsites of Europe, hoping it would be on a par with the ones we already had for France and Spain and would see us through Italy and Croatia. But the most up-to-date version available was 2013 and clearly many sites had closed or relocated since it was written. I resolved in future to ensure that we brought all the necessary literature with us from the start of any trip.

Unlike Pisa there were absolutely no signs for motorhome parking on the approach. Consequently we drove almost all the way into the centre in three or four lanes of traffic, or six or seven if you count the drivers who drove between two lanes just to keep a constant eye on which one was faster. Scooters darted at speed, dodging traffic and not in the least perturbed by an eight-metre motorhome on their arse. I lost count of the number of times I jumped out of my skin, grabbing the edge of my seat and slamming the imaginary brake on as one suddenly dived back in almost right under our bumper to avoid oncoming traffic.

True to form, our sat nav coordinates took us to a place that very obviously in no way resembled a motorhome car park despite being listed in our book. Eventually, for fear of killing someone, we got our campsite book out and headed to a campsite in the village of Troghi, twenty kilometres southeast of Florence.

What a contrast! Now we glimpsed the Tuscany we had imagined. The road was quiet, taking us up into hills with fabulous views. It was early April and wildflowers were beginning to appear, which made for some stunning hedgerows. Whatever I said back in northern Italy about houses and villages appearing cramped, this wasn't the case in Tuscany.

Having had that earlier insight into Florence, we initially planned to catch a bus in and out from the campsite the following morning. But it would take an hour each way and, being a Saturday, would be busy. None of us felt ready for another hectic day, so we booked an extra night and instead opted for a nice leisurely day walking in the countryside. We had a map with a suggested ten-kilometre route but we intended turning back halfway. We packed a picnic, binoculars, camera and Jackson's bug-hunting kit. The sky was blue and cloudless and it was wonderful to feel the warmth of the sun on our skin as we strolled through vineyards and along country lanes amid a riot of colour from wildflowers in the hedgerows and birdsong dominating our senses. Vineyards merged into olive groves where farmers laboured to collect and burn the dead wood as the trees sprouted new growth.

Wildflower meadows alive with bees and butterflies made for some wonderful photographs as we continued on through farms and past a private castle and a lovely quaint little church. The only anticlimax was a random dog who ran at us wagging his tail, played with a stick until he had had enough, and then, as he left, gave Jackson a bite, enough to bruise and shake him.

Almost without noticing we did the whole route. We have the bug kit to thank for Jackson walking all the way without a grumble. This was the point when I fell in love with Tuscany, and now we were ready to tackle Florence.

In a snap decision we decided that the bus journey did not appeal. We found an Aire a few kilometres outside the city, in a quiet rural area with a bus stop adjacent and a regular service directly into the centre. I had even done my homework and converted the coordinates to the correct format, and all was perfect until five minutes before our destination. At that point we reached a roundabout in a village with a choice of five narrow roads, whereupon our infallible sat nav kindly picked up our van on the screen and moved it off road into the middle of nowhere, as if to say: *Work the rest out yourself!*

We went straight on and a minute later found ourselves in a mess trying to turn around after the road got too narrow. None of the other roads looked any wider and for some unknown reason our sat nav was still out of action. With nobody to ask and a real fear of getting stuck under a low bridge or something just as bad, we gave up and began driving back down the hill towards Florence again, all the way witnessing the sat nav informing us that we were not on a road, just in the middle of a green space going round and round. We later learned, from people whose sat nav clearly does a better job than ours, that we must have narrowly missed the Aire we wanted. Apparently boasting magnificent views over the city, it certainly does exist and wasn't far away from where we were, but it just wasn't meant to be. Instead we parked on the roadside farther down next to an Italian motorhome where we caught a bus into Florence free of charge, as we hadn't realised we needed to go elsewhere to purchase a ticket. After a few attempts to explain that he couldn't sell us a ticket, the driver gave up and allowed us on for nothing. We'd understood but sometimes more can be gained from acting stupid.

Our first stop was the Ponte Vecchio over the river, which was plain mad. Between trying not to trip over pavement artists all over the bridge chalking up the most brilliant pictures of the Mona Lisa, or mime artists so good you thought they were made of stone, you dared not let go of each other's hands for fear of being swept away in the crowds. There was contrast in the extreme, with a solid line of jewellery shops on both sides of the road dripping with gold so extortionately expensive that you hardly even dared glance in the windows as you picked your way through the lines of touts in the road with their arrays of fake sunglasses and key rings, who randomly splatted blobs of jelly by your shoe that quickly reformed into a pig or whatever it had started out as. And then there, in the middle of all this mayhem, were a Chinese couple having their wedding photos taken, with an entourage of white umbrella carriers and people pulling suitcases, which I assume were full of props. One photograph was taken almost shoulder to shoulder with Geoff who was in a world of his own admiring some paintings on a stall. Another was timed beautifully to incorporate a passing road sweeper. Tips for how to make an unusual wedding album?

Knowing Florence is famed for the best ice cream in the world, we made a very costly mistake. At the end of the bridge we walked into an ice cream shop, ordered three small cones, one scoop each and took a photo of the selection. Then, offering a ten euro note and expecting change, we heard the waiter say: *24 euros please!* Oops, I'm sure the F word slipped out rather loudly. For that price we made damn sure we sat at a table for Jackson to make his mess all over and used the toilet and the Wi-Fi. Oh, and we asked for tap water too.

The next stop was the Duomo, which overwhelmed me. I'd had no idea of its scale or detail. It resembled a really intricate wedding cake with tiers of pink, green and cream icing towering high over everything else in Florence. You cannot do justice to it with a camera, since because of its great size you cannot stand far enough back to fit it all into a picture. Forget the camera, you can spend hours just admiring its detail.

Because the Duomo was fully booked for the day we decided to climb the 419-step tower next door instead. As we had no intention of carrying Jackson all the way up, we declared it a race: the first to the top would be King of the Castle! No kidding, he won hands down and would have run up if we had let him. At the top we were in a caged walkway at eye level with the groups who climbed the Duomo opposite. They, though, didn't have the luxury of a cage, only a waist-high railing. There was no way on earth I would have done that. One person told us it was even worse on the inside section when you spiral around the inside of the dome close up with the ceiling fresco in a clear Perspex walkway, giving the feeling of no floor or railing. Ugh! I felt sick just at the thought.

That climb and a stroll around enjoying the sights was all we managed in Florence, but we felt satisfied. To see any of these cities properly we would clearly have needed to spend several days in each, as well as finding time for the commute in and out each day. For anyone planning to explore Florence and its like properly it is also advisable to put some serious effort into pre- planning and booking entry tickets in advance if they want to avoid long queues or sell-out disappointment.

Now that we knew we needed to purchase a bus ticket before catching the bus, we headed for the ticket office at the central bus station. Right idea, wrong result. The man told us it was a different company and we had to buy the ticket somewhere else. Further information was not forthcoming so we asked him to elaborate. *Outside at the post office on the right*, he appeared to say, but there was no sign of any post office, so I boarded another bus and asked the driver. All she said was: *At the bar*, and again when probed about where the bar was, her reply was vague: *Over there somewhere*. Eventually we found a passenger waiting at a bus stop who told us we had to go to the *giornalaio*, which means 'newsagent'. Now why didn't I think of that in the first place?

After that we had to go through the whole procedure all over again just to find out where to catch the darned bus. An hour later we finally made it back to the van and decided to move on from our roadside parking space to Vinci, about an hour away, where our plan was simply to recover.

15. UNDER THE TUSCAN SUN

PRIOR TO ARRIVING in Tuscany we had been looking through our DVD collection for something to watch with a bottle of wine. We chose *Under the Tuscan Sun* to see if it would give us any insight into Tuscany. It turned out to be a rather soppy love story but an easy and pleasant watch, about a woman who goes through a messy marriage breakup and takes a holiday in Tuscany to get over it but ends up buying a derelict house in a moment of madness and relocating permanently. All of this will be relevant in a minute!

Vinci is the birthplace of Leonardo da Vinci, a little village set in the countryside with a few shops and cafés surrounded by olive groves and poppies. We slept in a free Aire alongside a sports field in the company of five other vans. It was so peaceful that the only noise was Jackson. In the morning we walked up to the village to buy our tickets for the museum and discovered that it is spread over four separate locations in the area.

We started in the Guidi castle where there was a display of scale models of Leonardo's inventions: those that worked, those that didn't, and unfinished concepts. I was surprised by how fascinated Jackson was and how it truly captured his attention. As he mulled over models of planes, machine guns, cranes and you name it, the questions flowed and he stayed there for hours.

It was mind-blowing to imagine Leonardo being one individual with a brain capable of dreaming up such a vast array of tools and equipment who at the same time had the artistic talent to put his ideas on paper so accurately that they could be developed into a finished product and change the course of history. For example, before he could design a plane, he first had to study the anatomy of birds in detail to understand the makeup and mechanics of their wings. He then translated this information into the languages of maths and science to come up with a design to enable people to fly. And then he switched back into artistic mode and drew it all out on paper. After numerous failed attempts and probably near-death experiences he eventually designed a plane resembling what we can still see today, before moving restlessly on to the next invention, which would be something wholly different. How, exactly how, can one person fit all this work into a lifetime? Not that it ended there!

We moved on to the museum housing the Human Body exhibition. Here there were explanations about how Leonardo applied mathematics to work out the proportions of every part of the human body to enable him to draw accurately, to scale, everyone from a baby to an adult. I discovered that your foot is equal in length to the length of your arm between your elbow and your wrist. Jackson again wanted to put it all to the test. In another experiment we had him lying on the floor, arms stretched out to either side, Geoff's foot marking his fingertips on one side and mine on the other. Then he had to stand up and lie back down lengthways between our feet. Sure enough, he was exactly the same length from head to toe. Now I challenge anyone to tell me a child can't learn as much from travelling as they can in a classroom. I am in no way a museum person but I enjoyed every minute and I'm quite sure I learned more of value here than I did in all my years of being taught from science books in school. Interestingly, over a year down the line when Jackson came back from school with homework on measurements, we reproduced this experiment. This delighted his teacher who told me she would demonstrate it for the entire class of five-year-olds. It left Jackson feeling elated, as if it was he who had come up with this theory rather than Leonardo.

If I could see glimpses of a science brain in Jackson, when we moved on to an art gallery to see digital images of the *Mona Lisa* and *The Last Supper*, to name but a few, he spent the whole time making police siren noises, tap dancing on the tile floor or bending over to look through his legs, declaring loudly that he was looking at the paintings through his bum — so maybe he doesn't have an artist's brain. But here again the genius of Leonardo shone through. How on earth did he combine being brilliant in art, science and mathematics, with a brain that must literally have been bursting to get all this information down on paper in one lifetime? How different must he have been to the average person of his time, and how did this impact on his relationships and mental state? Did he feel isolated and different?

The final stop was the house where Leonardo was born, a three-kilometre drive up into the hills. We had to stop en route to photograph the wildflowers. The village itself consisted of about four or five houses, a lovely car park with views across the countryside where we were very tempted to stay overnight, and a stall selling aniseed crisps, wine and cheese. We visited Leonardo's house and watched a film about his life, brilliantly done with a hologram of the great man giving you the impression he was in the room with you and you could reach out and touch him. Jackson was captivated and cried because we wouldn't let him stay to watch the Italian version after the English.

As we came out into the glorious sunshine the sight of an olive grove with artistically twisted trees caught our attention. We wandered among its long grasses interspersed with vivid splashes of red poppies, where the array of different wildflowers was too vast to count, as were the species of butterfly, while birdsong filled the air. I realised this was my idea of heaven. Geoff's too. We were both spellbound by the beauty and tranquillity of this place where time seemed to stand still. And then the sight of Jackson almost up at the top of an olive tree snapped us back into reality.

I have described the whole experience to make it easier for you to understand that this is where we almost made a life-changing decision based on that romantic DVD we had watched. We came across a derelict house standing alone on a rise looking down over the whole valley and within sight of da Vinci's house. It was falling down and overgrown and sitting in the middle of a sea of poppies and daisies, in its very own olive grove – and it was FOR SALE! We looked at one another and didn't need to say a word – our faces said it all. The next thing we knew we were discussing how we could make it into a holiday home… or a hotel… or a restaurant… or even our home. Then, and here's the scary thing, we walked away over an hour later having had a guided tour, with the price and phone number on a scrap of paper, courtesy of the man on the stall. It could be ours for a meagre 350,000 euros plus an estimated 200,000 more to rebuild it. Ah, bugger, another time maybe... But as I expect you will have noticed, thoughts of not returning home were undeniably starting to creep in. One thing's for sure: whatever we do we will undoubtedly visit Tuscany again. It had captured all of our hearts.

16. THE ROAD TO ROME

THE DISTANCE FROM Vinci to Rome was too great for one day so we had a stopover en route. Remember I said that we had returned to our van in Pisa in the early hours after an evening with our Belgian friends, with unspecified coordinates and a name on a piece of paper. And that neither of us could recall anything from our conversation but had stuck the note in our map book. Well, today, when we looked at our route on the map we spotted Pitigliano, the same name as on the scrap of paper. We tried typing in the coordinates, assuming they were for a recommended Aire or campsite and thinking we might stay there. Geoff thought he remembered it was in reference to *something good*. For me it was a complete blank, which I blame on that cheap but delicious bottle of local wine we drank.

So off we went, stopping for lunch near Siena, a place I'd have liked to visit but, with Rome on the horizon, we thought might be one city too many. From there our route took us inland for another hour to our mystery coordinates. As we drove farther into the countryside, in Chianti country now, the scenery changed completely. It was dominated first by large areas of flat farming land and then by strangely shaped hills that were greener than green. It seemed hard to believe now that back in the Alps the farmers would still be waiting for the snow to melt when here the barley and all kinds of other crops were already knee-high.

We got within a few minutes of our flagged destination on screen when once again our trusty @#£&ing sat nav treated us to yet another surprise announcement: *In a quarter mile, turn left and then leave the road!* Wonderful! Who are the comedians who programme these things? Maybe to those fortunate enough to be driving a four-by-four this statement has some value. But to the vast majority it serves little purpose. Forgive me for boring on, but wouldn't it be more helpful if the sat nav said whenever you first enter the coordinates unwittingly for an off-road location that your destination is not on a road of any description? That way you'd at least have the option of double-checking your coordinates or asking yourself whether you and your vehicle are up for an off-road adventure today.

By now Geoff was getting flashbacks to that drunken conversation. As we slowed for a chicken to cross the road, he blurted out: *Oh, animals everywhere, that's what they said, because that's why the kids loved it. It must be this place. Go back and ask!* That was as we were pulling in at a large house. Next thing I knew I was walking up the drive, Geoff having somehow convinced me that although he didn't speak any Italian, the sign on the gate was definitely for a camp site. I was met by an Italian woman who took one look at our van and said: *Oh my God, you English, oh my God, oh my God!* It was pretty obvious that was the only English she knew as this outburst was followed by a feature-length and very animated one-sided conversation in Italian. Not understanding a word I slowly walked her back in the direction of Geoff, hoping that he would either understand or just stop her talking. He was videoing us as we approached and, not that I'd noticed, he said I looked like the Pied Piper with about thirty chickens following me up the path. It turned out this wasn't the place.

We took our leave of her and then a right turn down a stupidly narrow track before finally changing our minds, returning to the road once again at this woman's house. This time Geoff re-read the sign again and retracted his initial statement, deciding that what it actually said was 'eggs for sale', not bloody camping. So off we went in the opposite direction and this time we spotted a sign with a picture of a tent. It was about two miles down a single-track road with a threatening ditch on either side, followed by a bumpy track, all with no idea whether this was a place where our Belgian acquaintances had ever stayed.

We ended up at an Agritourism site. This is a scheme across much of Europe, which promotes links between agricultural production and tourism, the idea being to educate and entertain the visitors while bringing in an income for the farm owner. A similar scheme in France known as France Passion allows you to subscribe and receive a list of participating sites ranging from vineyards or honey farms to recycling enterprises. Usually the cost of staying at one of these places is very low or sometimes even free. In return the polite thing to do is to purchase some of the produce directly from the land owner as a thank-you. For France Passion you have to be self-sufficient: in other words you must have a toilet on board as no facilities are available. We'd had every intention of joining and making use of the scheme but membership runs from March to March and we couldn't find any way of joining in advance in January before we left Wales. We'd assumed it would be possible to join en route but hadn't ever done so while we were in France. Now here we were in Italy about to embark on something very similar.

This particular site was a hazelnut and barley farm. We purchased some homemade minestrone soup mix and a bag of hazelnuts, after which a lovely gentleman showed us to our pitch. It was fantastically remote, so not surprisingly we had the whole site to ourselves unless you count the wildlife. The cost was only twelve euros per night included electricity and the use of a toilet and hot shower, as long as you didn't mind the spider encamped on the shower curtain and a living room full of ants.

While standing, for fear of ants biting our arses, in the living room, flicking through a dusty book, we discovered that Pitigliano itself was an incredibly interesting town, and then as if by fate another book revealed a picture of thermal springs nearby. At this point Geoff yelled out: *That's it, it's all coming back to me! The Belgians were talking about scorpions and I mentioned a place in Turkey, to which they replied there are thermal baths near Pitigliano that are very much like Pamukkale in Turkey!* So that was why we had these coordinates, though as for whether our friends ever actually camped on this hazelnut farm we will never know. It's amazing how so much information had entered Geoff's brain that night only to be erased by the morning and now, after a comedy of many errors, had bit by bit been dragged back out to the point where he could clearly remember every detail of the conversation. I still wait in hope for him to remember what item of mine it was he randomly pulled out of a cupboard to mop up heating fluid and then threw in the nearest bin. But I won't be holding my breath!

We drove to Pitigliano the next day. I will never forget our first glimpse of its skyline as we approached.

It is perched on top of a volcanic tufa ridge right on the edge of a cliff overlooking a gorge. It has an ancient past embracing many centuries of changes in civilisations and cultures. The Etruscans made cave houses all along the cliffs. Later on the Romans settled there. At one time it had a largely Jewish population, giving it the name 'Little Jerusalem'. Carved from volcanic stone, which resembles pumice stone, the town is like a historic timeline dating from the Bronze Age all the way through the ravages of World War Two and up to the present day. We spent a couple of hours exploring the picturesque hidden lanes and tiny winding streets, the little craft shops and cafés in the square and the lovely church.

From there we drove on to Saturnia, the home of the thermal springs. As we approached via a road that overlooked the river we caught a breathtaking glimpse of the town. A waterfall cascaded into a series of tiered pools carved into rock that was all smoothed and whitened by the minerals in the water. The pools went all the way down to the river and through my telephoto lens I could see people bathing in each pool. It's all completely natural and completely free. From now on I will begrudge paying for a thermal bath as this Jacuzzi in paradise beats anything I have ever seen. It wasn't even crowded and by 7 p.m. it was pretty empty. The water was a comfy bath temperature, but phew, did it stink!

We made use of a very large motorhome site close by with a park-and-ride service for a small fee. We could have paid extra to spend the night here but it was a fair bit more than twelve euros and we had grown to love our little private field at the hazelnut farm. Swimming gear on, we worked our way up from the river, discovering that each pool offered a different experience. Underfoot ranged from mud to pebbles to rough pumice stone and the higher up you got the deeper the pools got and the more powerful the current. Where water fell from one to the next you got the perfect neck, back and shoulder massage, while in the deeper ones you had an all-over bubble effect. If you had a three-year-old next to you fishing about in the mud in the lower pools, you could experience the hundreds of tiny blood-red worms wriggling around and, wait for it, ON you. Being the good mother, once I noticed them I totally freaked out and in an almost involuntary and certainly unladylike action I shot off scared stiff up the tiers of pools, leaving Jackson alone some twenty feet below wondering what on earth was going on. I did quickly return to my senses and go back and rescue him. He loved all of it and was swimming, putting his head under and generally having fun, all the while doing his skin the world of good.

We stayed in the water for three hours and I came up with a formula. Every hour you spend in this sulphur-rich water equals one day to rid yourself of the stink. I had no choice but to brave the bug-infested shower back at the farm where I washed and conditioned my hair and Jackson's that night. Even then every time I turned over in bed I smelt sulphur on the pillow. I think people must have kept a wide birth the next day. Our skin was noticeably soft, though, and when I told Jackson my arm was as soft as a baby's bum he asked me: *Does that mean your bum is as soft as a baby's arm, then?* I wish! There are times when it's best for a mother not to answer!

We left the following morning to a bill of sixty euros. Geoff had misread the information: it was twelve euros per adult per night plus something extra for Jackson, though we still felt it worth every cent for the experience. Evidently Agritourism didn't have the same pricing structure as France Passion.

Our next port of call was a campsite in Bracciano in the outskirts of Rome. It was a tip-off from a book I have previously mentioned, *Europe in a Motorhome*, which we had read before leaving home and had found to be packed with a healthy dose of humour as well as useful ratings on campsites and places to visit, so we often referred to it if we knew we would be crossing paths with their route. It had served to reassure us that we were not alone in our battles with our sat nav, enlightened us to the existence of the twelve-point turn, and guided me through the smoothest approach to dealing with the demands of the driver, shall I put it that way. It was written by Hazel Jackson (the name is pure coincidence) about travels with her husband and thirteen-year-old son who they took out of school and home-schooled along the way for a year. Much like us they were complete novices, but they took the bull by the horns and went one step higher than us, with a BIG American RV. In fact it was through reading the funniest parts of their journey that we made a firm decision to go for the smallest van that we could survive in. Okay, the salesman changed our mind; we opted for something in between and I have to give credit where credit is due, for he probably saved our marriage by giving us an extra few feet between the front and the back for those occasional moments of tension.

Hazel's book was all we could find when we looked for reassurance about travelling with children, although it quickly became apparent that we would be embarking on a very different journey to theirs. Her family relished all the history and art they could find along the way and, unlike us, they left no stone unturned when they explored a city. Still, her book was incredibly helpful on topics like getting around cities or reviews of tried and tested campsites, and we often felt reassured that if their vast vehicle could negotiate the approach roads we were taking, then we should be okay. It is also one of the inspirations for my writing this book, by way of offering families travelling with younger children an opportunity to compare an alternative experience.

In this case the Jacksons had highly rated this particular campsite and the owners for their friendly and helpful nature, so we decided to follow their example. After checking onto our pitch, we spent the rest of the day relaxing in the sun and studying other people's behaviour, or to put it more honestly, being nosey. I'll elaborate more on this favourite pastime at a later stage but suffice to say that I'm now able to hypothesise on the nationality of a person with no extra clues than either their method of establishing themselves on a pitch when they arrive or how they disestablish themselves when they leave; or, if they're already settled before we arrive, basing my observations solely on their behaviour and routine. There's nowt so queer as folk, as the saying goes...

We, of course, are as queer as any other folk, as evidenced by the distinctive way of preparing for an early start we displayed the following morning. Truthfully, anything before 9 a.m. had become 'early' for us. The only way we measured time was whenever Geoff had to refill his tablet box when he would exclaim: *God, another week gone!* whereupon we knew it was another Monday.

Armed (courtesy of our campsite owner, who was definitely living up to her helpful reputation) with a children's book, in English, with explanations of all the major attractions in Rome, which proved more useful to me than to Jackson, we caught the private campsite bus to the train station for the 9 a.m. train to Rome. The journey in its entirety took an hour and, aside from the increasing frequency of Roman ruins as we neared the Eternal City, the other indicator we were getting near was the amount of graffiti. It seemed a real shame as it wasn't particularly artistic graffiti, just scribbles and writing of names on everything. It engulfed trains, including their windows, inside and out, the seats, the tracks, the sidings and most buildings. Sadly our biggest observation as we headed to the south of Italy was how run down and in desperate need of repair everything was. The roads seemed likely to disintegrate soon if someone didn't resurface them, and it wasn't just here and there, it was every-where. The most you ever saw was a teacup-sized repair being done, where they literally stood in the road with a tiny pot of tar and filled a hole, as if they were filling a hole in the wall after taking a picture down. They seemed oblivious to the fact that, in effect, they were just adding another bump. Many buildings were at the point of becoming a safety hazard. Everything was dirty and defaced and again it was entire towns we were talking about, so I couldn't see how any council would have the money to put all this right. Litter too was a big problem, as were drunks on the streets, prostitutes and touts. Yet even so I'd come back to Rome without hesitation. We'd need to spend months in cities like Rome to even begin to understand them.

We had a short metro ride between the train station and our starting point. When we re-emerged into daylight again, right there in front of us was the Colosseum. It was certainly spectacular – but so were the crowds. We bought Jackson a gladiator costume from a street stall and he could hardly wait to get dressed up. From then on he became the focal point of strangers' holiday snaps worldwide, particularly in America, where they couldn't get enough of him. Every time we got him to pose for our family album countless complete strangers began snapping away.

As soon as we arrived we were hassled from every angle by touts selling anything and everything. We had been pre-warned about pickpockets and we were always concerned about becoming separated among crowds, so it wasn't that easy to relax and enjoy the experience. At least six different people offered us a guided tour bypassing the queuing system, and the prices varied greatly. A firm *No thanks!* got rid of them and we joined the queue for tickets. We reached the first gate only to be told that the queue inside before the security checks was 80 minutes. OMG, Jackson was driving us nuts already, so we backed out of the queue and negotiated a deal for an English tour due to start immediately, which had us queuing for less than 10 minutes. Hm, the part they omitted to tell us was that the tour would begin outside and last for a good 45 minutes (while someone else queued for us) before we then queued to go through security. At one point I fully suspected our guide would do a runner with our money before we got in, and in fact I could sense tension was building elsewhere in our tour party. In fairness, though, we were all wrong and, if we didn't get in much quicker, he was very funny and entertained us while we waited. Jackson spent the whole time attacking the ants on the pavement with his sword so he was quite happy.

Inside it was fabulous, particularly having just spent the evening before tucked up in bed watching *Gladiator* and preparing Jackson for the sights ahead of him. Standing there now in person, you could almost hear the roar of the crowd as the games (as they euphemistically called them) began. Imagine, the last thing most of those men saw was the inside of this place before they met their fate. We left our tour to continue without us because they were going on to another site, since this was the one we'd been interested in. We sat inside the Colosseum and ate our picnic while answering a host of questions about lions and bears from Jackson.

Next stop on the underground was the Trevi Fountain, which was very impressive but again you had to fight through crowds to see it. Legend has it that a coin thrown over your shoulder into the fountain ensures your return to Rome someday. There were certainly coins flying here, there and everywhere. Throw in a second if you're seeking love or a third for wedding bells. Who knows what Jackson was seeking? He wanted to throw hand loads of coins in there and in his excitement he somehow managed to throw his Spiderman cap in too. I wonder how many people will have a photograph of Geoff practically falling in attempting to fish it out. Apparently some 3,000 euros are thrown into the Trevi every day. They are collected every night and distributed to a charity, which gives rechargeable supermarket cards to Rome's needy to help them buy groceries.

From here we walked to the Spanish Steps only to find that they were surrounded by scaffolding and closed to the public. They had been undergoing a massive cleanup and large wooden boards obliterated any view of them. Many people were gathered around a fountain below but it wasn't quite the same thing.

By now it was 4 p.m. so we moved on to the Vatican. We walked around the immense square and sat in the sun taking in the atmosphere. I'm ashamed to say, though, that we couldn't face the queue to get in. We have since been told that this was probably one of our biggest mistakes. From countless reports from fellow travellers it really is a Must See, putting it on our To-Do list for the time when we are destined to return as a result of tossing a coin into that fountain. The length of the queue looked worse than the Colosseum so, wimps that we were, we decided that we had seen enough of Rome, feeling content without tipping the scales and regretting doing too much.

Instead we opted for a slow walk back to find a toy shop and some chips for Jackson. This was the turning point. Toy shops and chips are scarce commodities in Rome and we ended up walking miles to a general chorus of complaints from a tired child. Eventually we settled for some cheap guaranteed-to-last-five-minutes plastic cars from a newsagents. That said, they kept him awake all the way home, which in turn allowed us to enjoy a lovely bottle of Prosecco in peace later on.

Our feet and legs ached but although exhausted we had thoroughly enjoyed our day. How people have the stamina to repeat this again day after day, though, I will never know. It's not just the city itself and all the crowds and queues that wear you out; it's also the additional hour of travel at each end of the journey. I suppose that is a cost you pay for staying in such a pleasant campsite a little farther out and if I did it all again I would definitely make the same choice.

The next day was our recovery day so we pottered around the van sorting it out and tidying up. I thinned out Jackson's toy box a bit while he was preoccupied pedalling around on his bike and hatched a plan to sneak the contents to the campsite owner for her swap shop without him seeing and retrieving it all. I was fully prepared for World War Three if and when he should discover something missing. Jackson's position on the matter of toys was simple and consistent. He refused to understand that Dotty did not have expanding sides. And he insisted on collecting emergency vehicles of every description in every country. So something had to give. I resolved that on future trips we would set off with no toys and collect them en route, reasoning that there was way more fun to be had choosing something different in places where you've never been before than in being told you have to go without anything new because poor Dotty can't fit any more in.

My subterfuge paid off when he and Geoff decided to put wet suits on and brave the lake. Mummy, having more sense than that, took photographs. We then went up to the town on foot, found a hairdresser to cut Jackson's hair, had ice creams and generally idled the day away, which is always nice once in a while. Tomorrow would take us to Pompeii and we had a long drive ahead of us.

17. AROUND VESUVIUS

HAVING TWO OPTIONS for our route south, either straight down the motorway all the way, three hours max, or the scenic route across country and then along the coast, we opted for the latter. It took us over six hours and the state of the roads probably reduced the value of our van immensely.

About the driving near Naples, the closest I have ever seen to it was in Sri Lanka where they frequently have cows and monitor lizards the size of dogs to contend with. There's no such excuse here where they seem to have no rules. I'm not even sure if anyone sits a test, since we certainly never came across any learner drivers. Each junction is a free for all where the fastest wins. And lanes, what exactly are they? You either have three abreast, including a tractor and a bus at one point, on a bend, or else you have someone sitting in between the two lanes doing 15 m.p.h. They undertake on slip roads, toot for the sheer hell of it, don't wear seatbelts and think nothing of causing total gridlock by blocking the opposite carriageway in order to jump the queue at a red light. We even witnessed one brazen chap hurtling right past a police car in the middle of a town centre way above the speed limit without even batting an eyelid.

Service stations on the motorway serve wine and you'll be lucky to spot one table whose occupants are not partaking in this lunchtime activity with their meal, despite the majority being about to get back behind the wheel. The scariest we saw (which Jackson now imitates) was a bus driver having a very animated conversation on his mobile, involving the use of his spare hand to wildly gesture, apparently unaware that the person he was talking to couldn't actually see down the phone, while paying not the slightest bit of attention to the road and occasionally correcting the steering with his knees.

I recall a conversation with my friend Naomi in Varese who told me she had once been reprimanded by a complete stranger on the street, an Italian lady, for not having her kids, who are used to UK temperatures, dressed warmly enough for her liking. Naomi had not had time to gather her thoughts and react before the woman slammed the car door and shot off with her toddler not belted in on the front seat. And this is common practice. In that lady's eyes it was far more detrimental to a child to catch a cold than to venture into this mayhem without being belted up.

At least we got to have lunch on a beach rather than a service station. By 'lunch' I mean a cold slice of pizza base with tomato puree but no sign of cheese, which was all the café sold.

We arrived, exhausted and starving. We had planned to use a campsite recommended in Hazel Jackson's book. She and her family had been travelling in a Winnebago so we felt reassured that where a Winnebago can go Dotty should be able to go with ease. To our great surprise one of the three British couples we met on this campsite turned out to be close relatives of Hazel and they too produced a copy from their motorhome.

I completed the paperwork and was instructed to park up and walk in to choose a suitable pitch before taking the motorhome in. In the entire trip we had only been asked to do this twice. The last time was at the previous campsite outside Rome, where having entered on foot we just found an empty field. This time a very tired Geoff said: *Sod that, I'll drive in to find a pitch.* We spotted a British number plate and drove towards them only to find that we couldn't squeeze between the trees just there, so we either had to make a sharp left turn or reverse.

I voted to reverse but Geoff overruled me, claiming he could make it. Which he might have done had it not been for a very stubborn French man who parked in the pitch right by the turning circle and left twenty feet in front of his van while its rear end protruded out into the road. He then stood guarding his bumper and attempting to guide us round inch by inch rather than move forward himself. By now I was sweating as we were wedged at an angle between heavily laden orange trees on either side and his van. Thankfully the Brits came to our rescue, because otherwise there might have been a teeny-weeny row in our van. Ollie, our new neighbour, kindly spent the next ten minutes, which felt like an hour with all eyes on us, guiding us out of the trees and round the corner. Credit where credit is due, this is not as easy as it sounds, and Geoff was mightily relieved that it wasn't purely down to my guidance to rescue him. Given the length of the van, you needed to have a really good sense of spatial awareness to anticipate what effect a relatively minimal turn of the front wheels would have on the rear end of the van. In this case there were also low trees to contend with and if it had been left to me it probably wouldn't have ended well.

We attempted another pitch, where we even contemplated driving right over the top of a bush, but still there were overhanging branches. Finally, by stealth and animal cunning, we managed to magically 'disappear' the red and white tape blocking a suitable pitch, which was presumably there to allow the grass time to rejuvenate or reserve it for someone, both bridges that we'd cross when and if we had to. And in we went.

Moments like this were the reason I had opted not to drive the van thus far and I must give Geoff credit for generally remaining calm in these situations. We were the second van helped by Ollie, who himself had only arrived two hours before us. The rest of the evening was carnage with a convoy of people getting stuck behind that stubborn Frenchman. We made a swift getaway to buy some beer and wine as a thank-you to Ollie and then we joined him and Nicky, his wife, for a drink, right opposite the offending van. We lost track of time as we all got on brilliantly, while the kids ran riot having mud ball fights and our raucous laughter became unrestrained. Our French neighbour came out and gestured angrily for us to be quiet so that he could sleep at, er, 1.30 a.m. He left the next morning but we missed a trick there: one of us should have decorated his bumper with a big makeup scratch to teach him for being so selfish.

It's very rare to encounter this sort of attitude. Up to now we had been taken aback by the kindness of our fellow motorhomers, the friendliness of complete strangers, and the easy way everyone would come and go and slot into close proximity to neighbours and immediately spark up properly interesting conversations. Back home that happens all too rarely with neighbours near whom you've lived for years.

There is something very refreshing about being able to lose all your inhibitions on trips like this. Maybe it's because you very rarely wake up to the same people more than two days in a row.

When this particular night began little did I realise I would be hanging on its every word for years to come. Our newfound friends were living proof of a thought that had already popped into my head along the way: world schooling! Ollie, Nicky and their eight-year-old daughter and ten-year-old son had been travelling since the previous October. They initially planned to remove the kids from school for just a year in between exams, homeschool them while they travelled, then return to the same school one academic year later. However, guidelines from the local authority revealed that because they intended to leave the UK they could neither keep a school place for either child nor be offered any guidance on the syllabus to take with them. Eventually their head teacher provided some encouragement by putting together a few emails for them outlining the syllabus, listing study books to help and suggesting that realistically an hour of intense study each day would equate to a whole school day by eliminating the breaks, lunch, assemblies, physical education, registration and shared lesson time with thirty other pupils. They also discovered that if you are a 'traveller' you are provided with all your learning materials free of charge, whereas if you are 'travelling' and paying tax it all comes at your own expense – £800 in their case. With all this against them but refusing to be defeated, they took the decision to sell their house and say goodbye to their school once and for all and find out where the journey carried them without any restraints. By Christmas they had unanimously decided not to stop after one year but to travel indefinitely. Their long-term plan, when the time was right, was to settle in a favourite spot in Spain and set up a business based on motorhoming.

I felt instantly on their wavelength and found myself struggling to mask my jealousy. I thoroughly admired the whole family's determination to make it work, their self-belief and refusal to be talked out of their dream. Seeing their two children sitting in the shade under a tree writing their notes on Pompeii inspired me. The lessons and knowledge they were gaining might be different but seemed in no way less beneficial to them than what they would learn in school, while this lifestyle seemed so much healthier both for them and their family.

Nicky told me that an average day for them would often begin with an early drive still in pyjamas to get some distance covered, before taking in some sightseeing wherever they might be. The children would be set age-appropriate challenges to glean from these activities and, without fail, an hour would be set aside in the late afternoon when the two of them would sit at a table undisturbed to write up an account of their day. To complement this they both had laptops and an array of downloaded materials to practise their maths and various other aspects of their curriculum. Based on what I had already seen with Jackson, I found it easy to imagine how much their language skills, socialising skills and general knowledge were improving.

I could see how much self-discipline would be demanded from the parents to make this really work and I wondered whether Geoff and I would have the stamina. We had fallen by the wayside long ago, sleeping in until mid morning, allowing Jackson to be up until midnight and prioritising fun over education. I had left home with the best of intentions and part of the weight we were carrying was a vast selection of books including wipe-clean phonics, arithmetic and writing materials, but had any of them left the cupboard? I'm ashamed to say NO! And I was fairly certain that if there were waves or the snow was good there would be little chance of talking Geoff out of his plans to accommodate a study session. Still, no matter how much I tried to dismiss it, a seed had been planted that night and it would continue to grow inside me.

Ollie worked one month on, one month off on oil rigs, so he would travel with the family for a month, then set them all up somewhere suitable while he flew off to work for the next month, thereby giving them the means to fund this endless journey. We parted company at this site but kept in touch throughout the duration of our trip. Later we were very saddened to hear that, following a traumatic break-in soon after in a supermarket car park on the outskirts of Rome, which caused extensive damage to the interior of their van when it was literally torn apart and emptied in broad daylight, they retreated back to the UK to recover and carry out necessary repairs to their home. After that they felt forced by the pressures of exams and school to shelve their plans for the time being. It just goes to show you don't know what lies around the corner. I'm pretty certain that were it not for the fact that Ollie had to be away a lot and that understandably Nicky's confidence must have been knocked by the fear of something like this happening again during his absence, they would probably still be travelling the world somewhere. I'm sure, though, that it's only a matter of time.

Meanwhile we based ourselves in this campsite, getting a break from manoeuvring back out through the trees and facing the drivers on the roads again, for five whole days. This was the greatest length of time we had stayed in one place since the ski resort in the Alps, and it offered us a very different perspective to be afforded the time to get to know an area and our neighbours in more depth. At this point we still hadn't appreciated the impact this one particular site would have on our journey and our future. We now realise that it was one of the places that sparked the most interesting and lasting friendships and that it will remain, in every detail, in our minds forever.

We had five jam-packed days beginning with the ruins of Pompeii. The entrance was 200 metres from our campsite and, after the usual late start, we joined the queue for tickets at noon with Jackson in mid-tantrum about not being allowed to bring his scooter. No matter how many ways I tried to explain that the streets we were about to walk on in this heritage site were thousands of years old and that a wild child on a scooter would not be allowed in, it fell on deaf ears and I was met by a torrent of abuse from Jackson along with comments from an American tourist in the queue, who took it upon himself to judge me a bad parent for bringing a child here in the heat of the day when he was too young to enjoy it. I wished he could have seen Jackson ten minutes later, and indeed for the next six hours, loving every bit of it and still running around long after we were ready to drop.

We chose not to take a guided tour and so we didn't really fully understand what we were looking at. But we got the general gist from a guidebook and it somehow added to the adventure that we were free to wander through the streets as we wished, as if the town were still standing today. We allowed Jackson to decide which turns we took, so we saw some places three times over as we went round in circles. But he was just as excited at discovering something for the tenth time as he was the first time, and it gave him a sense of importance to be our tour guide for the day. It was pretty hard on the legs, though. The cobbled streets were slippery with wear and so uneven that every muscle was used in a bid to maintain balance.

Again, and I don't know what it was with these Romans, there were some pretty big willies on display, which of course amused Jackson no end. Me too. We stood inside the villas of rich people where paintings on the walls were still visible, while in other streets shop counters stood in otherwise collapsed buildings, giving a clear indication of what was once the shopping area. If you closed your eyes it was easy to imagine a whole community going about their business here as in any other town until that dark mountain that cast its shadow over the streets suddenly erupted, burying the whole town and all its occupants under several feet of ash. In one part, casts of actual bodies showed the exact positions they were found in, including the sleeping embrace between a mother and her child who stood no chance, the only consolation being that they died in each other's arms. It was very moving to see that embrace, which every mother on earth would immediately relate to. There is a strong sense of sadness and yet peace about Pompeii and, at times, it is unnerving to raise your eyes and realise that you are still walking in the shadow of Mount Vesuvius.

The outspoken American in the queue could hardly have been more wrong. This day impacted on Jackson's mind more than most and, a few years down the line, he remembers details and still asks lots of questions about volcanoes and death and all sorts of related subjects. I'm sure that one day in the future when they study this subject in school he will have gained immensely from having seen it for himself. For me there were so many subjects in school, particularly history and geography, that I simply couldn't relate to because I was unable to conjure anything up in my imagination. Reading about Pompeii in a book would have lost my attention from an early point, and yet walking through its streets had quite the opposite effect, sparking an ever-deeper interest. Thinking back to Nicky and Ollie's two children on the campsite the night before, writing their own accounts of their day in Pompeii, I knew for sure that they would have learned and, more importantly, would remember, so much more than a child sat behind a desk with a book. Suddenly my mind was opened to the concept of homeschooling while travelling the world – or 'world schooling' as research has since led me to understand it is called.

No rest for the wicked, the next morning we caught the train, again just outside our campsite, to Naples where we took a taxi to the port and a ferry to the island of Procida, about half an hour by sea. Since arriving at the campsite we had spoken to another British couple whose van had been broken into just outside Naples while parked at a supermarket. Our guidebook suggested that it was not the safest of cities to visit and probably not the most interesting either, after experiencing Rome and Florence, so we decided not to go into the centre and just to pass through on the way to the port.

Years ago when I was heavily pregnant we had had the unfortunate experience of being followed in Cádiz, which left me with a lasting sense of anxiety and heightened awareness around such busy places. Although in most places I feel naturally at ease, the slightest hint of doubt prevents me from enjoying my day, so all things considered we preferred to relax on this small fishing island than tackle the urban mayhem. Friends of ours couldn't believe it when we told them that we had been so close and not actually visited Naples, insisting that it was one of the best, most exciting cities in Europe. I guess it's another case of each to their own.

The train journey was certainly different, standing room only and a live band for our entertainment and money. My naivety immediately showed as I went into my bag and produced my purse to tip the buskers. The conductor quietly warned us against repeating this mistake, alerting us to the realisation that I had now provided countless beady eyes aboard the train with the exact location of my purse when I returned it to my bag. Needless to say this cemented our decision to bypass Naples itself. We subsequently heard a number of tales of people waiting until the train is just about to pull out of a station and then grabbing someone's necklace and jumping off before anyone could do anything to help. Another ploy is people carrying a doll wrapped to look like a baby. They trip and drop the 'baby', you react in horror and rush to help, quite likely dropping your belongings in a bid to save the poor child, whereupon you are robbed. Anyway, we enjoyed the band and went on to take several more train journeys, each with different musicians who jump on for a few stations, just long enough to walk the length of the train with a hat and then jump off and wait for the next train back to where they started so they can repeat the process.

The taxi through Naples gave us a taste of the city and regardless of what our friends say I will have to get a lot braver before I tackle it. We saw a drug deal taking place in broad daylight, prostitutes were a common sight and the driving was atrocious. In stark contrast we spent the day feeling like we were a million miles from anywhere, revelling in the peace and sunshine. Procida is the smallest island in the Bay of Naples and is somewhat off the tourist radar, being overshadowed by its neighbours Capri and Ischia. We stationed ourselves in the sun at a quiet little fish restaurant in a lovely peaceful harbour watching the fishermen repair their nets while we sipped cold beer. To keep Jackson quiet for a while we bought him a fishing net and he and a newly made friend, a nine-year-old French girl, happily fished for jellyfish. She spoke excellent English, to the point where when a fish escaped her net she shouted: *I got one! I got one! SHIT it's escaped!* I fell about laughing. On the boat trip back we sat on the deck, just us and one other couple up on the lifebuoy storage chest, with the wind in our hair. What a contrast this part of Italy was to the north and to the cities, and yet so far everything we had seen had its own appeal in abundance.

The next morning, nicely rested after that lovely day, we felt the urge to clean and tidy Dotty – my new form of housework. I just loved the fact that I could clean my entire home in fifteen minutes flat. On this occasion, though, we decided to rearrange the garage yet again. One of the main criteria in choosing this particular motorhome, the size of its garage, was now proving to be its downfall. Jackson could actually stand up and walk through it. It was accessible from either side and, being German-built, Knaus use a double floor system with a large gap between the two layers adding to its winterisation capabilities. It was entirely our fault for taking too much clutter, but we were put off bike rides by the sheer effort of reaching and removing the bikes from the garage. We had an inflatable three-seater kayak still neatly packed in its bag because we were afraid to open it in case we couldn't fit it back in, while buried completely underneath all of this, running lengthways down the van in between the double floor system, was Geoff's stand-up paddle board, which at this rate seemed unlikely to ever enter foreign waters. We still couldn't see a way to arrange our belongings so that we could access them easily and still drive safely without damaging them, and none of it was helped by Jackson's ever-growing collection of pebbles, bits of drift wood and souvenirs. And all this was destined to get worse as we hadn't even started to buy wine yet.

With some small degree of satisfaction that we had slightly improved things, we caught an afternoon train to Sorrento. We walked through the old town, which was incredibly pretty but heaving with tourists, many of them from cruise ships. All the shops were touristy but, if you had plenty of money, they had very nice clothing, and the air was filled with the heady scent of limoncello. The town is high above the sea and there is a lift down to the harbour. In our case we had ice creams and cakes to burn off so we walked down and later back up hundreds of steps. The harbour was lovely, colourful and packed with restaurants. Jackson paddled until he got completely soaked. He looked like he had wet himself and insisted on walking like it too (ha ha, funny boy!), and out of embarrassment we had to buy him new shorts to make the train journey back.

We spent the evening chatting over a bottle of wine, this time in the company of David and Helen and their 18-month-old son. They too were planning to travel long term. They had quit their jobs in a snap decision to cram in as much travel as possible before their son reached school age. Their plan was to see how far they could get and where they got to before either their money or their time ran out, whichever came first. We kept in touch through the duration of our trip and saw them draw a line under Europe after some difficult times in Greece and Albania, where the road system was so undeveloped that they struggled to make progress. They returned briefly to the UK, where they arranged to ship their much-loved and already packed motorhome over to Canada and take a flight to join it to begin another adventure through Canada and the USA. We followed their blog for the duration of their trip and it blew our minds. North America was worlds apart from travelling in Europe. It brought new challenges but the sights they saw and the quality time they shared with their son was unequalled. Eventually their money ran out ahead of their time and they had to abandon their plans to over-winter in Florida. By then they also admitted to needing some quality time with friends and relatives, having been on the road for a lot longer than us with a younger child whose grandparents were missing out on his childhood.

I said earlier that it was at this particular campsite that we made some lasting friendships. There was more to it than that although it is difficult to put a finger on exactly what. It felt as if we were destined to be here at exactly this moment in time. A day or two either side, a different campsite and we would have never got to meet these people whom we now call our friends. All of us were travelling in a different direction and heading for different lands and yet our paths coincidentally crossed here. For a moment time stood still, long enough for us to delve into one another's lives and draw inspiration and ambition from one another before we went our separate ways again. It was as if it was meant to be, like a mysterious magnet drawing people to this point to unite them. From those few nights sitting around one table sharing one bottle of wine we soon found ourselves in three different countries heading in completely different directions on wholly different adventures. It brought home how small but at the same time big the world is, making us want to keep going forever and see all of it. I'll never understand why this didn't happen to us more often and why this place felt so special – was it something to do with the proximity of that volcano?

And I could never have believed the impact it would have on me personally. It got me seriously thinking about subjects like world schooling and thoughts of motorhoming as far afield as New Zealand. Now hardly a day goes by without me feeling the need to mention my thoughts to Geoff in the hope he will one day cave and just say: *Come on then, let's go.* And each time I think about all this I am immediately transported back to this place and that table and that bottle of wine and that ignorant Frenchman (and I still regret not faking a scratch on his bumper!).

Another thing that comes back to me is how everyone we met had their own store of hilarious stories of their trip and how much we all loved to share them. It seemed that without fail everyone had got stuck somewhere or other. We soon realised that we were not uniquely incompetent, which was just as well as our best was yet to come.

When we arrived in Pompeii we had every intention of driving along the Amalfi Coast en route to our next destination. In fact it was one of the few plans we had set in stone before setting off from Wales. However, research had then revealed that motorhomes are not allowed on the coast road anymore and that although some people have got away with it, the reviews suggested that it was a scary drive in a small car, let alone a very large box on wheels. So we opted to leave Dotty here, all set up, while we hired the smallest car we could get and took a day trip instead.

It had always been one of Geoff's dreams to drive this route in an open-topped sports car, tearing around the hairpins, wind in his hair, ha ha! Well, we did it, only in a Nissan Micra in a nose-to-tail queue of traffic at 15 m.p.h., with added wind and torrential rain on the return stretch. Oh, and his hair parted company with his head a long time ago, and even if it hadn't it would have by the time we finished this drive.

Guidebooks describe this journey as a must, 'one of the best coastal drives in the world' and 'arguably the world's most beautiful and thrilling sightseeing road with breathtaking panoramic views at every bend.' What they don't tell you is that while you may be lucky enough to catch a fleeting glimpse of those spectacular vistas you can forget all your dreams of stopping to admire them or capture them on film, because you'll be sucked along in an endless traffic jam to a chorus of horn blowing and stressful aggressive gesturing by drivers. Stopping places are few and far between and are invariably full, so you are forced past the best viewpoints. Your progress is bumper to bumper with coaches and scooters jostling for space on the narrow hairpins and causing gridlock in the tunnels. It must be hell on earth in the middle of summer. Worse, the road is infamous for its drivers' lack of caution, which on a narrow winding road like that is plain madness. I doubt Geoff really noticed any of the scenery as his eyes remained firmly on the narrow, zigzagging road with no railings, strung halfway up a cliff with waves crashing below. I have never been so glad that we hired a car. Talking of those stories motorhome people always like to share after the event, our poor friends who had helped us negotiate the trees at the campsite attempted it later in their motorhome and sent us a text about the mayhem they inflicted upon the whole of the Amalfi Coast when they reached a tunnel that wasn't high enough for them and got stuck for nearly half an hour while they had to turn their van around. Knowing them, they were quite possibly still wearing pyjamas and seeing the funny side. I can't even begin to imagine how they performed that manoeuvre on these roads. They were only half the size of us so I know for sure we wouldn't have managed it.

After getting back to the campsite, having lived to tell the tale and mostly seen only the general surroundings of clifftop lemon groves and extortionately expensive villas, we concluded that the hype is more about the Amalfi Coast road itself, which is unarguably a great feat of engineering, rather than the scenery. We had easily seen its equal back at Lake Ponçon in France, and we would do so elsewhere later on in our trip.

We did stop at a grotto at lunchtime, where we caught a lift down from the road and ended up in a cave. There we were ushered into a rowing boat whereupon it all got a bit desperate. A brief scan of the cave confirmed my suspicion that this would be little more than a disappointment as there didn't appear to be anywhere for the boat to go apart from round and round in a small circle, which the skipper proceeded to do for the next ten minutes while pointing out stalactites and colours and shapes that only he could see, and even a plastic nativity that someone had put underwater, I have no idea why. All this was interspersed with requests for the passengers not to forget a tip for the guide after the tour so he could enjoy a glass of wine. Geoff gave him a tip: *I think you have had one glass too many already, mate!*

Our return journey was completely viewless as the clouds rolled down off the mountain, although in the brief moments of transition it made for some very atmospheric scenes.

Absolutely exhausted from cramming so much into such a short space of time, we decided it was time to move on the next morning. We would be heading east.

18. STRANGE DWELLINGS

UNUSUALLY FOR THIS trip we had to drive through torrential rain and flooding as we left Pompeii. All we could think about was any poor souls who had arrived on coach trips or some other prearranged excursion and were now paddling around the ancient remains where there was not a scrap of shelter. Thankfully we soon left the bad weather behind us and the sky lightened as we drove across the arch of the foot of Italy.

The area seemed in stark contrast to anything we had seen since Tuscany. For the first time in weeks we found ourselves chatting while we drove. What was going on? I realised that I was not running up the aisle retrieving objects from the floor, nor was Jackson attempting to shout louder than the rattle as we bounced over potholes because, very noticeably, there were no potholes. For once Geoff was decidedly relaxed and wasn't cursing some lunatic with a death wish because, again very noticeably, there were no other cars on the road. We speculated about the reasons for having this beautifully tarmacced stretch of straight dual carriageway here when the rest of Italy seemed to be falling apart. It begged questions about how fairly funds were distributed across the country.

I had the impression this area was not fully on the tourist radar yet, which was just the way we liked it. All the cafés and campsites were still closed out of season and no tourist attractions were signposted. It even encouraged us to risk wild camping for a couple of nights to save some money, even though it is supposed to be illegal in Italy.

We spent the first night in a deserted beach car park outside a closed café and, after a sunset stroll collecting driftwood (another addition to our already packed garage), we settled in and tried not to feel too spooked in all this isolation. We packed everything in the van ready to make a swift getaway should we feel unsafe or get moved on, and I must admit I spent half the night listening out for noises. But all was fine and we woke up in a beautiful setting.

Before embarking on this journey we had come across several articles about motorhome occupants who had been burgled during the night while they slept and who believed they had been gassed. We even spoke first-hand to one couple who told us it had happened to them with six adults sleeping in the van and not one of them had heard a thing. For a while it really unnerved me, but more research reassured us that it is all but impossible to gas someone in such a large space. Frankly, judging by the enjoyable social activities we had been witnessing, a more likely story was that all six occupants were rendered comatose by alcohol. We had a good alarm, which was even connected to the garage doors, so that should any door or window be tampered with we would be alerted. We accidentally put it to the test any number of times and knew there was no way anyone could sleep through that din. On the other hand I had also noticed that on those occasions when we accidentally triggered the alarm in supermarket car parks or wherever, no one took any notice, so in our absence I doubt anyone would have rushed to rescue our van.

Along the way we had also devised our own internal security system by wrapping the front passenger seatbelt through the door handle and clipping it into its holder, ensuring that if the door was yanked open swiftly the seatbelt would jam as if in an emergency stop. We also usually positioned something that would make a noise if tripped over in front of the main entrance door and closed the fly screen to help stop someone in their tracks if they tried to break in. All of this gave us extra peace of mind at night.

In our preparations for this trip we had also read that buying a safe for our valuables can be counterproductive. Any competent thief would know the few places where a safe could be screwed down and would have the equipment to wreck the framework of the van in order to remove it. Instead we brought a spare wallet in which we put 20 or 30 euros and some unused store cards, which, together with an old mobile phone and an older watch, we put in the drawer nearest the door as if hidden, although purposely very badly, in the hope that if a thief spotted them quickly they might just grab the lot and make a run for it, believing they had what they came for without rummaging through the rest of our belongings to find anything else.

If we had doubts about the safety of a place, one of us would generally sit in the van while the other did the shopping. We also purchased a sign warning about a German Shepherd on board. Other advice we had read was to carry a dog water bowl and a hefty collar and lead, then, if leaving the van unattended, close the blinds just leaving the lead on display and the water bowl outside the door. This was supposed to suggest to a would-be thief that they might want to think again before meeting the occupants of this particular van.

The basic idea behind all this is that if there is an easier target most thieves will opt for that, so by making your van appear to have a few extra hurdles, which might slow a thief down, the chances are they will leave well alone.

As we were already packed, we left before breakfast and drove to Matera. Neither Geoff not I had a clue what we would find there, but it was highlighted as a place of interest on the map and we thought it might be worth a look. As we drove into the new town area, which was fairly nondescript, there was substantial motorhome parking available in a guarded car park. There was no way we could imagine the mind-blowing sight that awaited us, literally just round the corner. In fact for a while we wondered if we had come to the wrong town until we checked out where we were with the waiter over our late breakfast in a seedy little coffee shop. Matera turned out to be one of the most interesting and unusual places we had ever been to, yet, astonishingly, it seems that it is little visited by foreign travellers. Almost everyone there was Italian. To me it surpassed the Colosseum and yet you could pass through on its very doorstep and not be aware of its existence.

Steeped in history and a National Heritage site, Matera is one of the oldest continuously inhabited cities in the world. It dates back 250,000 years to Palaeolithic times, when it consisted of cave dwellings. Its history is too vast and detailed to cover here except to remark briefly that these caves were inhabited for centuries until the 1950s, when there were hundreds of families living in them in poor and crowded living conditions. An outbreak of malaria sparked national outrage and it was finally decreed that the cave residents should be moved to modern buildings on the plateau above. By the 1980s the abandoned caves were no longer considered to be reminders of a disgraceful scandal but fascinating reminders of the past. In due course a few of the more well-to-do residents of Matera moved back in and renovated some of the caves. Today this is increasingly the trend, and some have even been converted into hotels or restaurants.

It is hard to believe that entry to the caves is free. We spent four hours walking around the caves and the old streets of the city, which are now full of quaint little cafés and arty shops. There are show caves that you can enter that are furnished in the traditional manner exactly as they would have been when they were abandoned in the 1950s. With no natural light, running water or electricity it is quite obvious how disease became rampant. Small beds were not only expected to sleep multiple people but the space underneath them was used to house chickens. In the same room, for fear of theft, pigs or horses would be kept indoors. 'In the most extraordinary way, this history of squalor and poverty is now proving to be the making of Matera in the 21st century,' the Guardian reported recently. A study in 2017 by the University of Siena revealed that more than 25% of Matera's housing stock is now available to rent on Airbnb, more than anywhere else in Italy. Matera was also chosen as the European Capital of Culture for 2019.

As might be expected, all of this, and particularly the Capital of Culture award, has attracted some controversy. Many local people fear for the future of Matera and the possibility of being pushed out to make room for tourists and the resulting demands for supermarkets and other amenities. Having seen the place before all this publicity emerged, I share their concerns. It is difficult to see how it will not change and lose its soul and that seems a shame. I now understand why, as in the case of Lake Orta, the Italians like to keep some of their most beautiful countryside to themselves: a secret.

History aside, most of our enjoyment came from admiring the magnificent views across the canyon in which the city sits and the fun of exploring all its nooks and crannies. For the brave or insane there was a very precarious, long and high rope bridge to cross the canyon but my stomach couldn't live with that. I enjoyed it as much as Pompeii with one exception: painted clay whistles, a local tradition, are on sale everywhere and Jackson accompanied us musically (NOT!) the whole way.

This region of Southern Italy is known as Puglia and forms the heel of Italy's boot. Our next port of call for the day was Alberobello. When we had set off in the morning we never anticipated the impact of Matera and how long we would spend there. Now here we were driving to Alberobello wondering whether we could fit them both into the same day. The only information we had on the place was from our friend Pete back home who had read a previous blog of mine and, realising where we were headed, remembered that he had seen a TV series filmed in this area. He told us that there were some 'beehive houses' somewhere around here – whatever they might be. Our approach was a lovely, peaceful, relaxing drive through countryside and farming land and along deserted country lanes, with, sure enough, occasional sightings of what obviously had to be beehive houses due to their shape. Some were even new builds.

When we turned into the car park for the main site we were amazed to find thousands of other cars and people everywhere. Suddenly it seemed as if every man and his dog were here and yet we had barely passed a car or a person anywhere en route. Having said that, it was late afternoon by now and I suppose most normal people aim to get there a little earlier than we did.

It turned out Alberobello is famed for its *trulli*, as the beehive houses are correctly named. Pete's BBC series was *Two Greedy Italians* – presumably some culinary programme. It was yet another UNESCO World Heritage Site, and we were about to immerse ourselves in culture for the second time in one day, although that's not really very difficult anywhere in Italy. Truth be told, until then I'd had no idea just how much the country had to offer. I can't think of anywhere else in the world where so much history is right there at your fingertips everywhere you go.

A *trullo* is a traditional dry stone hut with a conical roof. They were constructed as general store houses, field shelters or dwellings for agricultural labourers. One theory has it that they were dry-stone-built as a means of tax evasion, enabling them to be quickly taken down should a tax inspector show up. The oldest *trulli* at Alberobello date back to the 14th century but they were probably being built long before that and taken down and rebuilt several times from scratch rather than being repaired. They are built from limestone from this area on bases that are usually square and whitewashed. The walls are thick with few windows, which gives them an ideal temperature in both summer and winter. They are built around a central room with one or two smaller rooms connected via archways. From the outside the roofs appear to be conical but internally you can see that they are actually dome-shaped.

Within the official UNESCO town there were many hundreds of *trulli* and, alas, many hundreds of tourists too, wandering the narrow streets and exploring what are now mainly tourist shops and cafés. Some of the *trulli* are still residential and, of course, taking full advantage of being featured on the BBC, we were welcomed inside the house that appeared in it, where we took pictures and talked to the family. They cheerfully enlightened us that they no longer live in this house, because being famous they now live in a big villa. I would say that an hour or so here is more than enough to see it all, although there is apparently another place close by that is much less visited and totally residential should you want to witness the authentic *trullo* lifestyle. One thing we noticed in Alberobello, not for the first time, was that although ridiculously popular with tourists we barely heard any languages other than Italian.

Again we wild camped near a beach and were not disturbed, although the village next to us had a Sunday evening market and was heaving with people. Oblivious, at least for now, to the reason for these vast numbers of Sunday night revellers, we settled in for the night. Little did we know we were about to learn the answer the hard way in the morning.

19. A WHOLE LOT OF HORN BLOWING

THE DAY STARTED well enough, eating egg butties while simultane-ously paddling on what felt like our very own private empty beach. I actually blogged a photograph of the idyllic scene, trumpeting my disbelief that it was possible to have a piece of paradise all to ourselves at no charge (and once again paying no heed to friends back home having to see our bliss just as they were leaving home to go to work).

We planned to visit Lecce, a fairly large historical town, which, way back in the snowy Alps, had been highly recommended by an Italian gentleman we met. Thinking back, I can see it now: one of those in-depth conversations between two gentlemen during the emptying of toilet cassettes, only this time with Geoff in full cassette-emptying mode. *Whatever you do, don't leave Italy without visiting Lecce*, this Italian had said, rigorously swilling the last bit of poo around in his plastic box. And those words of touristic wisdom were chiefly the reason we were now visiting the heel of Italy.

The map showed there was a ring road around the town. By now experience had taught me that this meant a town large enough for us to get lost in, which sure enough we did, trying to find a car park big enough to accommodate a large motorhome. After 20 minutes of sitting in traffic, followed by an epic toddler tantrum in a coffee shop, I took Jackson to the toilet. By the time we returned, Geoff had decided he wasn't doing this today. Instead we would be finding a campsite and having an easy day of it. We would do some better planning and then tackle this road system tomorrow, with a map. It seemed unnecessary to me as we had coordinates for an out-of-town motorhome site, which I had already suggested from the beginning and would allow us to catch a bus into town. But there was no changing Geoff's mind, so back we headed to the coast.

Perhaps more than I'd noticed at home, I encountered this sort of randomly inexplicable behaviour from my husband several times on this trip. It seemed to be his coping mechanism in stressful situations. But, bearing in mind that I'd never once ventured behind the wheel, I didn't feel like arguing with it.

We passed miles of beautiful beaches and coves with motorhomes parked on the roadside where I made endless suggestions to stop and park up at one of them and wild camp the night again. But no, Geoff was having none of it. He had passed a sign miles back that said 'no camping' and that was that as far as he was concerned. Our problem was that most campsites were still closed and he was pressing on while expecting me to magic something up out of thin air, which soon resulted in our first proper argument. Many passers-by probably enjoyed the spectacle, which took place beside the kerb in a busy urban area, with the windows down, at full volume and with many obscenities flung back and forth. When we had exhausted ourselves I took to my bed for a few minutes of private time while Geoff worked out what he really, really wanted. Jackson paced the length of the van between us: *Mummy, is daddy just doing your head in? Daddy, is mummy being naughty? Mummy, is your head done in now? Daddy, you are doing Mummy's head in!* How could we not laugh? And, just like that, the argument was over, all thanks to a three-year-old's super mediating skills.

I had expected rows like these to be much more frequent, sharing such a small space for so long. But instead we came to realise how genuinely happy and relaxed we all were and how, with most of the external pressures of life taken off our agenda, Geoff and I had got to know each other so much better than before. It was so rare for us to have a cross word that this brief explosion genuinely took us all by surprise. I put it down to sheer exhaustion from everything this country had thrown at us so far. And it wasn't done with us just yet.

It was a mile or two farther on that we really came unstuck. We didn't expect on a Monday to find ourselves in nose-to-tail traffic with cars parked everywhere, picnics, families and coaches. I remember thinking something really good must be going on around here to attract all these people.

If you have never witnessed an Italian picnic I had better elaborate slightly. For a picnic, you or I might take a quiet drive out into the countryside, look for a peaceful, remote spot, lay a blanket down on the grass and bring out the shop-bought pre-packed sandwiches. Accompanied by a packet of crisps and an apple and washed down with a swig of squash straight out of the bottle, I would consider that a decent picnic. Not in Italy, allow me to me assure you! For a start, Italians don't simply picnic on the grass. They do it in style. They take the whole shebang, filling their cars to the roof, and even onto the roof, with tables, chairs, tablecloth, a vase of flowers, a bread basket and copious amounts of wine. Not to mention the entire family – whole generations of them. In fact their idea of a picnic looks more like my idea of a five-course banquet.

Next we come to their location of choice for partaking in this activity. Evidently the presence of cushioned chairs and a well-dressed table negates any need for soft, lush grass. So, with so much stuff to carry from car to site, any concept of being at one with Mother Nature is forgotten about and they set themselves up by the side of the road, in mud or gravel and amid traffic fumes and, these days, in the company of several thousand of their fellow diners.

Fearing that we might be missing out on whatever it was they knew about around here that we still didn't, we swung into action looking for a spot to park up. We noticed some motorhomes in a lovely picturesque cove down below the road and decided that this would be our destination. But things are never that simple in Italy. Straight ahead we encountered a 'no entry' sign where all the traffic was directed through a one-way system before rejoining the main road just up ahead. We could see coaches far ahead of us back on the main road, so with no further thought we took the sharp right turn into the one-way loop and, crucially, beyond the point of return.

Immediately someone pulled in and stopped right in front of us on the corner. Geoff tooted like an Italian, a few obscene gestures were exchanged and they moved on. Round we went cautiously with about thirty impatient drivers behind us. Then we turned left and it got narrower, just about leaving room for us to squeeze through, clipping wing mirrors with parked cars on either side of us. By now I was full-on sweating, sensing that this was not the end and knowing that there was no way back.

We reached the final left turn, where again some thoughtful folk had parked on both the inside and outside corners, leaving just enough room for a car at most to squeeze by at a push. I got out to a chorus of horn-blowing like you have never heard and made an extremely feeble attempt to guide Geoff around. But it was blatantly obvious it was impossible, and I mean IMPOSSIBLE! Still fresh from our earlier argument, he bellowed: *DO SOMETHING!!!* out of the window at me. I just wanted the ground to open up, swallow us all and save us from this shame.

Just then from the car behind us emerged a young and rather easy-on-the-eye Italian man who hastened to come to my rescue. Running a scornful eye over the parked cars, he announced: *Stupid bloody Italian drivers, they don't know how to park!* which instantly made me feel a bit better. I can't say the same for Geoff who was still sat behind the wheel with a hyped-up toddler in his ear, watching his wife eying up the muscles on this dark stranger who proceeded to wrench a huge lump of concrete, which supported a road sign, right out of the ground and move it to one side.

There followed ten minutes of inch-by-inch manoeuvring at the end of which we were truly in the deepest shit, having completely blocked the road and no doubt caused traffic to build up for miles. Behind us the nearest drivers were sitting with their hands permanently attached to their horns. Geoff was sweating and I was blushing crimson, but our superman wasn't done yet. He rounded up several drivers from their cars plus a couple of local passers-by who, sensing that this racket was more than just your average Italian road conversation, couldn't resist coming over for a nose-around. Discovering that one of the offending vehicles on the corner was unlocked, they proceeded to lift it up and carry it backwards up a bank. While I was still trying to pick my jaw up off the floor, Geoff inched his way round the obstacle and by the time I had jumped back into my seat they had put the car back where it had come from to a chorus of laughter and cheers.

On the final stretch we nearly took a wing mirror off but once we could breathe again we saw a car park right ahead. Abandoning our previous plans to return to our idyllic cove, we paid the attendant an extra two euros to let us camp for the night, which of course went straight into his pocket, and that, thank God, was the driving done for the day. Truth be told, we would have paid him 100 euros if he'd asked for it right then just to get us off the road and end our shame. It felt like we had held up half of Italy for all of eternity.

We sat and observed this traffic chaos for a while while recovering from our ordeal. Soon we realised that buses and coaches were simply ignoring the 'no entry' sign, waiting for a gap in the oncoming traffic and then driving the wrong way through that small section. Now if we had tried that trick, what's the betting that we would have met an oncoming bus whose driver had no hands on the wheel and whose attention was anywhere but on the road? Looking on the bright side, the next time a campsite conversation about impressive messes to get yourself into in a motorhome arose, we'd be able to take our story up several notches.

Our nightmare over, and still wondering why there were so many people about on a Monday, we walked down to the cove with our beach stuff. I lay down on the sand in my bikini while Geoff and Jackson paddled. Within minutes a group of young men turned up with a football, police siren, loudhailer and drum, and a friendly match got underway. Every time the excitement built, so too did the volume as the siren was sounded and the drummer beat out a rhythm. I looked around myself from the sand and wondered, for a split second, if I had died and was looking down on myself in this surreal world where I was the only person not clad in winter coat and jeans. Was this football match *really* happening in this tiny cove with crowds gathering, or had I imagined my whole day from start to finish? At one point the volume rose dramatically when the ball ended up in the sea and the wind carried it away. A volunteer jumped on an abandoned pedalo in an attempt to retrieve it, then discovered that the craft wasn't seaworthy and started to sink fully clothed. The rest of his team looked on from dry land, laughing, cheering and drumming as loudly as they could as he made it back sitting on the upturned edge of the capsized vessel.

Eventually we found out that it was a public holiday to mark the end of Italy's involvement in World War Two. On any other day at this time of the year both Lecce and this cove would have been deserted. But then what fun would that have been? This is what public holidays should be all about: picnics, family, fun, an electric atmosphere... All totally unlike our nation's idea of what to do on a bank holiday: neglect your family and make a futile attempt to catch up with the housework or the gardening.

By early evening we found ourselves alone in our field, which earlier had been a makeshift car park, but we took the risk and nobody seemed bothered by one family of campers. We were saving ourselves a considerable amount of money with all this wild camping and enjoying the sensation of waking up on our own in natural settings. That said, every few days it was necessary to use the facilities of a campsite or Aire if only to catch up on the washing and empty our waste tanks.

We discovered a very handy tip for the everyday small washing, which saved us a few euros. We would fill a plastic bin with a tight-fitting lid with water, washing powder and dirty clothes, and the motion of the vehicle while driving was enough to give the clothes a good wash ready to be rinsed and hung out to dry when we stopped for the night. Believe it or not, sharing mundane practical conversations of this sort with our fellow travellers got us quite excited. In fact, before leaving Wales, I actually read a whole chapter in a book concerning the motorhome toilet. It elaborated on the best brands of toilet paper: which ones would disintegrate the quickest (apparently, the cheaper the better), which chemicals to use, even going on to discuss various tips for reducing the need for frequent emptying. I found myself reading (and discussing in horror with Geoff) that some folk choose to bag up used toilet paper and dispose of it in a bin so as to avoid filling the tank too quickly. In fact let me not spare you the details: one recommendation was to line the toilet with a plastic bag before use, so you could remove your business in the bag and dispose of it in a bin and thereby leave your toilet clean and empty.

Then there was a debate between those who believed that the on-board toilet should be for number twos only because it did no harm to water the bushes, as it were, and those who shockingly reversed this in order to eliminate smells in the bathroom. Before leaving home this one chapter alone had led me to question my own sanity in deciding to leave my home comforts behind and lead such a primitive style of life. Thankfully with service points and Aires so readily available, it was one worry I had been able to dismiss at an early stage. But it is true that you do find yourselves engaging in the weirdest conversations with total strangers, hoping to glean some novel tips. Then farther on you gloat as you smugly pass them on as your own invention.

We left yesterday's madness behind – or should I say it left us behind? – as everyone returned to work and the place was once again deserted. This enticed us to change our plans for the day and explore the beautiful countryside instead of paying a cultural visit to Lecce.

We drove along the coast stopping for a look at a thermal bath. Discovering that it was just four euros for a swim, it seemed rude not to sample the lovely outdoor pool. For a thermal pool it wasn't particularly warm but what it lacked in temperature it made up for in its setting in the cliffs looking out to sea. Next we discovered a grotto, this time minus a drunken sailor. We had a brief walk around the caves, then slowly made our way towards Santa Maria di Leuca, the southernmost tip of the heel of Italy. Apart from a lighthouse there is not much of interest here, but it is one of those things you feel the need to see, if only for a photograph to prove that you stood on the end of Italy.

The drive along this coast was far more enjoyable than the Amalfi Coast, with spectacular scenery and quiet roads inviting us to stop almost anywhere to appreciate the breathtaking views over the turquoise sea. As the road twisted and turned around the cliffs the wildflowers were more abundant than I had ever seen in my life. We agreed we couldn't rate Puglia highly enough. Even so we couldn't help wonder whether, if we had seen during our journey any of the other places through which we passed not as they were then but at this time of year, when everywhere is warm and full of colourful highlights, we might have picked a different favourite, or whether Puglia would still win. There's no doubt that spring puts its own beautiful stamp on any area and, once the snow melts and the grass recovers, those mountain meadows through which we had previously skied would be transformed into an irresistible mass of flowers and wildlife. All in all, though, for us on this particular trip, Puglia emerged as our favourite region purely because we had been lucky enough to catch it at its very best. And to cap it all, our bird list was growing rapidly by the day.

As I turned these thoughts over, I realised that if we were to do this trip again at another time of year we would have very different experiences, and this increased my longing to go on and on travelling now for fear of missing something. It wasn't that we don't see the change of seasons back at home, more a case of wondering realistically how many of us have the time to notice that this little detail or those flowers or that birdsong is better today than it was yesterday, and that maybe tomorrow it will be better again? When stress is subtracted from your life you discover you have time to stop and observe and wonder. I felt more convinced than ever that Jackson must be constantly learning completely naturally while on this trip.

We decided to go mad and booked ourselves into a campsite in order to charge our electrical items. We parked next to a Slovenian family with two young girls. There was an instant affiliation between them and Jackson as they all got their toys out and played outside for hours, building train tracks in the grass and completely ignoring the language barrier. As for the adults, we had barely had time to organise the interior of our van ready for the night, by which I mean get the kettle out of the cupboard, than we heard our neighbours calling us. They had laid out four glasses and had already opened some wine. After a hastily prepared pasta dish, supposed to soak up the alcohol, all the kids descended on our van to watch a DVD.

The next thing we knew our new neighbours had decided to stay an extra day, and we quickly opted to do the same because Jackson enjoyed their company so much. That day they cooked us lunch and we reciprocated with tea after heading down the road a little farther to a sandy beach where we had our first dip in the sea in beautiful, clear turquoise water with tropical temperatures. No, I'm telling a lie, it was friggin' freezing! I felt better having braved it, though, knowing it could only get warmer from here on. Of course we were the only maniacs in the water, the locals not having even shed their winter coats yet. In fact that very evening the Slovenian family received news that the spring garden with a blossom tree in full flower that they had left behind a week before was now under a foot of snow.

When we left we headed back along the eastern Adriatic Coast of Italy. Over the next few days we planned to work our way slowly up towards Bari where we were booked onto an overnight ferry to Croatia on Tuesday. We had slipped up somewhat by forgetting to check the crossings until it was too late and had belatedly discovered that we hadn't left enough time to catch the next ferry. The silver lining, though, was that since there were only two crossings a week at this time of year, we now had time to play with. On this day we had planned finally to visit Lecce, but we allowed ourselves to get side-tracked to that little cove that a few days ago had eluded us in the bank holiday mayhem. We decided to allow ourselves an extra day of relaxation and set ourselves up ready to wild camp there for the night.

After a lovely lunch in the local restaurant, which kept the neighbours onside about the parked van, we took a clifftop walk through mile after mile of the most stunning wildflowers I had ever seen and added bee-eaters, pied flycatchers and great spotted cuckoos to our ever-growing bird list. Words can't do any of this justice but, as far as our eyes could see, the cliffs were smothered in a luxurious carpet of colour, like the best painting I had ever seen. Red poppies, white daisies, purples, pinks, blues and yellows were splashed abstractly over every inch of ground, sometimes knee high all around you and leaving only the gently winding green grass path uncovered. I started counting the different varieties of flower but lost track at somewhere around the fifty mark. All was alive with butterflies, the only noise was birdsong and bees and there was hardly a soul around. I don't suppose we will ever better this walk, which for me deservedly won top spot in my list of favourite moments on our journey.

Once again all this was totally unplanned and we would have missed it if we had just driven on past the cove towards Lecce. It really went to show how frequently these accidental adventures proved to be the most memorable. At this stage I hadn't yet fully understood about this. I still felt that we had all the time in the world ahead of us and was reluctant to rush through any area without leaving no stone unturned. I had the illusion that we could afford ourselves whatever time we needed for the delights of distractions and impromptu adventures. Later on I realised that this luxury should not be taken for granted when my appreciation of time changed in the latter stages of our travels.

A police car came by in the early evening by which time there were three other motorhomes parked up with us. Jackson was outside playing and Geoff and I spotted the flashing blue light. We braced ourselves to be moved but they drove off and an over-excited Jackson came running back shouting: *I waved to the police and they waved back and flashed their blue lights for me!* They didn't come back and were obviously not too concerned about it. I had the impression that wild camping was closely monitored but that if no harm was being done the police turned a blind eye a lot of the time.

The next day we had a slow drive because I was constantly making Geoff stop for me to take photographs of flowers. The sea views were fantastic all along this stretch of road. We stopped at a bauxite quarry near Otranto. Before us an emerald green lake surrounded by mountains of barren red earth made for a rather alien landscape but nonetheless beautiful. Bee-eaters circled above us and lizards rushed about their business around our feet. There looked to be some pleasant walks around here but we decided to move on into Otranto itself. A historic seaside town and port with a lovely castle, it had a warm holiday feel to it. It was probably the best kept of all the towns in Italy that we visited and stood out for all the right reasons – and this was seeing it on a pretty grey day, so I can only imagine it in blue sky and sunshine. The beach was white sand with a crystal-clear sea and even a couple of people braving the cold water – British, of course. We walked round the walled town before moving on to our campsite, where we left the van and went for a dip ourselves – of course!

Deciding we were too tired to drive the next day, we booked an extra night and spent the day walking the cliffs and picnicking, along with half of Italy because it was bank holiday weekend once again. We relaxed in the sun watching the general holiday antics of the local youngsters who were cliff diving and having fun. Again entire families with all generations were gathered together. A little procession of some sort from the local church nearly deafened us with all its honking of horns as they passed. The campsite here was quite basic, one of those ones where I questioned Geoff's judgement in opting to venture into the bug-ridden showers and toilet when we had a perfectly clean one of our own, but even so it was grassy and peaceful and within easy walking distance of the beach. The next morning, unless we got distracted yet again, we aimed to actually make it to Lecce.

20. A SOGGY FAREWELL TO ITALY

MAY

GETTING A GRIP, we put our heads down in a bid to prevent any further distractions en route and finally get to see this place, Lecce, that had eluded us for the past week. Unfortunately we arrived in the middle of a torrential downpour. No matter how many different forecasts we checked, desperately wishing for one to give us a glimmer of hope, they all clearly confirmed that this weather had settled in for three days. We sat it out in the van in a car park in the centre of town for as long as we could but eventually, with no sign of any improvement, we donned our waterproofs and braved the elements.

It was a Sunday so of course no shops were open. It was in that car park in a dismal mood that it dawned on me that every time my loving husband has generously surprised me by saying: *We could have a look around the shops, if you like*, this had coincidentally been on a Sunday. The feeling of empowerment from knowing that I had one up on him brought a smile to my face as we wandered the empty streets. But it was like a ghost town. On Sundays, towns in Italy, wherever you might be, are usually filled with families creating a very upbeat atmosphere. But today we were the only fools in sight, which shows you how heavy this downpour was. We could see numerous beautiful churches and archaeological sites around the place including a small amphitheatre, and it clearly oozed charm if only the sun would shine. We battled on but after an hour we were soaked to the skin and, totally disheartened, we decided to abandon it.

On the way back to the van we spotted a large hotel and thought we would ask whether they had a swimming pool that the public could use. A trade fair was taking place inside with stands demonstrating nail art, hair-dressing, massage and all things beautiful. We mingled, wandering around in our dripping wet waterproofs, imagining that we could blend in and acquire some freebies – until we saw ourselves in a mirror! Right in the middle of the room was an orange woman laid out on a table, topless in just her knickers (what there were of them!), smothered in oil and having a full body massage. I stooped to pick Geoff's jaw up off the floor. We were quoted 70 euros for a swim. After our thermal baths for 4 euros we just laughed and instead nicked their toilet roll on the way back to the van. We would have to resort to an afternoon of board games and DVDs.

Without actually noticing it creeping up on us, we had reached a point of exhaustion during these last few days. Now, with the change in the weather combined with the sense of hanging around waiting for our ferry crossing, we found it difficult to muster up the energy to do very much. Exploring Italy in a month is extremely tiring. There is so much to do. The cities are very demanding with their crowds and queues and transport links to be negotiated. Even the journey between one destination and the next leaves you feeling frazzled through the sheer stress of the roads and the absurd behaviour of other drivers. Your senses are constantly on high alert wherever you go, usually for the best of reasons. But there comes a point when you just have to stop and take a breath, and we had reached that point. Thankfully, Croatia was on the horizon.

All that said, we knew we would have so many reasons to return to Italy one day and that our trip would never have been half of what it was without our experiences there. It was by far the most varied, exciting, mad country I had ever visited. And, although we felt a little disappointed that we had not got to appreciate Lecce in its full glory after making such a big deal about getting there, we felt thankful for all the unforgettable sights and experiences we had been granted in taking this route specifically to add this one town to our agenda.

It was free to stay overnight in this car park on the Sunday and we were joined there by another eight motorhomes. However, it became apparent that we would be paying in other ways when a mobile snack bar set up just feet from our van in the early evening. We watched its owner setting up tables and chairs between him and us and decided on a strategic move to the far end of the line of campers. At about 8 p.m. the car park came alive. Hundreds of cars arrived from which emerged smartly dressed people of all ages who started walking into town and then returned an hour or so later. We had no idea what we could be missing but it was still raining and we simply didn't care. That, though, was just the lull before the storm, because at 3.30 a.m. it felt like a festival in the car park with much shouting and singing and the snack bar doing a roaring trade. Yet by 7 a.m. it again started filling up with cars and people going to work. If only we had drunk some wine we might have slept...

It was still raining when we set off, making a beeline for the coast in the direction of Bari. It was only half an hour away so we decided to do a big supermarket shop en route and then called in to a large outdoor shop to purchase a table, having realised we were the only people eating inside our van at campsites and thought: *What's one more thing to squeeze into our garage?* All we lacked now was a BBQ, but what with the rain bouncing off the road outside it hardly inspired us to rush into all of that.

We found a quiet beach car park in Polignano a Mare, a suburb of Bari, far enough away from the town and the port to feel safe and spend our last night in Italy. This time we had wine. But we also seemed to have some interesting company and a constant turnover of vehicles, which parked up in the rain, in the dark, with their lights off, then left half an hour later. It left very little to the imagination. I couldn't help feeling sorry for them all as we sat in our nice warm van, drinking wine and watching ruddy *Fireman Sam* for the umpteenth time, our king-size bed wasted on us while they no doubt settled for the back seat.

Polignano turned out to be a lovely town in daylight, with shades of Cuba in its architecture and design. There was poetry painted all over steps and doors and buildings, and paintwork deliberately left to fade and peel added to the charm of the place. Yet it was treated with no significance on the map, demonstrating once again that if you allow yourself time to explore you never know what you might find. We had begun our trip with this carefree approach four months ago but now, without even realising it, we were gradually becoming more rushed trying to fit everything in. Sometimes – not always – we were starting to find ourselves moving from A to B without allowing ourselves time to be spontaneous. These were signs that we were becoming aware of time constraints and that they were having an effect on us. It suddenly became obvious to us, as we approached our halfway mark, that this was bound to become increasingly apparent. For a moment we imagined just how different we would feel on the return stretch. It was not a good feeling.

After lunch we made the final drive to the port. As we approached Bari we noticed there were women on both sides of the road, one every couple of hundred metres, smartly dressed and sitting on white plastic garden chairs. With no evidence of stalls selling any wares it became obvious that they were in fact selling their bodies. One in black suspenders and lace stockings and what appeared to be a shirt but no sign of a skirt kind of gave the game away. Cars were pulling in, so they obviously had business. It sparked questions like: where do they go in the middle of the day? Do they use a hotel? If so, does some bloke actually walk in with that half-naked woman and ask for a room? And was it they who were using our car park last night? We discussed all this while momentarily forgetting that we had an extra pair of ears sitting behind us, quietly taking it all in. He would no doubt save his questions on this subject for when I was in a queue in a bank or an art gallery or a posh restaurant.

I confess I was a bit taken aback by these scenes. It was all so blatant. There was nothing to stop a police car driving past at any moment or someone's wife driving down the road and questioning why her husband's car was parked in the bushes. The fact that the chairs remained in position, marking someone's patch from one day to the next, just like closing the door on your office until the next day, indicated that there was little fear of any repercussions. There is one particular stretch of road on the Adriatic Coast named 'road of love' where this form of slave trade is rife. Nigerian women, who have been trafficked into the country believing that a babysitting or cleaning job awaits them, are forced into this line of work, saddled with unpayable debts and often terrified into silence by voodoo rituals. Maybe I am naive but I did not expect to come face to face with this sort of thing in this day and age, and I certainly did not expect to subject Jackson to it.

We sat the rest of the day out at the dock in Bari waiting for our 10 p.m. sailing. There were some seriously strange people hanging around here and the police sprang into action and cornered one car near us. It didn't do much for my nerves, which were already on edge thinking about the hours at sea that lay ahead of us. On the bright side, what a luxury it is to queue for a ferry in the comforts of a motorhome. We cooked a meal, washed up, watched DVDs, and we could even have gone to bed for an hour if we fancied it, while all around us people sat in cars in the discomfort we had always been used to.

Next stop, Croatia!

21. LAND OF A THOUSAND ISLANDS

I WOULD BE lying if I didn't admit to being a little anxious about this next phase of our journey. The prospect of ten hours or more at sea did not appeal on any level. But the wonder of new unknown shores enticed and so, dosed up with anti-sickness tablets and sporting the latest in travel wrist bands, we waved goodbye to Italy. In the moments I braved it on deck as we cast off from Bari we all got to witness the braveness and skill of the pilot who, having steered us safely out of the port into deeper waters, was soon climbing down a very precarious looking rope ladder on the outside of our ferry in readiness to step across the black void separating him from the pilot boat speeding alongside us waiting to transport him back to dry land. To a round of applause he was gone and I retreated to the comfort of our cabin with our own personal toilet for me to retch in private.

Having never had the need to use a cabin before, as I had never agreed to any sea crossing exceeding two hours, the fact that we were required to make our own beds from plastic bags containing a towel, sheet and pillowcase immediately had me questioning my level of expectations. The crossing was rough, the cabin cramped and the floor probably more comfortable than the beds. That I docked in the calm waters of Dubrovnik with my stomach contents still where they should be was a triumph, of sorts, but should not distract from the reality that I had been unable to lift my head off the pillow for the entire crossing. My resolve never to book a cruise was sealed.

Our first sighting of Dubrovnik was one I will never forget. Stepping up on deck into glorious morning sunshine to be presented with the spectacle laid out before us rendered us speechless. We were sailing into port surrounded by more islands than it was possible to count. It was exactly as I imagined the Norwegian Fjords, but nothing had prepared me for this. The sea was the deepest blue I had ever seen. Sparkling blindingly in the light, it was crystal clear and in the countless pebbly coves it took on an intensely inviting green hue reflected from the densely vegetated islands.

Once on land we found Dubrovnik immaculate after Italy, with its neat little red roofs and freshly painted houses, and everywhere litter-free and well cared for. It was only 8 a.m. and we wanted to make full use of the day to visit the city before moving farther on to camp. I suggested we should park near the port and catch a bus into town, but Geoff decided to drive in. After passing right through the main area and failing to find a parking space we found ourselves on a road heading out of the city with nowhere to turn round. If we turned off left we would be entering Bosnia, for which we were not insured, and if we went much farther along this road we would find ourselves in Albania. Luckily we managed to turn in a lay-by just in time.

We retraced our steps to the port, where we parked and caught a bus in. Geoff felt in control, though, because he had overridden my initial suggestion and this time around it was his idea. As a passenger I have learned when to shut up and smirk privately.

We hadn't realised that Croatia had its own currency and with a purse full of euros but not a single *kuna* to our name we parked outside the old walled city and went to change some euros. We had our first indication of prices in Croatia when we were charged the equivalent of 22 euros to park for the day in Dubrovnik, quite a shock after the free car parking we had pretty much encountered since leaving the UK.

Let me rewind back to my study of the differing standards of the toilet facilities we encountered along the way, because Croatian toilets deserve a mention. Throughout Italy the toilets were nowhere near as entertaining as in France. They were also generally unclean, invariably lacked a seat, usually wouldn't lock, never had toilet paper or soap and rarely had hand-driers, and for the pleasure of all this you were generally required to pay about 50 pence a time. At one point an attendant tried to charge me double because Jackson was with me. I offered him the toilet paper and suggested he could wipe Jackson's bum. Both he and Jackson stared at me in horror and we got our usual two-for-one deal. In Croatia we now found early indications that we could expect toilet seats, locking doors, toilet paper, hot water, soap and hand-driers. But this would come at the inflated price of about 70 pence a go. It was almost cheaper to use a café and pay for a coffee first.

Dubrovnik's Old Town, encircled by massive stone walls, was mightily impressive. It was buzzing with people but, unlike Rome or Florence, we did not feel in the least edgy and there were no beggars or lookie lookie men. It was all so relaxed and friendly that it was easy to lose track of time listening to live music and people-watching while enjoying a coffee in a pavement café. We had hoped to walk the city walls, a mile all round. But we found it would cost £35 for the three of us, which seemed a bit steep on top of the car parking, considering we had only been here for an hour or so. So instead we settled for a good old roam around inside the walls. There was a wonderful central square with on one side an arch through which you could walk out to the port. On the other side were a series of connecting passageways and steep stone steps, which took us on a journey surrounded by four- or five-storey-high buildings with washing strung out to dry high above our heads like bunting and elderly locals enjoying the sun outside their houses, while thousands of tourists of every nationality walked past.

There seemed to be nothing to dislike about Dubrovnik, and I would recommend it as a compulsory visit for anyone's Croatian agenda. For us, though, feeling the contrast with the emptiness of Puglia, it was just too overrun with tourists and, beautiful though its architecture was, it did not feel like the real Croatia we were eager to see. If you visited this city alone you would go away with very little idea of what Croatian life is really like, which would be a shame.

We left in the late afternoon and drove fifteen kilometres to our campsite. It is illegal to wild camp anywhere in Croatia and we had been advised by frequent travellers that the police would be on our case within an hour should we ever attempt it, so we aimed to stay out of trouble at least on day one and had booked a campsite. Our first impressions were that there was a slightly clinical feel to the country. The roads seemed purposely designed to keep one moving without any viewing points or picnic sites, and everything felt almost too neat and with too many rules. And yet, despite the lack of character, at least in this area, it was undeniably beautiful.

We had booked a small site, the sort that requires you to manoeuvre between olive trees, but it was clean and cheap and only cost £10 per night all in. We complimented the owner on its cleanliness, which, by Italian standards, was immaculate. We found ourselves parked next to David and Valerie, a couple from Leicestershire, who were caravanning and had years of experience in Croatia and gave us lists of recommendations. Quite unlike us, they researched an area for months before setting out on their travels and arrived armed with itineraries, pre-planned campsites and knowledge of public holiday dates. They supplied answers to every question we asked.

Needing to catch up on our sleep after the last few days, we resorted to our alternative approach to travelling and spontaneously decided to stay an extra lazy day here, which we shared with a family from Bavaria. In fact the wife had gone home as she had shorter holidays from work, but the man was bravely continuing for two more weeks in sole charge of two children aged three and six. This meant he was taking on the work of both of us, driving, cooking, cleaning and sorting the kids out, but he took it all in his stride.

It was inspiring to see how confident Jackson was when he asked me if he could go and see the kids as soon as he spotted them. I told him that they might not speak English. *It's ok, mummy,* he said, *I'll tell them I'm Jackson and ask if they want to play with me* and off he went on his own. I would never have done that when I was his age.

The kids' dad hit the nail on the head when he remarked that the most enjoyable part of travelling with children was the way they inadvertently initiate conversations between adults from opposite sides of the campsite who otherwise would probably never meet. Coincidentally he had done aid work in Kosovo at the same time as Geoff so they had plenty to chat about, while all three kids whizzed about the campsite on balance bikes and set up train sets on the grass. Their motorhome was an off-road converted army truck and they had been on a very exciting cross-country adventure through Albania. Jackson would never allow us to hear the end of it and wanted to swap our van for an army vehicle.

For the afternoon we took ourselves down for a picnic on what turned out to be our own private beach. It was a shock to test the sea temperature but although drastically colder than Italy it could not deter us fools. I measured it this way: in Italy the pain caused by the cold water eased after a few minutes and then the water was bearable for about five to ten minutes (though not enjoyable, I hasten to add), whereas here the pain stayed with you for a good ten minutes and then your body just went numb.

Next morning it was like a mass evacuation from the campsite. It seemed that everyone was leaving at the same time. Together with our Leicestershire neighbours, we were heading for a peninsula about two hours along the coast.

22. WINE ON THE ROCKS

THE DRIVE TO the Pelješac peninsula was outstandingly beautiful. We hardly went round a bend without another photo opportunity presenting itself. We were greatly disorientated by all the islands and this confusion never left us the entire time we were in Croatia. Between the sat nav, the map and the view from the window we had no concept of what was mainland and what was an island. Were we on one of those narrow peninsulas? Were we looking across the sea to an island? Or were we looking back at the mainland? After a while we gave up trying to fathom it out. Studying the map later back at home revealed that on both sides those were proper islands too numerous to count as we zigzagged from coast to coast along the length of this jutting piece of land.

Although it was still early days, it was clear that we hadn't yet really experienced much of Croatian life. Finding it was not as easy as we'd expected: it seemed to be a case of either wall-to-wall tourists as in Dubrovnik or everywhere being deserted. In our two-hour drive we passed two cafés and one petrol station, all three of them closed, with very little other sign of life.

This peninsula is famed for its wine production. As we got nearer to our campsite, every other building had a sign up outside enticing us to sample their produce. There were at least fifty of them but almost all were closed. Eventually we stopped to photograph the view and parked right outside a small wine-taster with tables set up like a café. But we found that unless we wanted wine, which I generally don't at 11 a.m., it was hard luck as they sold neither soft drinks nor coffee.

Looking at the vineyards it was hard to believe that anything grew. The vines literally appeared to be sprouting from rocks. Compared to the rich fertile red earth we had seen in Tuscany these vines had to survive near-drought conditions, never mind the poor farmers who had to build and maintain these rock terraces up the steep mountainsides. We had a date to sample their wares that evening as we had been assured by David and Valerie, our well-informed companions from our last stop, that this campsite had a quality restaurant and if we took our own bottles we could purchase house wine for a mere three euros per litre. My two plastic water bottles and a milk bottle were all rinsed out and at the ready.

En route we drove through an area that gave us some cause for concern as we suddenly witnessed the utter devastation caused by forest fires and realised this was a very real danger over the coming months. A vast swathe of land at least five miles long had been completely burnt to the ground fairly recently. The fire had destroyed everything in its path on both sides of the road all the way down to the coast, thankfully sparing a few houses right on the edge of the cliffs and leaving them sitting isolated in a blackened and lifeless landscape. It occurred to us that if we had travelled this route a week or so earlier and had found ourselves caught up in a fire in a vehicle like ours we might have been in real danger. The road ran straight for miles along the entire length of the peninsula and offered no turning places or escape routes to the left or right, so finding ourselves faced with a wall of advancing flames would have been absolutely terrifying. Today workmen were deep in black ash attempting to secure the steep banks above the road, since with all the trees destroyed their roots would no longer stabilise the earth and landslides might follow.

While reading about the frequency of forest fires as a result of this experience, I learned another interesting fact. Apparently the second most destructive plague to destroy pine forests, next to wild fires, is the pine processionary caterpillar. Since mid January we had seen evidence of these in their zillions all over Europe and had come very close to having a poke around with a stick at one stage, being curious about what sort of creature built these grapefruit-sized nests resembling ball-shaped webs that hung in their thousands from pine trees. At that stage we didn't know what they were or how dangerous they could be but thankfully the fear of spiders possibly running out at us had prevailed and deterred us from applying our stick test. It turned out that the caterpillars – not spiders – spend the winter in these nests, then in spring they all link up to form a chain often several metres long and move down to the ground where they bury themselves and later hatch as a harmless moth. The danger comes when they are still caterpillars. They shed venomous hairs, which on contact with skin causes a severe burning rash and if inhaled, or licked in the case of dogs, can be deadly. Everywhere I go now I look up just to be sure I am not close to one. Believe me, there is no shortage of them in Croatia, although thankfully by the time we were there they should in theory have been underground by now.

What a difference we found here in the standard of campsites compared to what we had been used to. We were greeted by very helpful staff who took us all on a tour of the site on their golf buggy so that we could select a nice pitch: none of this walking business. David and Valerie, needless to say, were well and truly settled and relaxing in the sun by the time we arrived, in a lovely pitch overlooking the sea. Opposite the site were a handful of small islands dotted about in a glistening bay, most of them uninhabited and one of them a 15-minute ferry ride away.

We opted for a pitch a short distance from them, overlooking the pool and just far enough away to give them some peace from Jackson. This was the first swimming pool we had found open since the indoor pool in the snowy Alps. In contrast this one was not heated as evidenced by the squeals when unsuspecting souls entered. The restaurant looked lovely, there was the all important swing park, a supermarket across the road and the most immaculately beautiful showers, toilets and washing-up rooms we had ever seen. It was actually the first shower we'd seen in three months where someone thought to build a separate dressing area per shower, so you could hang your clothes in the dry. They even had a state-of-the-art, futuristic chemical toilet disposal unit, which did all the work. All you had to do was take the lid off and place your cassette in the machine. It returned it to you emptied, cleaned and even ready with fresh chemicals inside. I didn't know they existed, and did I give it a go? Er, no – no chance! Why? Because under no circumstances did I want to lull Geoff into a false sense of hope that I might be willing to take on this role for a change. I let *him* have fun playing with it instead.

To show off a bit, we even got our awning out for the first time, although we had to enlist the help of David, for Geoff's memory didn't recall much of our three-hour familiarisation session on the garage forecourt back in Wales in December. I hadn't even known what colour it was until now, and thought that with our new table, chairs and citronella candle we were finally beginning to look the part.

With wall-to-wall sunshine and no wind we decided to tackle the job of unearthing our inflatable kayak from the tip that was our garage. We paddled, with Jackson in the middle of us like Lord Muck, across to a couple of the islands in the hope of a picnic, Robinson Crusoe style. There was no easy landing site and an army of sea urchins underfoot and with Jackson now fast asleep in the kayak we revised our plans and settled for a floating dining experience in the kayak instead. That lasted all of five minutes before Jackson awoke declaring he felt seasick.

This was how we spent the next two days, either in the pool, the sea or the kayak, but I have no idea what everyone else on that site was doing as we were always alone. I think most people just sat in the privacy of their own patches next to their vans all day. We did make a costly mistake here, being lulled into a false sense of security by all the peace and tranquillity of the scene. We had been mooring our fully inflated kayak at the water's edge near what appeared to be the caravan of some full-timers, judging by the array of beachcombing decor that adorned their plot. This one particular day we had got lazy and left our pump and the bag for the kayak in a nearby empty building too, and of course, being easy to carry, we returned to find that they had walked. For an awful moment we thought we needed the pump to deflate the kayak and I had visions of spending the next few days with a fully inflated boat on our bed, but luckily it deflated without it. Although we felt a bit let down and annoyed with ourselves for taking an unnecessary risk, it could have been worse: it could have been the kayak itself, so a lesson was learned, which would not be forgotten. In fairness we had done well on this trip. Four months in and this was the first theft we had encountered in spite of all the tales we had heard and all the wild camping we had done, so we didn't allow this experience to bother us too much.

One evening we joined David and Valerie for a meal at the campsite restaurant I mentioned previously. We sampled the house wine, found it good and made a hasty run to the van to pour our last bottle of milk down the drain to give us an extra vessel for our takeaway purchases. With all these soft drinks bottles now full of alcohol I needed to remember that if Jackson suddenly started acting strange maybe I had mixed one up with his cherry syrup. And we may have been a bit over-exuberant in our purchase as we woke up with stinking headaches the next morning, suggesting the wine might be full of chemicals and the need for an element of caution before sampling again.

It wasn't hard to fall in love with this site and it was quite a challenge to drag ourselves away. We were just getting used to relaxing properly after Italy and reminding ourselves that it was possible to make lasting memories by simply enjoying life right outside our van from time to time. But there was so much we wanted to see and we felt we ought to move on, so finally we left to head farther up the coast. By the time we got ourselves together and put all the toys away it was already nearing lunchtime and we had a long hot drive ahead of us.

Yet again, and quite unplanned, we found ourselves going in the same direction as David and Valerie. We were all using the same ACSI campsite book, which offers such good discounts that it's probably no surprise really. We had a couple of options in mind including a recommendation from them. They were always organised hours ahead of us, probably due to the fact that they actually knew before they left their home that on this particular day they would be vacating this campsite and instead of sitting staring at wall-to-wall mess the previous evening they actually got ready for their forthcoming departure. This was in sharp contrast to us who, four months in, were still almost always driving off site with me on my feet negotiating a moving van as I shut cupboards and threw all remaining loose objects onto the beds, in a bid to leave before we had to pay for an extra day. That was us, our style never changed, and our relaxed approach to things is what made it fun for us.

On leaving David shouted from his window: *It's about five hours away!* I didn't mention that part to Geoff. When I entered the coordinates into the sat nav and it announced: *You will reach your destination in two hours* I smelt a rat and hastily altered the settings to exclude motorways, which would have meant us missing all the beautiful coastline. Pleased with myself for having come such a long way as a sat nav operator and recalling the day I took Geoff up and down a mountain by mistake, which was a whole lot worse than it sounds, I sat in the passenger seat enjoying the scenery and feeling very smug that we clearly still knew something that David didn't, because even with motorways off the radar this journey that was to take them five hours would still only be taking us three.

Half an hour later Geoff aroused me from my daydream with a very good question: *Why is the screen all blue up ahead?* To this day that image is still with me! That was the sea, that was, and it taught us that there was yet another secret quirk the *&£@#ing sat nav had up its sleeve. Would I ever get to grips with the settings on the thing? What I now discovered was that you needed to cancel ferry crossings from your route options if you wanted to avoid being guided to the nearest port with no questions asked. As we sat in silence looking across the water with not a ship in sight and no idea of sailing times or costs, staring at our destination for the night, we were faced with no choice but to turn round and retrace our steps all the way back along the length of the peninsula, round the coast and then back along the opposite coast. And yes, funnily enough, David was right, it did take five hours.

Despite all this it was just about the best five-hour journey you could ever wish for. The roads were empty and in great condition and ran along just a stone's throw from the sea the whole way. I wish I could paint you a picture of the scenery because it had to be seen to be believed. Croatia was, quite simply, breathtaking. Heavily pine-clad mountainous slopes rose sharply from an ocean so clear and flat that every colour was vividly reflected in its waters. In places it was so green you could be forgiven for mistaking it for land. In others it was the deepest blue while in the countless hidden coves its shores were flanked by white pebbles that were clearly visible even at considerable depth through the cleanest of water. Rugged rocky outcrops protruded above the trees and the whole landscape screamed wilderness and unspoiled beauty.

Gratifyingly, the entire country seems to put respect for nature above commercial pressures to construct large-scale tourist resorts. Some call it The Land of a Thousand Islands but you would struggle to count each one visible at any point along its coastline. Each island seems as alluring as the next and although this time it wasn't on our agenda, island-hopping definitely appeals. No other place on earth has afforded us the ability to repetitively remark on its wonders as many times a day for as many days in succession as Croatia did. The nearest comparison I could make would be a blend of Switzerland, Norway and New Zealand.

We had one minor panic en route as we approached a customs point and discovered that we were about to enter Bosnia. Until then I was unaware that Croatia is actually split into two by a twelve-mile strip of coastline that belongs to Bosnia, though looking at the map it is clear to see why Bosnia would want to hold on to their only tiny port. Our vehicle insurance didn't cover us for Bosnia but we got through customs with no hassle and were the only vehicle on the road. Ten minutes later we were back in Croatia.

We were a little disappointed when we arrived at our next campsite, which had a very high rating. We caught them in the middle of building work making pre-season improvements and adding a new swimming pool. The work they had completed so far was really nice but it didn't alter the fact that the beach was markedly more building site than beach and doubled up as a car park for diggers and piles of building materials. Our main reason for choosing this site had been that the guidebook had boasted of its sandy beach, which was a rarity in Croatia, and our feet had had enough of stone by now. Sadly there wasn't a grain of sand in sight.

Split was only about five kilometres away so we caught a bus in. We managed to replace the pump for the kayak and enjoyed a pleasant enough walk around the harbour and old town. After some of the places we had been to, though, Split wasn't exactly spectacular. I think that after a certain point you just can't get very enthusiastic about yet another city unless it is something truly unique, and Italy had given us so much that by now we were very hard to please.

The weather forecast was for rain over the next few days. With this and with the state of the campsite in mind, we made a decision to move on the following day in the hope of finding somewhere with more activities to occupy us in bad weather. Once again it was a long drive, with the temperature dropping and the wind picking up, which made for choppy waters instead of the pristine lake-like azure seas we had become used to. This was a different side of Croatia.

We made a half-hour detour across a bridge onto a small island called Murter, where it's safe to say there are more boats than people. And we're not just talking wooden fishing boats here. There's also no shortage of luxury yachts.

Our final destination was close to Zadar. We arrived at a massive campsite, more like a holiday village actually, with on-site restaurants, shops, hairdressers, heated pool and no less than seven swing parks. I don't usually rate these big places because I prefer privacy and natural surroundings whereas here, as soon as you entered, you could be just about anywhere and everything around you was designed to keep you there and prevent you from being tempted to wander elsewhere. But we needed to remember Jackson's needs on this trip too and this place was just heaven on earth for him. Whatever the sky threw at us we could keep ourselves busy here, which was just as well because, believe you me, we saw some torrential storms over the next few days.

It is not easy to sleep in a vehicle with rain drumming loudly on your metal roof all night long. A brief respite from the rain the following day afforded us the chance to explore our site, revealing two beaches, one useable, the other as much a building site as the previous place or, as one German camper described it to me: *Catastrophic!* We couldn't actually decide whether the dark soft stuff full of digger tracks was sand or indeed mud but either way, bless them, there were kids playing in it trying their best to make sandcastles.

We opted for a late buffet breakfast just to kill time until the next rain storm passed. I think we did quite well out of it, creating a six meals for the price of two deal. Jackson's was free and, breakfast being his favourite meal of the day and the first bacon for months being on the menu, he ate like a horse. Then we managed to stuff our pockets full of rolls, cheese and fruit for lunch too, so we were happy campers.

By the time we arrived back at our van, guess who was walking around scouting a nice pitch? Yes, it was David and Valerie. The weather hadn't improved by the next morning, we were the only people in the pool, and eventually in sheer desperation we set off in Dotty to look up a place called Razanac, which a Croatian lady we met in Italy had implored us to visit. It was the home of her mother and she described it to us as having simply the best view in the world. All I can say is more fool us to expect anything to come of this, on such a crappy day. We could see absolutely nothing through the rain and instead we drove into the city of Zadar.

It turned out that Zadar had just been elected Best European City of 2016. I beg to differ, not wishing to take anything from Zadar, which was very pleasant, but really, how could you compare it with the likes of Rome or Florence? At least the rain finally stopped and before we knew it we were sitting on the pavement eating mojito ice cream in a street in the centre of the walled town, which was lined on both sides with ice cream shops. There was an interesting mix of modern buildings, Roman ruins and an 8th-century church, but the highlight was back outside the walls on the promenade. Set within marble steps that descend into the sea were a series of 35 organ pipes over a distance of 70 metres along the prom, creating a sea organ. An ever-changing, unpredictable series of musical notes was formed by the motion of the sea and the strength of the wind and was clear for all to hear as you strolled along the pavement or allowed yourself to become entranced while you sat staring at the horizon. The performer was nature itself. Jackson, of course, was fascinated and insisted on kneeling down with his ear to a hole and then poking an obligatory stick or dropping a stone into it. If we had hung around until dark and if the weather had been on our side there was another attraction in this area. There was a large circular area on the ground paved with solar panels, where apparently a combination of energy from the sun and the sea creates an impressive light show in the dark sky from dusk until dawn. Again nature was allowed to play such an important role in the architecture of this country and it definitely made it special.

Stepping up to the plate, we entertained not only David and Valerie but also Bill and Doreen, our other campsite neighbours, in our van that night. Of course we were not equipped for it, but everyone arrived with their own glass in hand and an enjoyable evening of wine, conversation and fun ensued. We felt inspired by Bill who, though you would never have believed it, turned out to be 80 years young. They had moved to France a few years before and now they travelled for several months at a time in a tiny little camper van, really quite hardcore. If this lifestyle could do that much for your health I'd be packing Geoff and myself into a van in years to come. Jackson would be visiting us on a campsite, never mind an old people's home.

Finally the sun made an appearance, but much as we had wanted to visit Nin, a lovely little town on a tiny island, which you walk onto and which has a picture postcard lagoon, we decided it wouldn't be fair to Jackson to drag him away from a beautiful campsite full of children and kids' activities on the only day when the weather behaved itself. So we will return one day with Nin to look forward to. Instead we had a fun-packed day starting with a bicycle race between Jackson and his new girlfriend Mia from Germany. The pair of them were literally screeching round the bends on their stabilizers, one wheel off the ground, laughing their heads off. Then it was sandcastles on the beach until we got invaded by a large number of very loud, very drunk Germans. It was school holidays in Germany and being only a 600-kilometre drive away Croatia is a popular destination, so the campsite was full.

The afternoon kicked off with a pool party for Mia and Jackson followed by a mini disco in the evening, although someone forgot to tell them that disco generally suggests one should dance. The pair of them stood motionless shoulder to shoulder the whole way through. No amount of encouragement could get them dancing until Mia sat the last two songs out and Jackson started jumping, I would say, rather than dancing. Their strategy became apparent not long after.

To everyone's dismay an evening of spontaneous entertainment courtesy of an American square dance group who happened to be holidaying at this campsite was forced upon us. It was just desperate! The youngest member must have been 70 if they were a day and to say they took it seriously would be a major understatement. Step by step, with not so much as a glimmer of a smile and without any sign of enjoyment or humour, they walked or stamped their way through one routine after another while a gentleman on the microphone talked the audience through every move as if we were taking notes (and as if we cared). The only exception was a white-haired old dear who truly applied meaning to the term 'mutton dressed as lamb'. A shameless display of flirtatious behaviour involving anyone who dared to glance in her direction continued throughout the performance while all the time she repeatedly hoisted up her white cut-off jeans and readjusted her bra.

Finally they got an obligatory round of applause and that was the moment when Jackson and Mia came into their own. They took to the stage with two balloons each and danced their way with gusto through each routine, waving their balloons about like cheerleaders. Everyone's attention was diverted in their direction as the dance group battled on in the background. At last, with no less than six balloons and two completely hyperactive children in tow, we returned for a long night's sleep ready to move inland tomorrow.

23. A MAGICAL PLACE

JACKSON SAID A tearful farewell to his friend Mia, leaving her with a bar of chocolate. She was to stay on for another week with her grandparents who were experimenting with motorhoming for the first time with a view to purchasing their own. Unfortunately, no doubt not helped by the weather and the need to entertain a toddler full time, the experience had really put them off and this new day promised nothing different. I can honestly say I have never seen rain like it. We counted our blessings that we were fortunate enough to have formed lasting first impressions of Croatia in the sunshine, which will draw us back for more.

But as for anyone arriving in the subsequent week, I felt sorry for them. Croatia, beautiful as it is, centres around the outdoor life and caters very little for persistent bad weather. In its defence, we have been told by many people who understandably return for holidays there year after year that over a twenty-year period it sounds like this one was a freak summer. The couple we had been following in the past few days had been to Croatia fifteen times and had never encountered rain until now. Not that any of this helped just then.

We left the coast for the first time since arriving in Dubrovnik and took a three-hour drive through the mountains to the Plitvice Lakes National Park. We had caught a brief glimpse of this place on a postcard in Dubrovnik and purposely averted our eyes in order to enjoy the surprise when we actually saw it. It had just stopped raining by the time we left but the sky ahead was black and judging by the floods we drove through we were following the storm. The fields were waterlogged and had overflowed to create a torrent of red mud, which turned the roads into what looked like rivers of blood, barely passable in places and very probably seeping into all our outside lockers. As we crawled forward trying to minimise spray we witnessed a magnificent display of forked lightning ahead and were deafened by huge bolts of thunder whose noise seemed magnified in our metal box. Nor was it long before we caught up with the teeming rain.

By now we were right up in the mountains, alone and barely able to see the road in front of us. The wind was so strong that at one point it moved the van right across the road. I'm painting a vivid picture here partly to explain the tense mood and ensuing argument. Just before we reached our campsite the rain stopped and the sky lightened. As our visibility returned we came to a stop right in the middle of the road, unable to believe our eyes, for the mountains all around us were covered in snow. Yesterday we had been sunbathing on the beach. Now here we were contemplating the thought of having to track down our winter clothing again. We passed a sheep farmer huddled up with three large mountain dogs guarding his flock, a reminder that we were now in wolf country.

The campsite was the polar opposite of the previous one and, in truth, much more to our liking. There were no formal pitches and you were left to choose your patch of grass amid the quiet, natural setting of trees, mountains – and snow. Sadly these serene surroundings did nothing to prevent a shouting match between Geoff and me when a rash choice of words left me feeling instantly resentful, whereupon, on the back of bad weather and late nights, neither of us bit our tongues.

Inevitably, any arrival at any campsite, irrespective of the trials that might have been associated with the journey there, signalled two conflicting versions of *I need* to two of the three inhabitants of the van. To the fed-up three-year-old it meant playtime. To the exhausted driver it meant downtime. To me it generally meant treading a path between the two of them, trying to keep them both happy – and quiet – which I tried to do with as good grace as I could manage. Today, though, truth be told I was as desperate as anyone else for some 'me time'.

It was no more than a case of being ignorant of one another's roles. Until now I had simply chickened out of driving and allocated, by default, that job to Geoff, without ever actually asking if he was tired of it. To balance this I had happily taken on the role of homemaker. Five months in, these had become habits. We might find ourselves settled in a campsite for days with no driving, and then covering long distances over several days. Either way our behaviour never varied. Neither of us made any effort to accommodate one another's needs even when the circumstances changed.

In this instance it led to a heated exchange of words, starting with a strop (mine) about the tediously impractical nature of carrying out certain normally simple procedures such as washing up. This was counterbalanced by a somewhat rude statement (his) about how stressful it would be as a passenger if I was at the wheel. This clinched it for me remaining as a passenger for the duration of the trip, thus absolving myself of any responsibility for any current or future damage to the van. Not that I mean to make myself sound as if I was doing nothing all the time we were motoring along. Very far from it: I was kept constantly busy, either acting as navigator in the front or up and down in the back attending to Jackson's many and varied needs, so that I invariably arrived at a campsite as tired as anyone else. Luckily at this point in the day this campsite was deserted and of course our row was all over and done with just as quickly as it started. Jackson meanwhile was still happily building some unidentifiable structure from dirty sand, oblivious of the whole thing.

Judging by the temperature here it was obvious that we would not be walking around the lakes in shorts, as I had fondly imagined. For the first time since we left France we needed the heating on in the van and even an extra blanket on the bed. We reached the lakes at 11 a.m. the next day by bus from the campsite. On arrival our options were explained depending on our ability and the length of time we intended to spend there. Following advice we caught the land train up to the highest lake and then began the descent on foot.

It was an exhilarating walk along a series of boardwalks over, through, across and, in some places, even under waterfalls and lakes. Despite having read up a little about this area before visiting it, we were still bowled over by it. There were a series of 16 interconnected lakes and over 90 different waterfalls, which came about because of a very complicated phenomenon that I gave up trying to understand. It had something to do with water dissolving the limestone that formed the lakes, but in the process doing so at different rates so that it re-emerged all over the place, resulting in streams flowing in every direction and a whole series of dramatic waterfalls at every turn. The water reacted with an algae, which caused a calcium-type deposit on the surface of plants and rocks, which then built up to form the waterfalls.

It was an area full of rare and endangered plants including carnivorous plants, as well as bears, wolves, deer and a huge array of bird life. Having been told all this, I kindly requested Jackson, on this one occasion, not, and I repeated not, to pick mummy any lovely flowers , although I could just imagine him presenting me with an extremely rare orchid or something. We armed ourselves with binoculars, pen and paper to add to our ever-increasing list of birds. And after all this careful preparation we went on to see ABSOLUTELY NOTHING of any flora or fauna.

I can only put this down to the sheer volume of people. Technically this was out of season but in fact it was absolutely heaving. Try to imagine those really long, really old, unevenly rickety boardwalks, inches above or, in some places due to yesterday's heavy rain, inches beneath the water. Imagine no sides or handrails anywhere, even though in places we found ourselves literally walking across the top of a waterfall within touching distance of the water gushing over the edge and crashing into a lake far below us. Then factor in hundreds, no, thousands of people walking in both directions attempting to squeeze past one another while all no doubt praying they didn't end up tumbling over. Add to the mix me trying to control Jackson for fear of him falling in, or worse still pushing someone else in. At the same time everyone, and I admit that included me, wanted to take photographs, ideally without another hundred people appearing in the background. Then there were the selfie addicts who caused utter chaos by concentrating more on perfecting their pouts than on the two-way traffic trying to negotiate safely around them. Top it all off with the bride, in full white meringue-style wedding dress and delicate white wedding slippers, her face saying: *This is NOT A GOOD DAY!* – bless her. And there you have all the reasons we had absolutely no chance of spotting any wildlife.

All that said, it was certainly the most spectacular walk we had ever done and one we will never forget. The colours were mind-blowing and barely seemed real. All around the lush green vegetation was interspersed with those lakes of the most spectacular turquoise blue water. I could almost swear that someone had gone along with a bottle of dye for effect, as they do on world championship golf courses. All told it is an absolute must, in my opinion – but be prepared to live with those crowds.

We were swept along in this great current of people for no less than three hours with no realistic way out other than turning round and going all the way back in the current flowing the other way. There was no way of stepping off the boardwalk for a rest unless you were prepared to take an unwanted dip. We were quite shocked at the complete lack of facilities such as drinks, toilets or even benches along the way and the fact that we had been given no prior warning about this. Indeed some poor people looked like they would never make it to the end. The simplest solution would be to make it one-way only, bus the groups to the top and set them off at half-hour intervals, thereby staggering them and making it a safer and much more enjoyable experience for everyone. In the height of summer in peak season surely some people must end up taking an unplanned bath.

At the end of this marathon we found ourselves by a large lake, halfway down the series. Here, following the plan we'd been recommended for the day, we caught a boat to the other side for lunch. This proved to be costly.

I made a careless mistake and we experienced our second theft of our trip, strangely both having taken place in Croatia, except that this time I was heartbroken because I lost my mobile phone along with all my photographs. Of course we tried everything like ringing it and reporting it but all to no avail. With a lump in my throat I spent lunchtime recounting all the lost contacts and more importantly all my forever lost Croatian photographs. Luckily we had backed everything up three weeks ago, otherwise it could have been much more devastating. I had only started a two-year contract a few months ago but as we were to be outside the UK for more than three months I could get no insurance, and now I faced the costly expense of replacing my handset too. That's no easy feat when you are travelling with no forwarding address.

I also used my phone to manage my blog and now with lost photographs, no camera connected to social media and all my contacts missing, my writing would suffer for weeks to come. Even while writing this book I have struggled to recall details to the same extent I was able to do before this loss. I had to play catch-up afterwards and with limited free time in the evenings I could sense mounting tension in the van, with either Geoff or Jackson vying for my attention or complaining about the excessive Wi-Fi usage while I tried to tell a week's worth of tales in one go. In fact for a while my blog became a chore and I almost gave it up, fearing that it had lost its appeal.

Yet here we were in this astoundingly beautiful place. I tried telling myself that nobody was going to prevent us from appreciating its sights for the rest of the day. Still feeling a little down in the mouth we continued our journey the length of this lake by boat and then again on foot to the end.

The lowest section looked similar to the rest, with an unprotected boardwalk made even more dramatic as it led through a steep-sided gorge with the walkway criss-crossing over the river barely an arm's length from spectacular waterfalls. However, we could only observe it from above as sections were closed for safety reasons in the aftermath of yesterday's storm. Even then the odd crazy few climbed over the danger signs and ventured down regardless.

In spite of my loss this was unquestionably a magical place. I feel truly privileged to be able to add this adventure to my top ten list of experiences. But I'm also not ashamed to admit that it didn't stop me wishing very bad things on the thief who robbed me of my treasured photographs of Jackson.

24. *LAST TANGO IN CROATIA*

DRIVING FROM THE mountains back to the coast was doubled in length and complexity due to some road works that sprung up overnight and required a diversion through narrow winding country roads. At one point the road was barely wide enough for us, never mind something else, but as usual the roads were empty. Unlike the traffic, the wildlife here was abundant, with hoopoes two a penny, a pair of hen harriers, a spotted nutcracker and an eagle whose identity remained unknown. As we reached the top of the mountain and rounded a hairpin we caught a spectacular glimpse of the coast with a magnificent view right across the valley below and out to the sea, which was dotted with barren-looking islands, appearing to the eye rather like a lunar landscape. We were heading for the largest island, Krk, which was connected to the mainland by a bridge.

Since we'd arrived in Croatia people had raved about the beauty of Krk. It was a shock, then, that our first sighting of the island was a bare, grey, rocky landscape resembling a quarry. Not far inland, though, it changed to a very green and heavily wooded environment, with country lanes, wildflowers everywhere and picturesque blue coves.

There were some seven or eight ACSI sites on the island but we had discounted the nudist ones – I got enough questions from Jackson in the shower without him encountering strangers in the supermarket with no clothes on. That left us with a choice of four. We had noticed it was important to properly read the description of campsites in the ACSI book because nudist sites were fairly common and often there was no indication of this until the final sentence, unless you found a picture of the beach that upon closer inspection revealed too much skin. We had chosen one that claimed to have a children's pool among other family-based facilities and, for the last hour of such a long drive, we had dangled this bribe in front of a particularly crotchety child.

We arrived to learn that here, apparently, mid-May was in peak season, so we could not use our discount card and had to pay full price, which was considerably more than we had expected. Too tired to argue that the ACSI book clearly listed peak season dates and that today was not one of them, we took this on the chin, manoeuvred Dotty into a very tight pitch, and immediately made a beeline for the pool. We found it covered for the winter with a season's worth of thick green slime growing in the stagnant water on the cover. When we confronted the reception about this we were told that the pool was closed because it was out of season. Talk about having it both ways! The campsite now had little else to offer us. The unattractive beach was all rocks and the pitches were cramped and gravelly. Even the kids' swing park was built on concrete. By now we were really tired, Jackson was thoroughly upset and we were still reeling from the previous day's phone theft, and all this came as one blow too many. There and then we made a joint decision to head back to Italy in the morning.

Croatia had baffled us and our opinions about it were divided. Despite a number of disappointments I found it astonishingly beautiful and my impression was that there was so much more waiting to be explored. But I could sense Geoff's disappointment. I think he found it a bit insincere. At first it had seemed perfect but then having scratched the surface we had found descriptions that were deliberately designed to mislead, campsites that boasted of beautiful beaches but were actually covered in building works, or peak-season rates being charged when all the seasonal facilities were still closed. Very possibly a couple of months later all these works would have been completed and we would have found pristine campsites. But that's not the point. You are entitled to be made aware of these limitations before you make a long journey and are asked to pay for something that's not there. I also struggle to understand why, when so much attention to detail is spent trying to keep their campsites undeniably clean, they then opt to carry out their building work and renovations not when they're closed but after opening, so that their guests have to share the idyllic surroundings with an array of building materials and the buzz of machinery.

For most of our visit too the weather had been against us and as first-timers we hadn't fully appreciated how unusual this was. Against that we had found faultless roads, generally friendly people and spectacular scenery. But there was a kind of uniformity to the place. Everywhere felt pretty much the same. It was a bit like having several good cups of tea: the first one was fabulous and maybe the second, but after five or six you felt you couldn't face another.

Perhaps we made a fundamental mistake in trying to tackle Croatia in exactly the same way as Italy by starting at one end, moving on every couple of days and trying to see the whole country in a month. This approach had worked so well for us in Italy because every city was completely different and a day or two in each place was sufficient. But Croatia seemed to demand a completely different approach.

If we return to Croatia in the future we will select three or four campsites and stay a week in each, giving ourselves plenty of time to settle in and get a proper feel for the area while exploring the surroundings and enjoying all the facilities. Croatia should be all about sitting still to appreciate its beauty and making best use of outdoor activities such as walking, rather than rushing along from one town to the next hoping that something great will leap out at you. I also think that island hopping would probably be a good thing to do, although that would take some planning. What seemed clear, though, was that rushing along, battling rain most of the way, had not enabled us to get very far into the authentic Croatia experience.

You live and learn. For us now it was time to make the most of the luxury of being free to go with the flow, as they say. So we would head to Spain for some sun, taking in a couple more points of interest in Italy en route. The spontaneous side of us was back – so look out, we could end up anywhere…

25. THIS WAY? OR THAT WAY?

IT ONLY REALLY dawned on us in the morning, as we were packing to leave, that we had only actually been in Croatia for two weeks. It felt much longer than that and for a moment I felt a bit guilty about giving up on it so quickly without somehow giving it a fair chance. Yet wasn't this what motor homing was supposed to be all about: the ability to be fluid and change your plans at a whim when you felt the need to do so? And, I reminded myself, with no improvement forecast in the weather, what was the point in battling on when we could be sunbathing elsewhere? One day in the future we might return to Croatia. But today it was back to Northern Italy – first stop, Venice.

Our route took us briefly into Slovenia where our appetites were strongly whetted for a proper visit one day. At a true crossroads in our journey we were strongly tempted to have a complete change of heart and not turn back towards Western Europe but venture east to countries about which we knew little. Dreams filled our heads of where a turn to the East might take us and what adventures it might bring. Sitting at this one particular spot on the road, faced with the luxury of choice, we suddenly felt very small. Whichever direction we took would lead to an entirely different experience.

In hindsight I can see that the pull to turn east was a message about what our journey was craving. Of course it didn't happen. We turned left, not right, to the west, not the east. It was a turning point, bringing us the harsh realisation that from here on we knew in advance the route we would take: down along the coast of Spain, through Portugal and Northern Spain, then through France and back home. In theory we could choose to detour inland, but it seemed highly unlikely with a surfer in our midst. Very suddenly it dawned on me that our whole mindset had changed. Without even realising what was happening to us, we had now turned around and, like it or not, we were heading homeward. Back at home it wouldn't be dreams but reality that would face us. And though we still had three whole months ahead of us, for the first time on this trip I felt the end in sight and experienced a slightly sinking feeling that I could not shake off.

The map showed the scale of the countries that lay before us. Even averaging a month in each one, we became uncomfortably aware that time was no longer on our side. We might have eluded these thoughts if we had turned right instead of left at these crossroads and headed off somewhere completely unplanned. But what really overwhelmed me, not for the first time but now more strongly than ever, was the thought of never going home, and wondering how it would feel to have no time limits whatsoever.

This brought a sense of division. Geoff was the realist of the pair of us, aware of having a budget, a time limit and responsibilities awaiting us back home. He would not give in to unachievable thoughts, or at least never showed it if he did. I, on the other hand, had let myself dream up endless possibilities from a very early point in this trip. I sincerely believed that anything was possible if we set our minds to it. If someone had suggested to me three years ago that we would sell our business, quit working, opt to keep our son out of nursery and run away like teenagers in a motorhome even for just one year, I'd have thought them mad. But we had done that part and now who could tell us that we couldn't keep on doing anything that we wanted?

Something life-changing had occurred on this journey that had caught us both out. While we were planning our trip I felt very strongly that we needed to have everything mapped out ahead of us: where we would go, how long we would spend in each place, when we would come back, which ferries to book, what jobs we would do when we returned, how much money we could spend... the list went on. It was Geoff who took me out of my comfort zone. He insisted, and now I understand how right he was, that travelling didn't work like that, that flexibility was the key, and that the more you were surprised or tested the more you would benefit from the experience. He saw in me a quite risky mix of uncontrolled excitement, sheer fear and inflated expectations and he worried that I would end up feeling let down by the reality of the experience and thinking that travelling fell short of what had been promised.

Certainly what neither of us expected was that I would fall in love with the travelling life in the way that I did. We were supposed to do our trip and then return home happy and satisfied, ready to move on to the next chapter in our lives. Geoff based his own expectations on his experiences when he was young. When he had travelled before he had done it the hard way. He had slept rough, carried his belongings on his back and eventually, and understandably, craved a proper home and a settled routine. But what we were doing now was something entirely different. We took our home with us wherever we went. Physically all that was missing were the people we loved and for me I hadn't yet been away long enough for that to become an issue. To be honest, I was a bit selfish about this. Unlike Geoff, I had no parents to worry about and our son was with us, whereas Geoff had left his daughter and grand-daughter behind. Jackson too was missing out on them as much as they were missing out on him. I believe it was for all these reasons that Geoff would not allow himself to waiver and tried not to give me a false sense of hope that he knew he could not fulfil. So it was that on this particular day Geoff indicated left and our journey in that direction began.

At this point we had planned a brief detour to Lake Bled to visit some friends from Slovenia whom we had met in Italy. But their contact details were on my phone in some stranger's pocket, somewhere in Croatia, so that ruled that idea out. So instead we just pressed on towards Italy.

From our brief glimpse of Slovenia, it seemed a green and fertile land, natural and unspoiled, with incredibly friendly people. Like Croatia almost every house had a garden devoted entirely to home-grown vegetables or crops. It seemed that most people were either self-sufficient or operated a barter system with their neighbours. We were intrigued and charmed by Slovenia and made a mental note to come back some day.

We found crossing the borders more entertaining than usual. Entering Slovenia from Croatia, we were also re-entering the EU. There were two adjoining kiosks. At the Croatian one the border guard carefully checked each passport. He then moved me on to the Slovenian checkpoint literally three paces away, where the guard took all three passports off me and then handed them straight back unopened. As for entering Italy, there was nobody there. They were all on siesta.

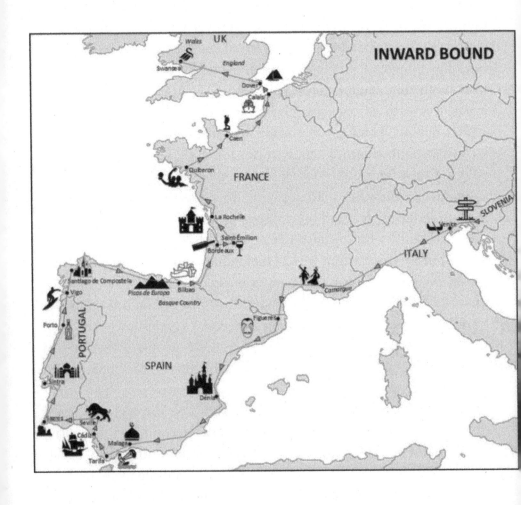

PART 2

INWARD BOUND

Italy

France

Spain

Portugal

Spain (again)

Basque Country

France

Wales

26. THE FLOATING CITY

AFTER SOME TRAFFIC delays on the road from the Slovenian border we arrived at teatime at Camping Europa in Lido di Jesolo, just across the lagoon from Venice. Straight away we lost Jackson who found a German family with four children to entertain him. We had chosen this location because we thought it would be a novel experience to arrive by boat from across the water. We also had access to a beach.

Campsites don't come much better than this one, which felt like being on holiday within a holiday. It was a large site with about 400 motorhomes including those enormous coach-built models with expanding sides, which we hadn't seen since leaving France, and motorhomes towing cars and boats. At least 95% of them were German. And oh boy, do they know how to camp in style? I will describe just one typical couple in the knowledge that many – not all – German motorhomers fit this description.

The motorhome arrives and immediately the occupants spring into action. Out comes the awning complete with safari sides, providing them with a completely enclosed tent on one side of their van; the matting to go underfoot in the tent; the table, chairs, tablecloth, potted silk flowers and artificial hanging baskets; the cube covered in artificial grass to hold the umbrella should there be a freak moment when either occupant might actually leave the security of their tent and venture into the outside world twenty feet from their door; the solar lights, BBQ, hanging fruit-and-veg baskets; and the list goes on. And from what we saw, once they're set up, they seldom move. They seem to eat, sleep, eat and sleep some more, all from the comfort of their reclining loungers within the shade of the tent attached to the van. To us it looked too much like being at home. Why bother with a motorhome when you don't use it to change anything?

In this instance we had walked in to select our pitch and had deliberately chosen one surrounded by vans with children so that Jackson would have company. At this point we hadn't realised that our immediate neighbours on one side were the only childless campers in what otherwise was a sea of kids. It soon became obvious that they were neither particularly sociable nor tolerant. Further enquiries revealed that they had arrived after the other four vans full of children were already set up and in full swing and had chosen this pitch because they always have the same pitch each year. They came to the same plot of grass on the same campsite for the same week every year and sat within the confines of their four walls of tent, scowling at all the kids for the duration.

For those of us who actually made use of the campsite facilities, your every need was catered for. The toilets and showers were cleaned after every use. The seating area outside the toilets was so pristine I would have happily eaten my food there. The kids had their own block, designed like a castle, with bright sinks, mini-toilets, family showers and even deep oversized sinks big enough for them to have a bath. There was an impressive swimming pool, well, several actually, all of them heated, and a Jacuzzi. These did come at a price, though, *and* you had to wear a swimming cap. Geoff, being bald, got away without one and spent the next few days taking the mickey out of me. We were also right on the beach, which, for the first time in ages, was lovely sand.

Unbelievably, though, we awoke to rain again the next morning. So much for fleeing from sodden Croatia! Undeterred, Jackson decided he wanted to join the kids' club, though being the only English speaker there this only lasted a day. He spent the morning drawing and in the afternoon insisted that I stay to keep him company, as they had a lesson in the importance of fruit. They began by drawing their favourite fruits. There was then a demonstration of how to clean and prepare various fruit. First they demonstrated with an orange, the excitement escalating when, with a slight squeeze of the peel, enough to send out a fine spray of juice, a balloon went BANG! This was meant to make clear the dangers to your eyes. Next it was on to the innocent apple, but maybe not as innocent as I'd been led to believe my entire life. Jackson was taught that washing it is not enough because shops wax them, so unless you have grown it yourself you should *never* eat an apple without peeling it. Really?

I gave up listening after that but once everything was prepared, each child, though by now they were all bored and misbehaving, was given a sharp wooden stick to skewer their fruit with. But they weren't allowed to eat any fruit until everyone was ready, at which point the staff came round and covered every piece of fruit with chocolate spread. This was supposed to demonstrate that because kids won't eat fruit it's a good idea to encourage them with chocolate. I must have been looking at the wrong children because I would swear that every one of them would have happily eaten every piece of their fruit prior to the chocolate spread if they had been allowed to.

That night we experienced the mother of all thunderstorms. Half the campsite were on the beach photographing the jet black sky and attempting and failing to capture the forked lightning. We returned to our van with seconds to spare before the rain arrived, which went on to drown out the volume of the TV and condemned us once again to a long night of no sleep.

The next morning it felt like a miracle that we arose to a sunny day and could spend the entire day on the beach. The sea was lovely and warm and very pleasant – at least it was until I spotted jellyfish… We shared a few beers with our neighbours in the evening and watched Jackson grow up right before our eyes. He went off on his bike to the mini-disco without us, in the company of other kids. I thought travelling with one child was hard but our neighbours had four of them all in one van, with all their toys, although they seemed to handle it with ease. They had a wagon on wheels like a giant wheelbarrow into which they threw everything from chairs to picnic things, beach toys to even some of the smallest children, then simply wheeled it to the beach or the pool and unloaded it.

Another day we took the boat across the water straight into St Mark's Square in Venice. I think Geoff, who had previously been to Venice, could see the illusion I was under beforehand and all my expectations of a romantic watery dream. He tried to forewarn me that, depending on the weather and the wind, it could get to smell quite rancid, though in fact this didn't occur. What really shocked me, though, was the surprising size of the place and the scale of commercialism arising from such huge crowds of visitors. Even so I was blown away by Venice, though I cannot find words to describe adequately what I felt about it.

As far as I could see, though, it was anything but romantic. Gondolas started at 80 euros for 20 minutes, there seemed to be constant gondola traffic jams, and they looked distinctly unsafe to me, rocking due to all the boat traffic so much I knew I'd be seasick. There was one 'You've Been Framed' moment when a young couple passed beneath the Bridge of Sighs in a gondola and about 50 cameras pointed directly at them from above, no question of asking for consent, in an all-out bid by each tourist photographer to grab an idealistic image of Venice before they left. To complete the poor couple's romantic experience, a hen party on the bridge, British of course and all done up in the usual hen-do gear, serenaded them with all their might to the strains of *Just One Cornetto!*

We deliberately didn't take a map, preferring to see where our feet took us. Consequently we thoroughly enjoyed ourselves exploring the back streets, crossing back and forth over the bridges and nosing about in the shops. We caught a water bus along the main canal, which gave us another different view of the city and an insight into the vast scale of the cruise ships anchored in dock. We stayed until 9 p.m. and it was all a fabulous experience, yet another reminder of all that Italy has to offer in so much variety.

We felt sad about moving on the next morning. There is an incredible amount to do here and I could see us returning to this area again some day. From here we had hoped to head up to Verona and Lake Garda, which had evaded us some months earlier due to inclement weather. But it proved impossible at this time of year when every campsite I phoned was fully booked.

But things always happen for a reason. We had been promising for years and particularly on this journey to visit some friends who lived in Spain. A phone call now revealed that they had accepted an offer on their house and were due to move out in a couple of weeks. So if we were to have any chance of seeing them it had to be now or never. A brief study of the map revealed that from the east coast of Italy where we were, in order to reach Málaga in Spain, we merely had to cross the top of Italy, pass through the south of France and then cover over a thousand kilometres through Spain all during the next week. Quite simple, really! We'd also need to include a few stops of interest along the way. We decided we'd formulate our plans as we drove.

27. SURPRISE ENCOUNTERS

FROM THE OFF, really, we faced some harsh realisations. We had planned a whole day of driving, expecting to cross Italy into France, and had earmarked a couple of places in the book of Aires, depending on how far we got. Of course we had totally underestimated the distance. We also had to adjust to a sharp improvement in the weather. By halfway through the day, Dotty was doing her best to roast us alive in temperatures over 27C.

The Gulf of Genoa coast road was a difficult stretch to tackle in a motorhome, with one upmarket resort following the next. Motorhome owners were not the sort of clients they catered for and we could only find one site in our ACSI book, which was still a long way ahead. As we finally approached it after several more hours on the road we saw that the tunnel that should have led us straight to the entrance of the site was closed to all traffic, causing a massive tailback along the beach front. Worse still, the signposted diversion said it was suitable only for cars. A policeman directed us back along the motorway to make our approach from the other side of the tunnel. Fortunately one of us had noticed the stationery traffic and equally huge tailback on the opposite carriageway, which we had just driven past, so instead we opted to move still farther along the coast.

Geoff by now was exhausted, Jackson was at the far end of his tether from a whole day stuck in his seat, and I already knew what efforts would be needed by me to accommodate their individual needs if and when we ever reached a campsite. While one would demand rest and peace, the other would want to play and run wild. At the same time we would all need food and an early night. At times like this I wished I could split myself in two. It wasn't as if tomorrow would be much more pleasant because we still had several days of driving to get through, and at this point it was essential to try to remain upbeat and civilised.

We passed hundreds of motorhomes heading the other way, all stuck in a jam that I estimated was about fifteen miles long and stationary, and it was already 7 p.m. They would all be feeling the pressure by now because campsites closed for the night and you couldn't just wild camp around here, nor would it be very safe to do so. Friends of ours had had their van broken into the previous week in the middle of the day, right in the middle of a busy car park.

We finally arrived at a site near Pietra Ligure, about sixty kilometres west of Genoa. There we were issued with one shower token each for Geoff and myself as part of the price. Jackson wasn't a paying guest so didn't qualify. This would enable us to access hot water. In stark contrast to the last camp site we were now back to reality: four toilets, three of them just a hole in the floor. I mean, come on, we had paid twenty euros for this luxury – for no toilet paper, no soap and a limit of three minutes' hot water. Reading this back, mind, it sounds as if I had forgotten that we had a perfectly clean, hot shower and a toilet with a seat and paper in the comfort of our own van. That just goes to show how much Geoff had brainwashed me into following his rules in order to minimise his chores around the van.

Now when I'm back at home, when in a rush I can shower in less than three minutes. But that's without the pressure of a hot-water deadline hanging over me and stressing me out. It must have been the least relaxing shower of my life! First I had to get completely ready, line up all my bathroom products and stash my clothes and towels in the waterproof bag, which I had to take to hang in the shower with me. Then I had to insert the token, whereupon the countdown began. While attempting to keep a vague count of 3 x 60 seconds I allowed myself 10 seconds to shave each leg, deciding to leave my armpits until last in case my time ran out. Then it was on with the shampoo and immediately off for fear of not having enough time to get the bubbles out. Shower gel next and yes, just time for the armpits, nearly cutting myself in the rush. Then 5 seconds to ponder: Do I risk conditioner or will it still be in my hair when the water stops? I risked it and, literally as the last of it was rinsed out, with no fancy alarm or anything, BAM, there was freezing cold water: my 3 minutes was up! What a wonderful experience *that* was… To spite Geoff for being awkward about using our own shower I convinced Jackson how much fun it would be to share Daddy's shower tonight. Double trouble for Geoff!

What this campsite lacked in luxury, though, it did more than compensate for in another way. My walk back from the shower was lit by hundreds of fireflies flashing and twinkling all around me. Jackson was mesmerised by them, like a curtain of green glitter sparkling all around him, and the sound of a toad croaking in the darkness rounded it all off perfectly. Looking back, I realise that this sort of experience is what you miss out on in a really busy campsite, and it is what I love most about this lifestyle. What you will encounter or experience in each place is a mystery, but it's the element of surprise that makes for an unforgettable adventure. I'm quite sure that it is the humbler campsites like this one rather than the five-star sites that we will remember with most affection in years to come.

The Camargue region of France, to the south of Arles, was not initially on our agenda for this trip. But our improvised plans of the previous day had put it conveniently within driving distance and suddenly it looked interesting for a one-night stop. It is a wide expanse of wetland, naturally formed between the Mediterranean and the Rhône river delta. The guidebooks refer to its rich bird life, including flamingos, and the wild white horses and black bulls that roam the marshland. It sounded like a perfect retreat for us to enjoy a day off from the road, relaxing amid the wildlife. I had already pictured in my head a nice bike ride armed with a picnic, camera and binoculars and the obligatory bug-hunting kit of which Jackson never tired.

So, we arrived after a very long motorway drive dodging all the super-rich coastal centres such as Monaco. I had visited Monaco once before when staying there with a friend. An evening drink in a pavement bar came to the jaw-dropping price of 90 euros for one bottle of house rosé. I still keep the bottle on a shelf at home as a rip-off memento and reminder that we had enjoyed better wine for 3 euros on this trip. Today, armed with this knowledge, we had refused to go anywhere near Monaco for fear of Jackson demanding an ice cream that could equate to a week's worth of Aire fees. Even by motorway it took us over five hours and after the cheap but terrible roads in Italy, the immaculate roads in France came at a price: 100 euros in tolls! But the last half-hour made the whole day worthwhile as we drove along a quiet little road across the marsh.

We immediately spotted the white horses and an endless choice of riding stables open to the public. Then we saw the bulls, which were small by bull standards, and all sorts of birds, including a stork, a bee-eater and flocks of unidentified long-legged water birds taking flight.

Approaching the campsite, we passed two massive car parks right on the beach where we noticed thousands of motorhomes parked up. For a moment after such an expensive day's driving we forgot about the campsite and enquired about the price of the car park. A group of French guys, gathered around their van with guitars, told us it was free and suggested we park next to them in what was pretty much the only space left. They pointed out that the adjacent car park cost twelve euros without offering anything extra, then in the next breath they commented on how nice our van was. Something didn't feel quite right and, keeping one eye on Dotty, we hopped over the fence to the paying car park to ask about the difference. The security guard collecting cash was only too happy to engage us in conversation but the only two words Geoff could decipher from it were 'guard' and 'gypsies'. We decided to move ourselves there, since we planned to leave the van while we went off bird-watching the following day and would feel safer knowing that someone was patrolling the site.

We did make a quick two-minute trip down the road to check out the campsite because it was only an extra five euros and had a swimming pool. However, it was fully booked and as motorhomes were now beginning to queue on the road we made a hasty retreat to the paying car park to grab one of the last spaces.

This was another of those moments when we felt that everyone else knew something that we didn't. We had expected this to be a fairly quiet region on the motorhome, or even general tourist, map, yet here we were at exactly the same moment as vast numbers of people, with more and more arriving and being turned back and with every available parking space, and we are talking many hundreds, now taken.

We took a brief walk across the road to see the flamingos and found ourselves chatting to a Dutch lady. When we asked her what she thought about the the safety of these two car parks she informed us that we had no choice because every single campsite in the entire Camargue was full. *The big Aire in town has been taken over by gypsies*, she said. *I'm afraid you have arrived a bit late and you have a two-kilometre walk from here, but it's all there is.* A bit surprised, I replied: *Oh, can't we bird-watch around here?* This was when we learned that, unless we were completely mad, bird-watching was not after all going to be on our agenda the next day.

By sheer coincidence we had managed to arrive on the eve of the Gypsy Festival, the biggest occasion of the year in the Camargue. This lady had travelled a great distance specifically to tick this event off her bucket list. We must have been the only idiots there who until that moment had absolutely no idea what was going on, and she could probably see the confusion written all over our faces. The place had been taken over by true Romany gypsies, many of whom had undertaken a religious pilgrimage to reach this destination. So no, we would not be spending the next day watching birds. Instead we would grasp this opportunity with both hands and join in the festivities while pretending it was all a part of our carefully prepared cunning plan.

This annual pilgrimage takes place every May when various processions take place over a few days, most of them incorporating religious ceremonies attended by entire Romany families, often spanning four generations. Sad to say, over time most of them have traded their colourful horse-drawn wagons for the most luxurious imaginable motorhomes and caravans, large enough to house whole families in their traditional dress. Seeing the great numbers exiting some of these vehicles, they had to be be sleeping in the aisle and on the kitchen units, and I bet it made for a highly entertaining journey travelling with everyone from great grandma to the newborn in one small space.

We did see some traditional horse-drawn caravans, which always drew a crowd, and also some dress fashion that would feel right at home on *My Big Fat Gypsy Wedding*. This particular day was greatly significant in their calendar when, among other church services and prayers, they held a massive procession through the town, led by gypsy men in traditional costume, on horseback, with thousands of gypsies and priests following on foot, singing, playing music, praying and reading aloud.

This was followed by an unforgettable night of gypsy music on every street corner, in bars and restaurants. Wherever a space could be found a band or soloist would be there to busk the night away. Most of the music was of such a high standard that I had to pinch myself to believe we were hearing it for free. And there was no trouble despite the presence of large crowds, much beer and live music. Such police as were present took a very relaxed role and allowed the night to flow.

They were the most polite, well-mannered people – well, apart from a few old ladies who insisted on trying to pin good-luck charms including rabbits' feet on you. They had travelled from all over Europe, and some even from other continents, to be here. Disappointingly we had to miss an event that is on my own bucket list, when on the Friday of the festival they run bulls through the streets chasing anyone brave or dumb enough to run in front of them. Then in the evening they hold a bull fight but with the only risk being to the matador as they attempt to remove a coloured garland from the bull's horns. We simply didn't have time to stay here until then, and at this stage I probably valued my life a little too much and didn't fancy ending this trip with two horn-shaped holes in my arse.

As a family we remember this event as the festival of chipsies, as Jackson called it. When we explained to him that we were going to see a gypsy festival instead of going out on our bikes I asked him if he had any idea what to expect. In true Jackson style he replied: *Lots of chip shops and toy shops.* No matter how I tried he still didn't understand that a gypsy is not a chip, and because he'd had chips in town that day for lunch he seemed to think that the thousands of people were here for the chips. He even asked me the next day if there were going to be chips in Spain too.

The Camargue easily made it into my top ten places to revisit. It would be ridiculously hot in the summer months and full of mosquitos, but in April or May the list of activities to keep you busy would be endless. Everything would be at hand from horse-riding to quad-biking and four-wheel-drive adventures. There would be organised bird-watching trips, boat trips, kayaks to hire, helicopter experiences, children's activities and even a lovely sandy white beach to relax on. It was another magical place we considered ourselves fortunate to have stumbled upon. But now we had to head onwards towards sunny Spain.

28. ON DALÍ'S HOME TURF

WE KNEW NOTHING about Roses until it was recommended by someone we met in the Camargue. As we were hot-footing without any prior planning to catch up with friends near Málaga, anywhere en route that was conveniently positioned to break up our driving was worth considering.

Before that, of course, we had to get out of France, which we only just managed by the skin of our teeth. Desperate for fuel and not having passed a garage for ages, we resorted to searching for petrol stations using the sat nav and made a detour. When we finally found a garage we couldn't believe the size of the queue. We had to wait over half an hour to reach the pump and then learned that there was a restriction on the amount of fuel you could have. But it got us across the border to Spain where we turned the news on and heard that there was a fuel strike in France. It seemed that our fuel station had been one of the few still open as most of them had no fuel left. For once luck had been on our side.

The border was in the mountains. We caught a glimpse from afar but then each hairpin dashed our hopes that we were almost there. Eventually, with Jackson turning from white to green, we reached an ugly, graffiti-strewn building where officials stood outside enjoying the sun. One of them waved us through without particularly even raising his head.

Roses itself was a joy. It had a very old centre and a fishing port but also a fairly modern town and seafront. We also discovered there that fifteen kilometres up the road was the home of Salvador Dalí and a museum that showcased his work and also housed his tomb. Geoff has always been a fan of Dalí and we could hardly miss this opportunity, so that became our plan for the next day.

The museum was in the lovely bustling town of Figueres, which we caught on market day. After a picnic of bread, cheese and fresh fruit next to a fountain in the park we walked through the town being very cleverly led to the museum by Dalí's interactive sculptures. From the outside it didn't disappoint, a striking building painted in bright red and gold with hundreds of egg-shaped structures along its roof. Shall we just say it was impossible to mistake it.

Inside the centrepiece, underneath a spectacular glass dome, was a black Cadillac suspended, as you do, underneath an upturned boat. Again encouraging you to touch, interact and fund it, if you inserted a coin it would rain inside the car, which on closer inspection was full of passengers and plants. There was surely a profound meaning to all of this but, having one as a sister, I never try to understand an artist's mind: it's dangerous! A particular favourite of mine was a beautiful large mosaic-style painting depicting a naked woman standing with her back to you looking out of a window. It was a masterpiece: a closer inspection revealed each individual square of the mosaic to be a miniature painting in its own right. Another coin allowed you to view this picture through an inverted telescope, making it appear much farther away, the distance completely altering the image from a naked woman to a head-and-shoulder portrait of Abraham Lincoln. I was mesmerised, unable to believe my own eyes, because even when I looked through the viewfinder of my camera and saw only a naked woman, when I viewed the photograph on my screen it was definitely Abraham Lincoln. Dalí had then taken this up another level by also incorporating this new image as one single square of the mosaic in the big painting. I will never understand how any of this works but I instantly knew this was my type of gallery — something to get those brain cells working. I couldn't even begin to answer Jackson's rush of questions. He thought it was magic and expected us as adults to have all the answers. But it was equally as mind-blowing to everyone witnessing it, whether adult or child.

Another piece was a self-portrait of Dalí painting a portrait of his wife. At first glance it did not seem that special but then you began to understand the complexity. He had painted it to show both their faces in a mirror. For a skilled artist this should be easy enough, but Dalí had actually painted it as though he were a bystander stood behind himself, so that the back of his head was in the picture too.

The entire exhibition drew you in, making you stop and try to fathom everything out. Jackson totally loved it. There was a mix of sculptures and paintings and things that suddenly changed their appearance right in front of your eyes – causing whole families to question one another's sanity because each person saw a completely different image. And the scale of some of his work was immense. I think you could visit the exhibition a hundred times over and still get something new from it each time. If you're ever in the vicinity it is well worth a detour, although I'm told that in summer queues can be lengthy.

By now we were strongly feeling the pull of time constraining us. These days we were only touching briefly on areas that deserved much fuller exploration, which, in the earlier stages of our trip, had been what we enjoyed doing so much. Four months ago it had felt as if we were in no rush at all. If a little village happened to appeal to us then we would stop there for a coffee or a walk. If a name on a map sounded nice we would take a detour and often stumble upon something beautiful and little known. But now we had become aware of the mileage we needed to cover in the coming months just to get Jackson home ready to start full-time school.

Even so, every now and again we reminded ourselves that we did still have a choice. Two approaches still remained possible. Either we could continue in the vein in which we had started, covering much smaller distances and allowing ourselves time to explore places fully, although in the last few days of the trip we would need to rush back along the cross-country motorways to get back to Wales. If we took that approach we could safely leave entire regions untouched and save them for another trip. Or we could attempt to cover the whole distance in less detail: an approach that would let us make informed decisions about areas that seemed worth revisiting on future trips and mentally relegate any areas we thought less attractive.

And in fact we changed our minds constantly. A long day on the road would have us regretting our decision to rush and vowing to take things more slowly, never mind how far we had got. Then two days spent in one place would see us getting itchy feet and wondering what lay around the next corner, and then before we knew it curiosity had got the better of us and off we went again. There seemed to be no right and no wrong way to do this. In the end I think we found a balance, as best we might, that worked for all of us.

Still, there was no doubt in our minds that without that school deadline hanging over us, we would have visited all of these places in a very different frame of mind. In that dream scenario we would have wandered like free spirits into a whole new chapter of adventures both east and west. And surely there are many who would join us in wishing for that carefree, footloose kind of existence.

It felt like we could travel for the rest of our lives without ever being contented that we had seen enough. I couldn't help imagining what a wonderful feeling it must be to know there was always another tomorrow, with no end, no rush, no responsibility. I felt deeply envious of some of the people we had met on our journey, who were living this itinerant life to its very maximum.

Clockwise from top:
Annecy; busy tractor;
Alpine campervans;
where's the road?;
Le Grand-Bornand.

Above and bottom right:
in winter and summer

Left: all mod cons and
curves inside.

Below left: navigator's
nightmare – how do v
get out of here?

Left: the willy pointer in Lyon.

Below: Lake Serre-Ponçon, and the same view with added family.

Bottom: sweeping off snow at Serre-Chevalier.

Right, from top, all in Serre-Chevalier: family and guest; Jackson's favourite toy piste-basher; fresh snow in unbelievable quantities.

Serre-Chevalier: Jackson
in a winter wonderland.

Lake Serre-Ponçon: views that
had me reaching for the tissues.

Lake Annecy: the moment before
the best jeans turned green and slimy.

Right: on the road to Les Carroz.

Below: Les Carroz, where Jackson's skiing overtook his mum's.

Opposite, top: wrong sat nav coordinates + mountaintop dead end = twenty-point turn...

Opposite, centre: what a view to wake up to!

Opposite, bottom: on top of the world at the Pila ski resort.

Top: Lake Orta.

Above: Sacro Monte di San Francesco, the 'sacred mountain of Orta'.

Left: emptying the toilet (men's work).

Above: Riomaggiore.

Right: 'The Leaning-over Tower'.

A wildflower meadow in Tuscany.

Florence *(above)*: Chinese wedding couple and entourage.

The Pitigliano skyline.

419 steps to a view of the Duomo.

On an Agritourism site in Tuscany, which we had all to ourselves.

Thermal springs at Saturnia;
Trevi Fountain in Rome.

Junior gladiator.

Top: play and relax time.

Above: ridiculously popular *trulli* in UNESCO World Heritage Alberobello.

Left: football match on a beach in Puglia.

Clifftop wildflowers *(above)* on the Adriatic coast of Puglia.

Narrow streets in Dubrovnik's Old Town.

Dubrovnik's harbour.

View from Nevio Camping, Orebic, on the Croatian Pelješac peninsula.

Rickety boardwalks
traversing the
Plitvice Lakes and
waterfalls.

Just one cornetto?

Gypsy festival, Camargue; Casa Dalí,
Figueres; sunflowers in Andalucía; and
insane numbers of kitesurfers in Tarifa.

Grumpy macaque in
Gibraltar; Jackson's fourth
birthday balloons; and
a fairytale in Sintra.

Below: São
Lourenço

Above: joy in Peniche.

Right: fishing from
the cliffs in Nazaré.

Left: fish display in Nazaré.

Below: fish genocide in Lavos.

Left: Vila Nova de Cerveira, all dressed in knitting.

Above: countless thousands at Vigo.

Above: taking the plunge.

Right: Santiago de Compostela.

Above: Guggenheim Museum Bilbao.

Below: multiple flavours of motorhome.

*Left: c*louds dropping
out of nowhere on the
Picos de Europa… ;
… not what you want
to see on a cliffside
road; almost added
another hay barn!

Kayaking in the Dordogne.

Prehistoric standing stones, Carnac.

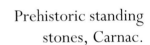

Entering La
Rochelle's
harbour.

All fade away…

29. FIRST BREAKDOWN,
OF THE MECHANICAL KIND

W HEN WE SET out in January our plans were, shall we say, fluid. But there were one or two places we definitely intended to visit. One of them was Barcelona, the next stop on our route.

But from the previous night's news we learned that the city was in the middle of five planned days of rioting. This would not be the first time we brushed up against unexpected events. We had left Disneyland Paris the day before the arrest of a gunman who had checked himself in to the Disney Hotel inside the theme park with a suitcase full of weaponry. In Rome we had visited the Colosseum a few days before terrorists were captured in possession of plans to attack it. In Florence we had stood on the very street that not long after fell into the river along with a whole row of parked cars. And before just recently crossing into Spain we had grabbed the last petrol available in France without even realising there was a fuel strike. Not wanting to push our luck yet again, we decided unanimously and with rather heavy hearts that we would bypass Barcelona. We promised ourselves that we would return when Jackson was older, and pushed on towards Málaga instead.

I had a feeling that the day had started too well. We had a lie-in, left our campsite at 11.30 a.m. and followed the motorway for three hours, a pleasant, quiet route. Then, perfectly timed for a break, we exited and picked up a straight road. Five minutes later we reached a dead end, right on a beautiful sandy beach with two people on it. We cooled off with a lovely impromptu swim followed by a quick picnic on the sand. From there, still keeping off the motorway network, we stopped for coffee in a pleasant café just five minutes on. By now you will know that when our day starts this well it sure as eggs won't end that way. True to form, relaxed and re-energised, off we went, whereupon, only an hour away from our overnight stop, our radiator blew up.

It was just as well it happened right at a junction with a deserted minor road. We were able to limp off the dual carriageway and pull into a lane without causing any traffic disruption or risking our lives while awaiting recovery. For a while it was almost pleasant, with Jackson hastily setting up his own rescue with all his toy cars on the grass verge and Geoff cleverly discovering a bird's nest low down in a tree next to the van where, incredibly, we were all lucky enough to actually watch them fledge. I mean, what are the chances of that? Or was it the noise of Jackson's mock rescue that drove them out of the nest? I gave myself a pedicure, shaped my eyebrows, wrote all my postcards and cooked us tea in the baking heat. There are worse ways to break down than in a motorhome, that's for sure.

Jobs all done, four hours had passed and still there was no recovery vehicle in sight. We realised how much less pleasant it could have been had we been stuck on the motorway or broken down in various much more awkward places on another day. At least we were safe and comfortable here, though a bit bored by now, not to say quite concerned about where we would end up sleeping tonight if this went on much longer. As the hours ticked by we thumbed through the pages in our book of Aires, realising that we should be looking for somewhere right here, not an hour away – assuming someone got us started again, or even actually turned up.

We repeatedly called the UK repair base. They would then refer it to their Spanish base, who would pass it on to a local firm of mechanics. The problem seemed to be the need for a garage able to deal with such a large vehicle as ours and with the necessary equipment if we needed to be towed anywhere. At least an hour would pass between each call to the UK and the eventual reply after it had worked its way back through the system. Eventually we got out of there at 9 p.m. in the dark, limping along behind the recovery vehicle with a patched-up radiator sufficient to last us the fifteen kilometres to a lorry park opposite a garage workshop, where we had to sleep (or, more to the point, *not sleep*) until the morning and await proper repairs.

As lorry parks went it felt very safe, although we did put our big 'German Shepherd on board' sign up in the window to boost our security. But in these places it's always the noise that is so hard to deal with. Trucks came and went all through the night, none of them quietly.

It was about 30 degrees in the van and all we dared open was the skylights, so what with the noise and the temperature we had a sleepless night despite our best attempts to knock ourselves out with a few beers.

The next day we couldn't praise the mechanic enough. The original radiator had corroded and we needed a completely new one. Dotty was ten years old so this was hardly a surprise. Our mechanical hero worked tirelessly by himself on a Saturday, long after the garage officially closed, to get the job finished. After all that, and as if that wasn't enough, he plied Jackson with gifts as a reward for being so patient.

We still managed to squeeze in a four-hour drive before dark, enabling us to reach Dénia, south of Valencia. It was pretty much a case of studying the map and finding a place off the motorway where we might be in with a chance of wild camping. This area looked promising, with various beaches marked and a series of small coastal roads linking various villages. After a brief exploration we were able to park up for the night near a lovely beach.

A month later we found out we had been all but on the doorstep of another pair of friends whom we had promised to visit on this trip. I had mistakenly thought they lived in an entirely different region. When we were returning north some weeks later I looked up their address and realised our mistake. We were really disappointed because this area looked properly interesting and, if we'd known, I'm sure we'd have stayed to explore for a day or so. As it was we had an enjoyable night and were up and back on the road again early the next day.

By now we were all suffering from cabin fever, having covered an insane distance during the past week. I felt particularly guilty about Jackson who for a three-year-old had been extremely tolerant of these lengthy drives when it really wasn't fair on him. The only logical thing to do now was to go for broke. Almuñécar, where our friends (who were also my previous employers who had introduced me to a life of working with dogs) lived, was easily a two-day drive from here. We decided to tackle it head on and use the fastest roads in an all-out attempt to get as close as possible this very day. We shamelessly dangled the lure of a swimming pool and a week of no driving, just playing as a carrot in front of Jackson's nose to keep his spirits up for this last leg.

30. CHILLED TO PERFECTION

JUNE

YES, THE DAY would certainly be challenging. From our rough calculation we had some 400 kilometres to cover, most of them on motorways.

Our route took us along the coast past Benidorm, which from a safe distance appeared as a mass of tower blocks on the skyline, then around Alicante, giving us plenty of scope to get lost, which of course we did. From there we headed inland in a more or less straight line to Murcia. This avoided a long stretch of toll motorway, using instead the E15, which was free, quieter and probably just as fast as the motorway but took us inland all the way to Almería.

The change of scenery was dramatic. Clearly there had been little rain for months. The dry, barren landscape stretched as far as the eye could see and inside the van the temperature was almost unbearable. On both sides, littering the countryside in a particularly unattractive way, we could see extensive use of plastic tunnels and tents for bringing crops on early and giving them protection from this intense sun. This was where I imagined cowboy films had been made.

Many hours later we connected with the coast again and with only one thing on our minds: a swim in the sea, by hook or by crook! We were in for a shock, though. As we approached the coast all hopes of pretty scenic towns were dashed as all we could see were ever-increasing amounts of plastic. All along the coast we found mile upon mile of dirty plastic tents resembling massive refugee camps on both sides of the road. Here and there in this plastic world a town would emerge with buildings poking out above it, the sea of plastic surrounding the town right up to its very doorstep. We later found out that Brits had been caught up in all this. Having purchased what were once lovely holiday villas in scenic coastal villages, they were now surrounded on all four sides by white plastic, drowning all evidence of nature and making their homes unsaleable – all this to enable us to purchase what should be seasonal produce all year round from our supermarkets, with little concern for any environmental impact. We drove right down to the beach but this scenario continued all the way to the sand dunes, totally obliterating all that may once have been pretty and replacing it with filthy, dusty, torn polythene flapping about in the wind. The word 'horrible' barely does it justice, sparking me into some brief internet research, which, to my horror, revealed that what I was looking at was a minuscule section of a vast 26,000-hectare swathe of, in my interpretation, 'plastic pollution' and 'slave labour'. In order to boost the local economy by in excess of £1 billion annually, these greenhouses were not merely home to the crops grown in them but, sadly, masked much darker truths. The working conditions were so brutal as to be a danger to life, with many Spanish workers opting to leave these positions to about 100,000 legal/illegal immigrants from Africa and Eastern Europe.

Desperate to cool off, we parked along a stretch of deserted windswept beach. Within the minutes it took Geoff to walk through the sand dunes to check out the sea, a car with two shifty-looking men drove past, clocked our van, immediately reversed, then spotted me and drove off again. Feeling very suspicious, we decided to take turns to walk to the water's edge while the other sat guard. The sea was dangerously rough. Violent waves crashed right onto a steep pebble bank, the sort that moves underfoot, sucking you into the swell. We couldn't even risk a paddle. Not surprisingly, the same two gentlemen from the car showed up again, this time on foot walking through the dunes. They passed us and then turned back along the road in front of us. No doubt if we had left the van even briefly we would have returned to a burglary.

After an in-house picnic and a quick coffee farther on, where the pretty scenery thankfully returned, we phoned Lesley and Rob and broke the news to them that we were unexpectedly within achievable driving distance and would be able to arrive a day earlier than planned, if they didn't mind. They assured us they didn't.

With what happened next, it seems a miracle that they ever received any Christmas cards from us. I confidently turned down their help with directions, insisting that I had their postcode and would rely on the sat nav. At this stage I was blissfully unaware that what I had written in my address book many years ago was at best only half correct. The sun had clearly fried my brain because, even if I actually had the correct postcode, which I didn't, and even if I had the correct address, which I also didn't, as a general rule I would still not rely on that sat nav of ours.

Half an hour later, with Rob apparently standing on his garden wall high up on a hill, my phone rang and he announced that he had just seen us go the wrong way through a tunnel. A swift U-turn seemed to put us back on track, but then the phone rang again informing us that we had just driven past their turning. It felt like being in *Big Brother*, as we had no concept of where Rob was that allowed him to watch our every move. But as we rounded a hairpin he jumped out onto the road in front of us, eager to guide us smoothly into their drive, which was supposed to be our bedroom for the next few days.

That plan had to be abandoned when a small dip in the ground between the road and the steep drive caught Dotty's very long rear end and threatened to rip her underneath off. There followed much scraping of metal and advice about reversing in, which would have been extremely tricky at such a sharp angle and steep incline and through very tight gates. It all fell on deaf ears anyway, because Geoff had just driven for eight hours and was in no mood to attempt a manoeuvre that could see Dotty acquiring a new pair of gate posts. Eventually we gave up: our third failed attempt to camp on friends' drives out of the three that we had planned. Either we needed a smaller home or they needed bigger ones.

We booked ourselves into a nearby campsite and left the van there for all of three euros a night. Rob very kindly followed us there so he could transport us back to their place, waiting patiently while we threw into any available bag whatever clothes, toys, medication and washing stuff we thought we might need over the next few days. We had never previously left Dotty alone and realised we had to consider what food would have rotted in the fridge by the time we returned and should be taken with us. We also swept up our passports, all our valuables and the all-important alcohol supply, which we very definitely owed to Lesley and Rob for causing them so much chaos.

What they wouldn't dream of telling us was that, having turned up a day earlier than planned and taken up an hour of their time because we couldn't park, we were now unwittingly side-tracking Rob in a campsite when ideally he should have been at home welcoming their dinner guests and helping Lesley, who was suddenly having to cater for three extras including a pescatarian (Geoff), when chicken was on the menu. Unlike what I'd do if I found myself in that situation, Lesley was taking it all in her stride, entertaining Jackson in our absence while hurriedly phoning her friends to request that they bring anything that wasn't meat from their fridge to cater for Geoff. When we finally realised all this, we were a bit red-faced. But soon it was ancient history when it came to light that these friends were the parents of a girl with whom I was in school and used to know well. So the evening was filled with memories and catching up on the past twenty years of the lives of a lot of names from our past. It just goes to show what a small world it is. If I had stayed at home I still wouldn't know the half of it, but send me to Spain and I find out more gossip than you'd believe.

Since selling the boarding kennels, which Rob and Lesley used to own and where I had worked for many years, they had retired and opted to spend six months of the year in Spain and six months back home. Thirteen years later their network of friends out here was as big if not bigger than back in the UK. Their house was absolutely gorgeous, I would even say palatial, bearing in mind the space we had been living in for the past 4½ months. It was built on a hillside running through a valley that wound down to the sea, so when we sat out on the veranda for breakfast we could look across to their neighbours on the opposite side of the valley. If you shouted loud enough you could hold a conversation. With balconies on all sides no ray of sunshine was ever wasted and this showed in the swimming pool, which was heated only by the sun to a balmy 29 degrees. It felt like we had walked into a five-star boutique hotel. It was our first night in the luxury of a bed that could be accessed from either side as opposed to our routine of one foot on a stool and the other on the sink to enable us to climb in at the foot end, our only point of entry. And this bed could be sat up on without whacking your head on a cupboard. The combination of this comfort with the long drive and a drop or two of wine made for the best night's sleep I could remember for ages.

Over the coming days we breakfasted outdoors on apricots freshly picked off the tree in the garden and spent many a relaxing hour sunbathing around the pool. Well, I use the word 'relaxing' lightly as one eye was permanently trained on a very excited, over-confident three-year-old who believed if he threw enough inflatables into the six-foot-deep pool he could walk on water. Sometimes we would muster enough energy to relocate to the beach and back in time for another al fresco sunset meal followed by a drink under the stars, all in the company of Peanut and Almond, the two resident hounds, who made us realise how much we were missing canine company.

We were experiencing the highest temperatures of our trip so far and with not a cloud in the sky we had no reason to venture far from the water. We did, though, sample two of the local beaches, both pebbly but picturesque and perfect for swimming. Geoff actually managed to get himself a job at one of the beaches, working for a man who turned out to be a consultant at a Swansea hospital. The task was to find not one but three lost bunches of keys on the pebble seabed in waist-deep water, which had fallen in when he was wading in from his boat. This chap had spent 24 hours on and off searching with a mask and snorkel, Geoff came up with two bunches in ten minutes but the last bunch, including the garage key to store the boat, evaded everyone and when we left a few days later the boat was still anchored offshore. Next time I need some peace I might try hiring someone to repeat this scenario and keep Geoff occupied for a couple of hours.

In this region of Spain it is customary to receive a free *tapas* with every alcoholic drink you order. Three beers at lunchtime gets you a free three-course mystery meal – and in my case, being out of practice, also gets you tipsy. Which is all very well if you don't have Jackson who, if he's not fed chicken nuggets, fish fingers or chips, turns his nose up and goes hungry. Something we had also noticed when visiting our friends in Italy was that many Brits living abroad tend to succumb all too easily to a lifestyle of eating and drinking in social circles at a level that Geoff and I simply could not keep up with.

Partly with this in mind, we took ourselves off to Almuñécar for a day to give our hosts some peace and visited the local aquarium. Jackson had been to Hastings aquarium several times from a very early age but obviously didn't remember it because he was demented with excitement at the sight of sharks and rays. He actually asked me the following morning when were we going to see a real live shark. When I told him those had been real sharks, he replied: *No, I mean in the wild, in the sea with surfers!* I hope it's not an omen now for Geoff. The town was a delight with its castle and varied array of little shops, but it was just too hot to walk far and instead we sat, ate some lunch and did some people-watching while we slowly slipped into the Spanish way of life and ticked the lazy box again for the day.

By the time we left, Lesley and Rob had showed us an unforgettable week. We were chilled to perfection. It had been so relaxing that it was too easy to forget that they too were making the most of their last week here. The following week they would be flat-out packing up their belongings to have them transported back to the UK while they stayed on holidaying for a couple more weeks before saying goodbye to Spain and closing this chapter in their lives. Their house had been on the market for years before it finally sold and now inconveniently it had happened just as the glorious Spanish summer was beginning. But Brexit was a word that was now on everyone's lips, for the UK was due to vote in the near future. With so much uncertainty lying ahead I imagine it came as some relief for them to know they would not be torn between their two countries.

We left them right at the beginning of June and returned to our van. Dotty seemed to have been well looked after in her campsite, which was extremely basic but hey, for three euros, what did I expect? After staying in so much luxury it was a relief to still feel instantly at home again as soon as we stepped inside Dotty. She continued to be our portal to this eight months of freedom we loved so much, and no amount of being spoiled would sway us from the choice we had made to do this trip in the style we had chosen.

We drove down the coast all the way to Zahora in the province of Cádiz, where we expected to meet up with two very close friends from Swansea out there for a week together at a campsite: a first for them. They would be flying in on Sunday.

Rob and Lesley's next and final guests were arriving on Tuesday, would you believe, but that's what happens when you have such a lovely place and you are also such wonderful hosts. After we parted company with them, Jackson added a new phrase to his dictionary. Now everything started with: *Good God!* When she first heard him say it, Lesley was reminded that whenever she heard a new word or phrase at his age she used to practise it by using it as much as possible, even out of context. We thought that this one came from hearing her favourite phrase: *Good God, Robert!* just a few times. She more than made up for leading Jackson astray by teaching him dominoes and cards and by giving all three of us a week to remember forever.

31. FIELDS OF GOLD

W E WERE ANTICIPATING another exciting week as two of our best friends from Swansea, with whom we often holiday, were coming out to join us and experience life on a Spanish campsite for the first time. Knowing some of the antics we had gotten up to, I had an underlying dread that unless luck was with us for the coming week, this might end up being their first and last campsite experience.

When we set off on our adventure back in January their holiday dates were already booked and as we had absolutely no idea where we would be by then, that was as far as anyone's planning could stretch. As far as Jeanette was concerned the only criteria that mattered were sun and a beach. Pete and Geoff, being surfing buddies, were a little harder to please. Any old beach would not do. It had to have waves, which was part of the reason we had made a dash to this coast, whose shores we had frequented in the past.

Conil de la Frontera is a small resort on the southwest tip of Spain along the stretch of coastline known as the Costa de la Luz. It sits halfway between Gibraltar and Cádiz. Booking for Conil proved much more difficult than expected as we discovered that most sites were fully booked over the weekends and it was not possible to guarantee us a space for our motorhome. This was useless to us. Our friends needed to book urgently in order to arrange their flight and we didn't want to arrive and find ourselves on different campsites. Eventually we settled on a site that appealed to all of us and Pete booked themselves a bungalow just days before they were due to leave. Explaining our own situation over the phone, we were fortunate to find a very understanding member of staff who told us that all they could do was try their best to squeeze us in on arrival, but the earlier we arrived, the better our chances. We rushed straight there, bypassing Gibraltar, which we had planned to visit en route, and, hoping to grab a space, arrived two days earlier than our friends. It was lucky we did because at 3 p.m. we were ushered into the only suitable space for a large van, which just happened to be more or less opposite our friends' bungalow. At that stage there appeared to us to be a wide choice of pitches. But the next six hours saw caravans, motorhomes and car loads of campers arriving in droves until every available space was taken and the once peaceful site was transformed into something resembling a scene from a *Carry On* film.

In the evening for some reason an almighty Spanish party got underway, with BBQs and music and kids running riot well into the night. We spent our first night there with our heads under the pillows trying to block out the noise and awoke with only one thought on our minds: what in God's name had we done to Pete and Jeanette? We spent the morning doing very overdue house work, Geoff in the garage rooting around for his surfboard, boxing away my driftwood collection and so on, while inside I made Dotty sparkle and freshened up our bedding and wardrobes at the laundrette.

We were within walking distance of the beach but our first impressions were disappointing. The tide was out, revealing nothing but rock pools, and with a cold gale blowing I just wished I could close my eyes and drift back to Málaga, where it was 40 degrees. Well, it was what it was: if Jeanette survived the campsite experience and didn't get blown away on the beach, there seemed zero chance of her doing any swimming with all these rocks, and this would definitely be the last holiday she would ever come on with us.

On Sunday we awaited their arrival packed like sardines around the pool, although now it was hot and sunny, the wind had dropped and the pool was a welcome sight. Jackson immediately got stuck in with the Spanish kids, dousing innocent sunbathers with water pistols, and everyone seemed to be looking on the brighter side again. By midday the campsite started to empty out and we breathed a sigh of relief as it dawned on us that they had just been weekend crowds. And in fact it then remained really quiet until the following Friday. If this had been explained to us over the phone we could have spent a few days in Gibraltar on the way down and booked ourselves in from Sunday afternoon: a case of miscommunication.

Pete and Jeanette arrived mid-afternoon and despite being tired they were keen to see the beach. What a pleasant surprise it was this time. The tide was in, covering the rocks and revealing only soft sand, and with no wind it was really warm. It seemed we had inadvertently saved face and Pete and Jeanette's first impressions were as good as anyone could wish for.

They had hired a car for a week, which allowed us to visit a few different beaches, chosen, of course, according to wind and wave conditions. It was a real joy to sit for hours catching up on all the gossip from back home and enjoying Jeanette's company while Geoff and Pete did likewise, perched with a leg either side of their drifting surfboards eagerly awaiting their next wave. By the time we ventured as far as El Palmar, the main beach resort around here, Pete and Jeanette were already sold on the place and were deep into discussing plans to return next year.

The roads were quiet and passed through large swathes of agricultural land, mostly planted at this time of year with freshly blooming sunflowers, making for golden fields stretching away for miles around. The image of millions of crisp yellow heads against a deep blue cloudless sky was stunning. It raised a question to which we still haven't found an answer: why, everywhere we went, did the flower heads all face away from the sun? All my life I had thought they turned towards the sun. I've still got a mental note to do some research, but there was a car load of us to back me up so it wasn't just me having too much sun.

Just up the road from the campsite there was a storks' nest perched on the stump of a palm tree whose top had been cut off. It housed three babies and the adult, an amazing sight for Jackson. There were fledgling sparrows all over the campsite and it was common to find them stumbling around on the ground trying to take flight. Sadly one or two hadn't made it and of course Jackson had to notice this. When I explained that the bird was dead but the parents were still hanging around so we had to leave it there until they gave up on it, he seemed genuinely sad. Unfortunately he returned half an hour later and said to me: *It's okay, Mummy. I rode over the bird on my bike to make sure it was okay and you are right, it's dead!* Horrified, I immediately removed the poor corpse before he thought of a worse plan.

We treated Pete and Jeanette to dinner in a fantastic Moroccan restaurant in Vejer de la Frontera, one of the white hilltop villages in this region. Geoff and I had stayed there on holiday when I was expecting Jackson and it was surreal to return now with the end product coated from head to toe in chocolate ice cream. We took some photos in identical spots so we could show him the before and after shots one day – except that this time I had no excuse for my big tummy other than the too-good-to-resist foreign cakes. The Califa restaurant didn't disappoint. Just like last time, the food was outstanding, as were the surroundings where we ate in the courtyard amid flowers and moody Moroccan lighting. Unfortunately our wonderful meal ended in an epic toddler tantrum. When asked to apologise for something very minor, Jackson, without any warning, screamed at ear-splitting pitch: *SORRY!* This shocked all the other diners into dropping their forks and I felt a hundred pairs of eyes on me. Thank goodness we were ready to leave anyway, allowing us to calmly pick up our belongings and leave in a composed fashion, giving the outward impression: *I've got this* while silently breathing out the words: *You little shit!* and attempting to pinch him under the arm without being noticed. He had his bike locked away for a day so he'll remember it well.

Geoff and I returned the following evening, making use of the hire car, to hunt out some birthday presents for Jackson who would turn four in a couple of weeks and hopefully put pay to the torturous threes. As we were to discover, this was no easy feat with said toddler in tow. The shopkeeper must have wondered which planet this bunch of weirdos had just come from as we walked around her shop subtly pointing things out to one another without touching anything, all the while telling Jackson to go and look for a new water pistol, knowing perfectly well she didn't sell them.

We finally gave each other the wink and asked the shopkeeper to confirm for Jackson's benefit that she didn't sell water pistols, where-upon I left Geoff in the shop to explain to someone who only spoke Spanish that he didn't actually want a water pistol but a number of toys that he now had to remember and relocate. Meanwhile I had to explain to a disappointed child that I had left Daddy in the shop because the lady had to go upstairs to look for a water pistol in the stock. To head off any rebellion I suggested we go and get an ice cream, and then realised I had left my purse in the shop. I didn't dare wander too far for fear of getting lost in the maze of white streets.

Next thing I knew, his eyes like a hawk, he'd spotted Daddy, who, having spent an age waiting for the woman to elaborately gift-wrap each purchase, was now making a dash back up to the car with not only the one bag we had taken into the shop but also the one that was secretly stashed inside it too, both of them now bulging at the seams. We managed to convince Jackson that the lady must have sent Daddy to try another shop for a water pistol, whereupon he instantly forgot about the bulging bags mystery. Eventually, our mission accomplished, we bought him a water pistol back at the campsite. That gave me two weeks to thin his current toys out sufficiently without him noticing before we added the new ones to an already tight space.

The week just flew by. We finally waved Pete and Jeanette off, me with a lump in my throat, with a promise to see them again in a couple of months. It suddenly hit me how much I missed everyone back home. Maybe we hadn't noticed it so much, being focused on new sights every day and, with the help of technology such as Skype and Facebook, keeping everyone up to date with our adventures. In fact, in recent months, what with phone calls and WhatsApp messaging, everyone seemed to be abreast of our news and photographs before they even appeared in my blog. Even so, it wasn't the same as seeing someone in person and catching up with all the details of their life.

It dawned on me that knowing from the outset that we would be returning after a maximum of eight months was what had prevented us from feeling homesick. If in future we were to do longer trips or be tempted to live abroad, we would naturally incorporate trips back to the UK into our plans and would enable our family to come and stay with us regularly. So, if anything, this experience had served to make me realise that distance should never be a barrier. You are only ever at most a day away from home and, realistically, by the time you work around school hours and everyone's work schedule you can easily have as much quality time in a few good holidays together every year as you ever do in those few half-hour coffee breaks at home.

This was the longest we had stayed put in one place since we set off in January but it was just what we needed to rejuvenate ourselves and be ready to continue. There were no time constraints, no driving. We just got up when we felt like it and sunbathed all day long – pure relaxation.

Still, I feel the need to set the scene at the campsite for you as the weekend came around again. It was 11.30 p.m. as we returned from the bar. I don't think one child, including ours, was in bed. Wide awake two-year-olds were eating ice lollies and charging around the place. Everywhere, whether in chalets or tents, people were cooking their evening meal. (We had eaten six hours ago!) The toilets were a sight to be seen, with all ten sinks occupied by girls aged between eight and about fifteen, most of them just showered, one in a bra and thong while drying her hair, another not even as far as the bra but busy applying makeup. One managed to spend longer than it took two of us to use the toilet and wash our hands, just deciding where the waistband on her pyjama trousers looked most flattering in the mirror. All of them were preening big time and all the while a group of young boys gathered outside and in the dish-washing room next door, probably wondering if the girls would ever appear. I felt glad I had a boy because all this stuff I could not cope with.

We managed to meet some really funny people in this place. Most impressive were a couple next to us, probably in their mid seventies, who had hired a motorhome from Malaga for two weeks to get used to again after five years since they last rented one. How that previous trip didn't put them off for life I'll never know. They went to Florida, hired a motorhome there that turned out to be falling apart, had no heating and not even a screen to close off the front windscreen to keep heat in, but hey, it was Florida, who needed a screen. Except that this was the year it snowed in Florida. They only had summer clothing and had booked a campsite right on the beach. When they arrived they couldn't even see the sea because the sky was black with vultures who were eating the 30-foot-wide stretch of dead fish on the sand, all frozen in the low temperatures. Even the geckos were falling out of the trees with the cold. They slept in layers of clothes and hats and turned the gas rings on when they needed to defrost. Now would you *ever* set foot in a motorhome again after that experience?

They had seen so much of the world. Maureen had walked around New Zealand and hated it. Peter had cycled it twice and loved it. Maureen had walked from Lands End to John o' Groats with Peter driving all the way behind her so she could sleep in the motorhome each night. On this latest occasion she had finally talked her husband into buying a motorhome so he gave in and allocated a budget. Next thing, armed with notepad and pen, they were first in and last out of the Birmingham Motorhome and Caravan Show. She came out having purchased a six-week motorhoming tour of Argentina but with no van. Having realised that living in a house with a very small drive on the Isle of Man, which involved a ferry crossing for every journey, perhaps didn't make them the most suitable candidates to own a motorhome, here they now were, having hired another van to practise ready for their big tour of Argentina.

By now, telling us their story, they were rolling about laughing as they divulged that when they retired they had bought a boat, a Baltic something-or-other. Neither could sail, so off they went, signed up for a course and then set off to the Mediterranean. That was when it dawned on them that their Baltic boat was not designed for the Mediterranean. It seemed a miracle that they lived to tell the tales of that trip, and they certainly made Geoff and me feel quite sane in comparison.

We also met a retired head of maths who watered the dangerous seed in my head by suggesting that we homeschool Jackson next year and travel round New Zealand, where he was now doing voluntary teaching. According to him, children learn more from travelling while being homeschooled than they do in a regular school. I confess this got me thinking.

Finally, just as we were filling up with water before leaving, Geoff got chatting to someone from Gibraltar, which is where Geoff had lived from the ages of 14 to 17. It turned out they were the same age. They had gone to different schools but had several friends in common. Geoff discovered that the class joker went on to become a head teacher and that his best spear-fishing mate was now a millionaire. It's a small world, indeed.

We left on the Sunday in a thick sea mist with red flags hoisted on the beach. It seemed that Pete and Jeanette had taken the sun back with them.

32. LET'S GO FLY A KITE

A LTHOUGH WE HAD passed Gibraltar by, it suddenly seemed important, after having that chance conversation about Geoff's childhood in Gibraltar back at the campsite, to show Jackson where his Daddy had once spent his evenings snorkelling after school. So we decided to retrace our steps.

We had to drive past Tarifa, which is the windiest place in Europe and hence home to an insane number of kitesurfers and windsurfers. It is also where the Mediterranean meets the Atlantic. We stopped for a quick look and ended up staying the night in a free sand dune car park with the wonderful company of about 200 other motorhomes. We approached one couple with British plates on their van and asked them, out of politeness prior to launching into fluent English, whether they were in fact British. At exactly the moment the words left my mouth our eyes converged on their teapot, covered in a very brightly coloured knitted tea cosy, which reminded me of my grandmother. There was no further need for them to respond.

They were one of those couples I keep referring to with envy, with no immediate plans and really no idea or concern about when or even whether this lifestyle will ever draw to a close for them. Passing by, they had decided to stop here for one night. Five weeks later they seemed perfectly at home here and had little intention of going anywhere soon. As they put it, they were currently earning more than they were spending by renting out their UK property while staying here for nothing, so why on earth would they want to change anything? I could hardly agree more, but it's the stupidest things that get in the way. Like, their campervan MOT was due to expire in September and enquiries had led them to understand that one of the criteria of their insurance was that the MOT had to be carried out in the UK. There were ways around it that weren't totally above board, so to properly legalise it, come September they would be driving to Dover to the nearest garage before performing a swift U-turn and heading straight back to the sun.

Unlike us, they were what I call hardcore campers, in a small, not to say tiny, convertible van in which you could not stand up. They had to make their bed up each night and then put it all away in the morning just to be able to sit down. They paid a local café twenty pence every time they wanted to use the toilet and they hung out a bag of water in the sun to use as a makeshift shower, but only at the point where they couldn't live with one another's smell any longer because, unlike us, they had no storage tanks for fresh water so had to use it sparingly – preferably for pots of tea. They managed without electricity or heating and would drive into the nearest town whenever they needed water, filling up an array of plastic bottles and returning pronto to bag their prime spot back in this car park.

Seeing them sat outside in the sun enjoying a fresh brew and looking very relaxed, happy and tanned, all the while knowing that while they were doing this their bank balance was steadily going up, I really didn't think the lack of a shower or fixed bed bothered them in the least. That said, I remained aware that in our case the reason we were enjoying our experience so much and finding it so easy was in great part thanks to our faultless choice of motorhome. I don't think we could have chosen a better one if we had tried. The beauty of a Knaus is the quality of workmanship, making it not just easy on the eye but also hard-wearing. As I've said before (though it's worth repeating), if a three-year-old hasn't broken it in six months, it won't break. Dotty, in fact, was as good as new inside despite Jackson's relentless efforts to destroy her. The bed was genuinely more comfortable and larger than our king-size one at home. We had adequate storage for every cooking utensil, item of clothing and toy that we required. I was again reminded that all the masses of stuff I had in storage at home was essentially surplus to requirements and only served to clutter up my life.

So, much as I considered myself well and truly hooked on the travelling lifestyle, would love to convince my husband that it was possible to continue like this for a few more years if we homeschooled Jackson, and would jump at the opportunity if he said yes, I was also aware that we needed our comfort and that space was crucial, particularly with a child. I felt I understood the salesman who convinced us to go for a bigger van when he said: *If you want to come home still married, go as big as you can cope with.* It really was very true.

The next morning we drove to Gibraltar, unaware that it was a bank holiday there for the Queen's birthday and that most of the shops would be closed. Or was this another of Geoff's ploys to save money...? Australia had had theirs the previous Monday but to my knowledge the UK wasn't bothering, so how's that for priorities?

We had hoped to drive across the border but having not found any evidence of motorhome parking anywhere in Gibraltar on the internet, we decided to park up in an Aire at the marina on the Spanish side and walk across the border. The traffic waiting to cross was backed up outside but foot passport control was simple enough. We had to walk right across the runway to enter, controlled by a barrier system much like a level crossing to protect you from incoming planes. The temperatures soared to 37 degrees that day and we strolled through the closed town thinking we would wait for it to cool down a bit before going up the Rock. I have visited Gibraltar before so it came as no surprise to see all the British shops like M&S or even C&A and others that have long disappeared back home. Poor Jackson got confused when he suddenly had to say *Please* and *Thank you* instead of *Gracias*, and our sterling got an airing again. We ate fish and chips and shopped in Morrisons. In the glorious weather at the time the inhabitants of Gibraltar must have thought the rest of us Brits had a screw loose to choose to live in the UK when they could have it all here, with the added bonuses of a tax-free haven and a warm climate. Gibraltar's not for me, though. I could happily live abroad but not there.

We enquired but were refused entry into the compound where Geoff used to live, which is still controlled by the Army. In fact Geoff barely recognised Gibraltar. So much land has been reclaimed from the sea and so many high-rise apartments built all over it that Gibraltar has been stretched out to become bigger and bigger. Where there used to be water you now find car parks and shops, which, in the opinion of many locals, has ruined the place. We were told that property prices were ridiculously high and that many locals were being priced out of the market. People were only too keen to stop and chat with us, with only one topic on everyone's minds, namely the big vote on whether Britain should stay or leave the EU, which was only a matter of weeks away. It was plain to see how much this could impact enormously on Gibraltar's future and there was an understandable air of worry and doubt around the place.

In the late afternoon, with little reprieve from the heat, we ascended the Rock via the cable car to see the Barbary macaques. Instantly we were greeted by one rather grumpy-looking specimen guarding his prime spot on the wall overlooking Gibraltar town, the coastline of Spain and all the way across to Africa. Everyone took turns to cautiously pose with him as close as they dared go for a photo. We witnessed three scuffles between human and monkey, usually over the contents of a bag, including one very narrowly averted attempt at a handbag snatch: apart from that one, the monkey always won. My closest encounter was while descending a spiral staircase when I was met head on by an ape coming up. I instantly tensed up and edged my way around him, making sure he knew he was the boss and that I was not about to challenge his authority. Then I legged it to the bottom, leaving Jackson and Geoff farther up to fend for themselves. I didn't win any Good Mother Awards on this trip, that's for sure! At the top we were hammered by hurricane-force winds blowing hot air so we decided not to go into the nature reserve, which would entail a three-hour walk back down. Instead we caught the cable car. Just as we were about to depart, in jumped a monkey through the window, causing a big commotion, particularly for a petrified woman next to me. The cable car operator calmly said the monkey didn't worry him because it would get out when it wanted to. I won't tell you what the woman said in reply and he probably didn't understand her anyway, which was just as well...

Trying to avoid returning to the oven that would be our van right now, we stopped for cold drinks and a swing park. Eventually we opened our door at 8 p.m. to be hit by a wave of escaping heat. There seemed no option except to swim. The only place for that was a tiny, very litter-strewn beach on the Spanish side of the border fence. It was certainly unusual to be swimming in amongst rubbish up against a concrete wall topped by three layers of barbed wire, separating us from Gibraltar. It wasn't enough to stop two young men climbing over it into Spain with three bags, probably full of duty-free cigarettes, right in front of us and a couple of fishermen, who looked just as surprised as we did.

We left the marina the following morning with every intention of driving across the border to fill up with half-price fuel in Gibraltar. But the queues were a good hour long. We abandoned that plan and headed back to our free sand dune car park in Tariffa, which we reached by lunchtime.

One of my favourite things and among the biggest surprises about our trip was the way we could glide smoothly from the luxury of a friend's house one night to a piece of rough ground all alone the next, where we would happily slum it amid the most beautiful nature, foregoing all amenities. I honestly didn't mind where I was: it was the variety that made it all so memorable. As for this particular site, the mix of characters ranged from young surf dudes to elderly couples who just seemed to enjoy sitting watching all the activity unfold around them. As for the vehicles, they ranged all the way from top-of-the-range motorhomes carrying motorbikes and every kind of luxury to tiny vans in which you couldn't stand up, but there was no sense of any competition between them, everyone seemed happy with their choice and they all looked out for one another. The sense of harmony extended to the locals too. In some places the locals can be quite territorial about their home stretch, but not here.

The wind was the main thing to contend with here. One day we made a mistake by trying to shelter our van behind another one, and when we opened our windows we realised they were perfectly aligned with next door's open windows. Within seconds our van was filled with the potent aroma of weed carried on the through draught. On the windiest days there could easily be 200 kitesurfers in the water at the same time. Sprinkle in some windsurfers and you were literally taking your life in your hands crossing the sand. Attempting a brief dip between all the overhead strings threatened to behead you, while the unpredictably fast-moving boards narrowly avoided contact with one another and with you. We heard a first-hand tale from a windsurfer who, years ago, had become becalmed here when the wind suddenly dropped. While sitting on his board, a fin popped up, circled him and one eye looked right at him. It later transpired that it was a blue shark, which are usually harmless, but even so it put him off for a bit.

It was very weird witnessing the occasions when the wind would suddenly drop. One minute the sky would be alive with a mosaic of colourful kites and sails and the whirring, humming sound of the wind catching the taught strings would be all around you like hundreds of bees. The next, a silence would hit you and your eyes would rise to see the sky clearing as the kites drifted silently down to land on the sea. Those that had happened to find themselves near the shore might paddle back in, but for the majority they would just sit on their boards bobbing about, no doubt unaware of the shark story, until a gust of wind would come to their rescue and the kites would take to the skies once more. The closest we got to joining them was flying Jackson's kite in the car park. The waves were not suitable for surfing but we could easily while away the hours sitting in the beach cafés in the sun. One day when we explored the sand dunes in an attempt to find shelter we marched straight into a nudist colony, to Jackson's huge amusement. We declined the invitation to join them.

We spent a day exploring Tariffa town, which must hold a record for the greatest number of surf shops in one street. We swam in the Mediterranean, then crossed the road and paddled in the Atlantic, which, although considerably choppier, was also surprisingly warmer. We managed to watch the Euro 2016 England–Wales football match in a pizza restaurant. Jackson declared he was supporting Spain, which was probably a sensible approach bearing in mind that we all had to return to the confines of our van when it was over.

Much as we loved this place there came a point where we told ourselves that we needed a wind-free day. But as we drove inland in the direction of Seville, boy, before long were we wishing for that wind to follow us. Windows wide open, hot air rushing in and *Jingle Bells* escaping at full volume courtesy of Jackson's Christmas CD, which he insisted on playing – that was how we tackled what felt like a long drive.

33. THE GHOST OF VICTOR MELDREW

THE DRIVE TO Seville took us only about two and a half hours but because of the heat it was one of the most unbearable yet. As soon as we left the coast the temperature increased by about ten degrees with absolutely no breeze. This called for regular coffee breaks in air-conditioned cafés to bring our core temperature back to a healthy level. We arrived at around 3 p.m. having had no choice but to allow the driver one last surf at his favourite spot, El Palmar, on the way past. That was the start of our misery because he managed to put his back out while waxing his board. Amazingly it didn't hurt too much to surf, but for the rest of the day he declared himself unable to do anything apart from sigh, gasp and whine about the pain.

Arriving at our Aire in Seville did nothing to lift his mood when we discovered that it was a car park, in the middle of a car garage, in the middle of an industrial park: all concrete, not a scrap of shade, diesel engines running constantly and filling the air with fumes, toilets and showers shared with mechanics, and nothing at all within easy walking distance. There were two Aires listed in the book but this one, on paper, had looked the most attractive, though at this point there was no moving Geoff never mind the hell hole we were in. Mr Grumpy went to bed and Jackson and I decided to be brave and make our own way into Seville.

Who was I kidding? I have no sense of direction at all. By the time we had made our way down the half-mile track to reach the main road I was already spooked by the number of empty discarded beer bottles and the groups of teenagers hanging out in the bushes on either side. Someone in a chauffeur-driven car with blacked-out windows stopped and offered us a lift to town. At that point, genuine though the offer might have been, we retreated in defeat back to the car park, having caught a brief and appealing glimpse of the city across the river.

The main purpose of visiting Seville was to surprise Jackson with a day at the Magic Island theme park, a few miles outside the city, as an early birthday treat, since we had no clue where we would be on his actual birthday. Clearly Geoff felt no more cheerful when he got up, having struggled to sleep in temperatures of 28 degrees at 2 a.m. He announced that since he couldn't drive we would have to catch a taxi. An hour later, having stood on the roadside in full sun attempting to flag one down, we were seriously considering giving up as we hadn't yet mentioned to Jackson where we were going. All our tempers were fraying: Geoff was in pain, Jackson was fed up, and I was blaming Geoff for causing this by refusing to drive just a few miles and giving us all sun stroke. Thankfully at that moment a taxi finally pulled up.

When we got there all we could see was lines of hundreds and hundreds of people waiting to buy a ticket. You can imagine how well that went down. Again Jackson and I stood in the full sun, now at 40 degrees, for long enough to have to apply sun screen twice. Meanwhile Geoff disappeared, I assumed to nurse his back and stand in the shade. Fair play, though, after a while he returned, moaning even more, this time about the incompetence of the staff and the lack of signs but with info that we should abandon the queue and follow him to the 'internet tickets only' booth. Strangely enough this worked, except that with tickets now in our hands and a mere 100 euros the poorer we still found ourselves outside but now facing a different queuing system to hand in our tickets and actually gain entry. I'm ashamed to say that Geoff devised his own speed-entry system, consisting of putting his head down and walking head-on directly to the front of the queue and straight in, handing the tickets over while still walking. For a split second I gave him the benefit of the doubt but when I asked him: *Didn't you see all those people queuing?* his reply was *Course I did but I've had enough of this bloody place already.* It seemed to be the moment to break the exciting news to Jackson that this was his birthday treat, simultaneously kicking Geoff to remind him why we were here and plead with him to at least pretend to be happy. All this was merely the preamble to a day spent in a swelteringly hot, expensive Seville theme park with the ghost of Victor Meldrew.

Our 'cheap' tickets bought us entry into both the aqua park and the theme park, but in 40 degrees there was no contest and we made an instant beeline for the water park. As soon as we got in we were faced with a queue for a locker. Five minutes later we were offered a choice between a lockable safe or a plastic tub behind a desk with no lid. Same price so no brainer really, except that as we tried to part with yet more cash we were informed that we couldn't pay there, oh no no no NO! We had to go to the shop and queue all over again and, guess what, they had run out of flaming lockers by then. So the box it was – for what that was worth. I might as well have stuck my purse on a sunbed with a sign saying 'Help yourself' because, despite the fact that I queued alone this time to hand my ticket over to get a box and in return was handed a wrist band with a number on it, when I returned later I was handed someone else's bag by mistake. In the time I was away, Geoff had laid two towels on sunbeds. But no sooner had I got my arse down than they were onto us: *Where are your tickets?* Geoff just laughed in their faces, not in a funny way. By now I was fully expecting to be thrown out but, instead, back to the shop I had to go, hand over another note and then at last we had permission to sit down.

Even then, bearing in mind I was only gone ten minutes, Geoff had managed to get into trouble yet again. He had committed the capital offence of standing in the kids' pool. By the time I got back he was ranting about the life guards and then literally, as I stood there, the whistle blew and yet again it was WE who had caused it because, heaven forbid, Jackson was wearing goggles. NO GOGGLES ALLOWED in this pool, only in the big pool, oh and NO RASH VEST in this pool either. This really was the final straw. I refused to take the vest off him: he was the only blonde, fair-skinned kid in sight and it was quite obvious he would burn up in half an hour. I was just about to demand our money back when someone advised me to ask the chief lifeguard if he would make an allowance. I mean, seriously? I can't even be sure I asked the right person. Some bloke answered in Spanish who might have been saying: *Has anyone ever said you look like a beached whale in that?* for all I knew, but I couldn't care less. For the rest of the day, every time a lifeguard blew the whistle and pointed to Jackson's vest, and that happened in double figures, I just said: *The boss said it's ok!*

Jackson was clearly frightened to attempt much on his own when we were not allowed to set foot in the kids' pool for moral support. We moved on to the larger pool where the men with overactive whistles were going bananas. Peep peep, NO INFLATABLES! Peep peep, NO BALLS! Peep peep, NO SPLASHING! Peep peep, NO JUMPING! The idea seemed to be that if you were having fun you were doing something wrong. Ok then, lunch seemed to be a good idea, and although we'd been bankrupted by Magic Island, we had luckily brought a picnic. Ah no, you guessed it, peep peep peep, NO FOOD BY THE SUNBEDS, which we had just paid for and which we would damned well stay sat on even though it meant hiding our sandwiches with one arm under the bed in between bites.

Once in the big pool it became clear that Jackson was too short for all the slides. We returned to the kids' pool where finally he enjoyed the baby slides despite still being petrified of the life guards. Each slide ended in an overly long, flat section slowing each child down to a stop. At that point the instinctive and commonsense reaction was to stand up and walk off the end. Peep peep! Cue endless whistle-blowing and demands for them to sit down and shuffle along on their bums. Poor Jackson, every time the whistle blew he squatted down and shuffled about even when he wasn't on the slide. Just when I had finally convinced him not to be scared because they weren't telling him off, he chose that moment to come down the slide on his tummy to a loud whistle and a finger wagging very crossly in his face.

Determined to get our money's worth I forced Geoff to man up to his back pain and go on every adult slide there was. We all did the lazy river, floating in a rubber ring. Later on Geoff returned from the slides, finally grinning from ear to ear. *I found a bloody great big shell Jackson gave me off the beach in my pocket*, he announced, *so I dropped it in the middle of the lazy river. You watch, they will have to hold a committee meeting tonight to discipline the poor sod who allowed a bloody great big shell past their beady eyes and into the lazy river.* He really was enormously pleased with himself.

We spent the next few hours in the theme park, which, apart from extremely long queues for everything, was rather good and I have to say we all enjoyed it. It was a cut-price version of Disneyland, here featuring grumpy staff. We endured the heat as long as we could and returned for one last swim before watching the closing show. At 10.30 p.m., ten minutes into the show, we made our escape – the show was beyond dire and we were ready for our beds.

How do I sum up the whole weird phenomenon of Magic Island? Let me start with three questions: Would we and Jackson remember this day? Would we come again? Would we still be laughing about it in years to come? To which I'll answer with three words: Yes! Never! Definitely!

I had high hopes that Geoff would wake up in a better mood next morning now that all that was over. But he had already made his mind up that he was *not* attempting the city in this heat. Since it happened to be Father's Day it seemed only fair to let him spend it as he wished, and Seville would have to wait for another trip in a cooler season.

34. COWBOY TOWN

G EOFF AWOKE TO an overexcited Jackson with a Father's Day card shouting: *It's a happy Father's Day!* in his earhole. We packed up and drove a short distance towards the coast heading for Hinojos, a town within a nature reserve. The Doñana National Park is vast, stretching for miles inland from the sea through marshland and pine and eucalyptus woods. Here we had chosen a campsite and booked ahead and it didn't disappoint. It was completely surrounded by woods and, apart from bird song, it was silent. It was everything we had craved yesterday, cool, shaded, quiet and with a very inviting swimming pool with no sign of any men with whistles. But this comfort came at a cost in the form of hungry swarms of mosquitos. It was a case of repelling, covering up, burning candles and constantly swatting in the van despite the fly screens.

We lay by the pool, bird-watching from our sunbeds, adding to our list the azure-winged magpie, which only lives on the Iberian peninsula. Jackson was still in Father's Day mode and insisted on bringing Daddy present after present, mainly sticks and stones. He was most pleased with his gift of a huge dead black beetle, which, to the amusement of two other British couples, he carried over and dropped onto Geoff's sunbed, singing loudly: *Happy Father's Day!* As one man said: *Well, it's more than I got!*

All this fun got us chatting to a couple from Scotland who ran a motorhome park but had never actually been motorhoming themselves. They had finally bought one and set off for six weeks in search of a nice place to live in Spain, but after five weeks they had pretty much scrapped that idea and now could honestly say they fully understood what their clients were on about. They had decided to buy a bigger motorhome, live in that and work from Europe via the internet.

We had a fantastic night with them although I swear they thought we had given Jackson drugs, since he talked nonstop rubbish to them the entire evening. He had been acting strangely the past few days, talking as if he had already been to a place that we were only just visiting for the first time and going into the details of a job that he used to do there, as if he'd had a previous life. I had to blame it on the blue ice creams. Heaven only knows what they put in the stuff but it always sends him round the twist and gives him bright green, not actually blue, poo the next day, which is alarming.

It turns out that our Scottish acquaintance, Ian, had sailed, surfed and windsurfed and that he was windsurfing competitively at the same time that Geoff was doing sports photography. They had many, many old friends in common. This prompted us all to drink a little too much wine, get eaten alive by mosquitos and have bad heads the following day. What a strange coincidence that Geoff had caught up more on his teenage years to his thirties at our last two campsites than he had in the last forty years.

Once our hangovers had abated we took a drive into a town deeper within the park by the name of El Rocío, which closely resembled a scene from any good western film. Riding into town in our eight-metre motorhome, I had never felt more out of place. White cowboy-style houses and a beautiful white church formed a perimeter around a huge central square, leading off into a couple of wide streets. Underfoot was sand and dust, with no sign of any paved areas. In the square were a handful of cafés and shops and wooden rails where you could tether your horse while you browsed. We sat outside in the sand drinking coffee and admiring spoonbills and flamingos on the lake in front of us. The owner of the café confirmed that it was 40 degrees and with few options of shade all we could manage was a wander around town. If you needed a new saddle, a pair of riding boots, a cowboy hat or various forms of horse decoration, you were in luck. Otherwise there really wasn't much else on offer apart from some antique guns and pistols, which Jackson refused to accept were not toys.

We ventured a further ten minutes down the road in the van and came to a lovely sandy beach front lined with cafés. But, and it pains me to say it now that we are back to reality, it was simply too hot to enjoy, so we made our way back to base to feed the mosquitos. They had a particular taste for Geoff because he left with over fifty bites while I had maybe five. We spent half the night sitting up in bed with a fly swat whacking the ceiling. To this day we have never worked out how they got in, since we had fly screens everywhere, but nothing seemed to stop them. To add to his continuing back pain Geoff now had a very swollen arm from all his bites.

We would be leaving the darned critters behind in the morning, when we aimed to cross the border into Portugal.

35. WOLF WHISTLES FROM THE NEIGHBOUR

CROSSING THE BORDER into Portugal on the Algarve, we continued a further twenty kilometres along the coast to Tavira, which had been recommended by someone at a previous campsite. But we could find nowhere to sleep, and neither of our books listed anything in this area. We resorted to following little wooden road signs to various campsites, and then turned to the sat nav, which allows you to search for campsites but doesn't elaborate on whether they are equipped to accommodate an eight-metre vehicle or just a tent. After several failed attempts we retraced our steps to a small village we had passed earlier, which had an Aire costing all of four euros per night.

It turned out to be a pleasant surprise when we got there. Each pitch backed onto a lovely grassy area, perfect for a kick-around for the kids, while you could still keep an eye on them from the van. Electricity and water were optional, we were within easy walking distance of shops and cafés and just a short boardwalk away from the sea. We chose a spot right next to the route to the beach.

Within ten minutes we were packed and hot-footing it across the sand. As we returned it became impossible to ignore the loud wolf-whistling. Not that I was under any illusion that it was aimed at this middle-aged woman with at least two spare tyres on display, sea-styled hair and crow's feet accentuated by the sun due to Alzheimer's causing me constantly to forget my sunglasses. But apart from myself, there was only Geoff — no need to elaborate — and Jackson. Nobody else was around. Who was it who fancied us?

Finally I spotted him, our next door neighbour: a very fine male specimen... of the feathered kind. He was an African grey parrot, perched on top of his cage in a tree outside his motorhome which, although only half the size of ours, housed four adults, three beautiful shaggy rescue dogs and Oscar the parrot, who went on to entertain us for three days with his early-morning imitation of an alarm clock and his singing and laughing. He constantly had us all reaching for our mobile phones as he mimicked incoming text alerts.

Next door on the other side were a lovely Portuguese couple, Beatrice and Pedro, and their two-year-old daughter Maria, much to Jackson's delight. Thankfully they spoke excellent English and in no time Jackson and Maria were joined at the hip right from their first game of ball on the grass. In general he was very good at playing big brother and responsibly taming his football game to a level at which Maria could join in safely. However, any attention that she received from Geoff or me was met with jealousy, which was rather amusing. Although only just two she seemed to be fearless, and she absorbed English like a sponge. She learned overnight to count in English from one to ten and was repeating words at ease. As soon as we woke up Jackson would want to know what Maria was doing, and apparently they had the same in their van, with Maria constantly calling out: *Jackie!*

We decided to stay on for an extra day to allow their relationship to blossom and spent plenty of time on the beautiful beach. The sea was rough with strong currents so it was paddling only, but the weather was perfect and the Aire seemed such a friendly place that you just didn't want to leave. This is how Maria and her family holidayed regularly, not that far from their home but in what felt like a real getaway. They preferred the peace and tranquillity of the Aires as opposed to the regime that often accompanied full-blown campsites, while of course the lower cost of Aires made them a more frequently affordable pleasure. There was a daily market just up the road where we could fill a carrier bag with fresh produce including hot bread, while really struggling to spend more than four euros.

These days we were finding we didn't need to refill our gas now that no heating was required. Realising we had forgotten in which country we had last filled up, we instantly checked the gauge at the back of the van just in case we couldn't use the cooker tonight. Water and emptying facilities were all provided and in all this glorious sunshine our solar was enough to keep our hot water and batteries permanently fully charged. We had even learned at last that we could also use our inverter to charge up the tablet and cameras, which I wished we had known a few months back. This reinforced our appetite to approach future holidays in this style. Who needs fancy hotels or all-inclusive packages when you can do it this way, get a real feel for an area and its people, make lasting memories and cement friendships?

Since Pedro and Beatrice were on holiday for two weeks with no fixed agenda, we mentioned Jackson's pending birthday and arranged to keep them informed of our whereabouts in case they could join the celebrations. Unfortunately every day now we felt the pressure of time and places that we still wanted to visit on our homeward journey. Even so we still found ourselves changing our agenda frequently when we came across little gems along the way that we simply couldn't miss. Keeping one eye constantly on the weather, we knew we always had the option of staying in the south to properly explore a smaller stretch of coast, saving all the rest of the country for a different trip – for we knew that as we headed farther north the temperature would drop. Yet somehow curiosity always seemed to get the better of us every time we studied the map, fancying just a quick look at this or that place. And so we still found ourselves on the move every few days.

So it was that soon we were on the road again heading for Lagos, a lively town we had visited before, where there promised to be some-where suitable for us to settle down for Jackson's birthday.

36. TURNING FOUR

LAGOS HAS ALWAYS been an interesting town, steeped in history and with buildings and facades that reflect its varied past, including evidence of its involvement in the slave trade. All this plus beautiful beaches and a vibrant marina helps to draw in both tourists and artists. We've found some of the best musicians we've ever seen busking here. Its old centre of cobbled streets and many culinary delights offer something for everyone, so it was little wonder that we found ourselves back here again. We looked at an Aire on the outskirts, but the circus was in town and the parking for motorhomes was right next to the tents in a dusty car park with no shade at all. It was also two kilometres from the nearest beach so we decided not to stop there. Instead we found a campsite in the next village, Praia da Luz.

This really was something special, immaculately clean, with a massive swimming pool, kids' pool, Jacuzzi and even a wellness centre. There was a full entertainment programme both for kids and adults, and it ticked all the boxes as a birthday party venue. A few text messages later we booked the pitch right next to us for a surprise visit by Maria and her family on Sunday. All the while we were doing this the name of the town seemed familiar to me, and then suddenly it dawned on me that this was the area where Madeleine McCann disappeared, as Google revealed, from a villa just down the road. This did nothing to calm my nerves when Jackson insisted on going off around the campsite with three older Polish boys from the next pitch, making it clear that he was a big boy and neither needed nor wanted Mummy to accompany him.

We spent an hour or two by the pool, which momentarily brought back the reincarnation of Victor Meldrew when a very miserable-looking lifeguard told us off for putting a Lilo in the pool, followed by no goggles in the Jacuzzi and no jumping anywhere. But apart from an hourly patrol around the pool to issue his orders there was rarely any sign of the life guard, so anyone planning on drowning just needed good timing. Joking aside, I soon began to understand the rules. While we were chatting in the Jacuzzi to an Irish man and his two children, between all five adults not one of us spotted his little girl in trouble, apart from him – luckily within seconds. She had slid off the seat into the deeper water and with no foothold she couldn't get her head above the water. I witnessed first-hand what I had often read and wondered about, namely, when someone is drowning there's often no splashing or shouting to alert you. This little girl looked still and calm just as if she was standing in the water, except that her feet were not touching the bottom and her mouth and nose were both underwater. It was a wake-up call to everyone that when kids are around water your chatting has to wait: they need your undivided attention. This time, thank goodness, all was fine.

As if that wasn't enough of a shock, we awoke to discover the referendum result and to learn that we Brits had voted to leave the EU. It knocked us for six and, probably quite unnecessarily, we suddenly felt embarrassed about having a British number plate. It felt strangely shaming to be enjoying all this European hospitality, as if from now on people would judge us personally on this decision. Inevitably it was a topic on everyone's lips, and, from the moment we first opened our door in the morning, several conversations with people of various nationalities ensued. Our thoughts returned instantly to the people of Gibraltar and to Lesley and Rob, whose future might have been very different had they not received payment for the sale of their house in Spain just a few weeks before the referendum. Then there was the couple we'd met from Scotland who had just settled on their plan to buy a big van and run their Scottish motorhome site while on the road in Europe. We recalled, from our drunken chat that evening, that the wife's job was totally reliant on European funding. With the prospect of losing that and quite likely her job as a result of this vote, I could imagine all their plans having to be instantly changed. We chatted for hours over coffee with our Polish neighbours who had many concerns of their own about the number of Polish workers employed in the UK. Surprisingly to us the general consensus seemed to be that no-one felt they would benefit from Britain leaving the EU, and many seemed to think it might spur on other countries to do likewise. One thing seemed certain: we should try to survive for as long as we could on what euros we had, because it seemed unlikely we would get much for our pounds right now.

We tried to put these thoughts to one side and to concentrate on the here and now. We spent some lazy times in the sun around the pool and went into Lagos for an evening hoping to find a Portugal football shirt for Jackson, for no better reason than that it was his colour. For seventy euros, though, I thought I'd prefer to dye a white shirt.

Finally the big day arrived. Jackson opened all his presents before breakfast and then we were occupied for the next three hours assembling a Playmobil police car and speed boat (the latter, by the way, sped very well in the paddling pool when the life guard wasn't looking), a Lego fire station, and a two-wheel scooter because he was a big boy now and wanted to do tricks. Give me strength, I already had the plasters ready!

While at the pool, Maria and her parents made a surprise entrance and Jackson's face instantly lit up. Children and adults had a fun-filled afternoon, to say the least. Coincidentally we managed to be on the one campsite in the whole trip just at the right time when they were holding a fun day with a bouncy castle, balloon modelling, face painting and even plate spinning. I do believe Jackson thought it was all specially arranged by us for his birthday. The staff spoiled him and he ended up with a sword, gun and belt, a pirate's hat and even a parrot on a swing, all sculpted out of balloons and all of which had to fit into our van. He had to shower with one arm held up in the air covered by a carrier bag to protect his red dragon tattoo.

The icing on the cake for him was when we returned to our van to find thirty balloons wound all the way up the awning support and across its canopy courtesy of Pedro and Beatrice. Funnily enough, the previous evening Geoff had been stealthily ordered to catch the bus to town – which turned out to be an ordeal involving some hitchhiking – in a desperate last-minute bid to find some balloons, because the campsite didn't have any. He had scoured the town and returned hot, bothered and empty-handed, and now here we were, drowning in the things without any warning. We were really moved by their thoughtfulness. We all ate together in the restaurant that evening and, when the chocolate cake arrived with what can only be described as a firework on the top, the whole restaurant joined in with not one but two renditions of 'Happy Birthday', first in English and then in Portuguese. Shortly after that, disco night commenced and boy, did Maria show the boy how to dance? She was up on stage and never stopped until well past any two-year-old's bedtime.

We had planned to move on the next day but we were all having too much fun, not to mention we had teeny-weeny hangovers. By general consensus we all decided to stay for one more day. Jackson had spent so much time around the pool here that he asked me to video him, and now he went on to swim a whole width unaided. He had started Water Babies at ten weeks old where they had always said that by the time he was four he should be able to swim a width. Now, true to their word, at four years and one day here he was doing it.

Eventually and reluctantly we all packed up together on Tuesday morning. For the first time in the entire trip I put the map away and we followed them, clueless where we were going exactly, to a beach they had fallen in love with nearly three years ago, which went by the same name as Maria's middle name. Let's just say we doubled the space between our vans that night.

It was only a half-hour drive to Boca do Rio, a beautiful unspoiled beach beneath high crumbling cliffs, with a river full of fish flowing across its expanse and into the sea. On this particular day the cliffs provided little shelter from the strong onshore wind whipping the sea into a frenzy, which threatened instant capsize if we attempted to launch our kayak as we had planned. Instead we settled for sandcastles and kites for the day. We celebrated our final evening together with a traditional meal in a local restaurant, beginning with snails — not the French type but tiny little things that looked as if they had been randomly collected from the garden, although, as long as I gave them no thought, they tasted very good. The kids were still playing outside in the swing park at 10 p.m., as was the norm here.

Since their previous visit to this beach, signs had appeared forbidding overnight parking. It seemed very unlikely due to the remote location, but it was always possible the police could pay a visit and issue spot fines of 200 euros.

Instead we followed a tip from Pedro that if we just moved 500 metres inland and there were no signs stating otherwise, we were welcome to camp wherever we liked. In the pitch dark we selected a picnic site encircled by woodland, then everyone descended on one van, opened the beers and subjected two toddlers to *The Gruffalo* on DVD. Thinking back to the spooky location, we should probably have chosen a more appropriate film, but no lasting toddler harm was done.

Maria and her family were heading home the following morning but generously said we were welcome to visit them when we passed their home town farther on in our travels. Sadly by then time would not be on our side and this was the last time we saw them.

We three set off for Arrifana, a surf beach we had visited on a previous holiday. By accident we detoured to Cape St Vincent, but there are some detours you can be grateful for. The cape at the southwesternmost point of Portugal was truly impressive. The 75-metre cliffs rose vertically from the crashing waves, topped by an impressive lighthouse, which guards one of the world's busiest shipping lanes. We knew the cape was renowned for its remarkable sunsets, but eager to reach the next beach we decided to settle for a slightly less impressive sunset elsewhere.

After all this Arrifana let us down a bit, excluding us by low barrier systems from all its car parks so that we could not sleep there. We parked by the roadside above the bay where the view revealed far from ideal surf conditions and a horribly steep walk to and from the beach. Undeterred and with the bare minimum of equipment we began our walk, one that I will always remember. Halfway down my phone rang and I found myself staring at one of the most beautiful views in the world while conversing with Jackson's soon-to-be head teacher. Funnily enough I had to decline his invitation to visit the school the following week to familiarise Jackson with his new teachers.

Although we appreciated how such a visit would benefit him, we had concluded months ago that his experiences from this trip far outweighed any gains from just paying a half-day visit to the school. After all, he was about to spend the rest of his childhood years at school and he would have plenty of time to get used to it. While out here we were paying particular attention to his interaction with other children and it was plain to us how much confidence he was gaining.

When I explained that we were travelling I was asked if we definitely intended to take the school place in September. To this day I will never know how I stopped myself saying: *Well, actually, now that you ask, can we just say he'll start the year after instead?* This entire fraught matter was something Geoff and I had talked about at great length over the previous months. Jackson was not legally required to be in full-time education until he turned five at the end of June, and it had crossed our minds to request that we start him one year later, when he would be the oldest in the class by a couple of months rather than one of the youngest. Maybe that thought caused me to stay my hand and those fateful words to remain unspoken. After the call had ended, we were both a little subdued with thoughts of hard work, daily routines and time constraints rushing back into our lives in the near future.

Maybe it was these gloomy thoughts that spurred us on to make another spontaneous decision as we walked back up, grasping with both hands the luxury of still having the option to act on the spur of the moment. Instead of following the coast road to find a suitable overnight stop, we headed inland, climbing and climbing past the spa town of Monchique to the top of the highest mountain in the Algarve, Mount Fóia in the Monchique Mountains. When we arrived we found an observatory and two designated motorhome spaces, one of them happily empty for us and the other occupied by a British van, and nothing else but the stars above. We watched the sunset in gale-force winds, grabbing a second layer for the first time in months to protect us from the decidedly cooler temperatures, and later we star-gazed from our cosy bed through the skylight – the wimps' way! Our surroundings were spoiled only by the very ugly, ill-conceived concrete tourist information building and café perched here on the top of the mountain. Having said that, the smell of coffee in the morning forced us to put them in further funds.

We learned more about our neighbours' journey the next morning and it filled me with sadness and admiration for their bravery. He had been diagnosed terminally ill and had refused intervention. Instead his wish was to buy their first motorhome, use it to see as much of the world as time would allow them and spend this precious time creating memories for his wife's future. It seemed to me a really wonderful attitude although I could imagine the tough decisions they'd had to make having chosen to leave behind their family and friends. I would like to think that they are still travelling and enjoying a magnificent view somewhere in the world right now. It goes to show that it really is never too late.

We set off in the opposite direction down the scenic winding route through the rest of the mountain range towards Setúbal. There was hardly time to blink before we found ourselves in trouble trying to wind our way through a tiny village at exactly the same time as the local supermarket took their delivery. After holding up the traffic in all three directions the delivery driver directed us inch by inch between his truck and the row of parked cars. I had my eyes shut throughout the whole process and by the time we got through we had acquired some more multicoloured wing-mirror paint. After that the road widened and took us through silver eucalyptus forests before we descended farther into beautiful twisted cork woods. It was a haven for wildlife here and at one stage we watched a polecat running alongside the van. The area was clearly prone to forest fires with evidence of large swathes of replanting having taken place in the aftermath.

By the time we stopped by a reservoir for a picnic lunch it was too hot for us to sit outside. I began to feel like a serial moaner: *Too cold! Too hot!* We hadn't seen a drop of rain for two months and still I was finding reason to complain about the weather. What hope would there be for me back home?

On the far side of Setúbal we hit some outstanding coastline of small white-sand coves and bays with scenically positioned rocks resembling oversized weather-smoothed pebbles dotted about the sand as if placed there on purpose to provide perfect photographs. The crystal-clear sea was calling to us and we stopped for a cool-off. Jackson went straight in, watching the fish swim around him through his goggles. We had tried to introduce him to a snorkel but panic would set in before he even got his feet wet. All our explanations that he could breathe through his mouth failed to register. Every time he took a first breath through his nose he would inhale all of the air from his mask, steam up his viewing window and immediately rip the whole thing off, insisting that we were suffocating him. Instead he preferred to hold his breath and look through his goggles.

Five minutes earlier on the road we had noted a potential car park to sleep in, but instead curiosity got the better of us and we thought we would first investigate just a little farther along the road. Big mistake! As usual I was in charge of the sat nav and after driving for five minutes I advised Geoff to revert to our original plan. As we turned around we spotted a no-entry sign. Unable to understand the Portuguese writing beneath it, I insisted that we play safe and not enter. Immediately we were reminded of that no-entry sign that had caused us so much grief back in Italy. Geoff reminded me of the rule we'd agreed: when in doubt, ignore the sign. In Italy that had made sense but here it seemed ridiculous to take the risk on such a narrow road with no sign of any vehicles going the other way. To be honest, I hen-pecked Geoff into doing it my way, having convinced myself that the sat nav depicted an alternative route.

One thing my driver repeatedly brought to my attention during this trip was that I could look at a map or screen and then issue very firm navigational instructions while somehow failing to observe the landscape all around me. And sure enough, half an hour later, when we were 500 metres up on a ridge looking down on where we wanted to end up, this matter was brought to my attention once more. What the sat nav *should* do, faced with sea on one side of the vehicle and a sheer cliff on the other side, is tell us that unless we turn round now and follow the road alongside the sea we will end up climbing, or descending, steeply.

Now the latter option, in any language, translates to hairpins... lots of them. In an eight-metre vehicle pulling the weight of contents of an entire house, lots of hairpins equates to slow – painfully slow – precision driving and intense concentration from the driver, whether you're going up or down. The hairpins option is rarely a popular choice, and this definitely wasn't the time (as I would soon find out) to be squealing with delight at the astounding view (it really was fantastic!) or requesting photo stops (*NO!*). Instead of ignoring the no-entry and taking the safe, sensible option, we argued all the way down through the hairpins and thankfully emerged at the bottom exactly where we would have been 45 minutes earlier if we had done it Geoff's way. Point noted!

Interestingly our guidebook later revealed a little more about this ridge and that the one-way system only operated from July to September. As we were there on 30th June we could legally have taken the coast road, but I didn't feel the need to share that knowledge with Geoff.

The car park we had seen from up above turned out to be a motorhome site, but it seemed to be unfinished. The guard on the gate quoted a very reasonable six euros for the night, which we gratefully accepted though on entry we found we were the only guests. There were temporary toilet blocks and showers with no doors and, interestingly, a ladies unmistakably labelled with a picture of a woman in a skirt and offering three urinals and one cubicle. I came back out twice just to check the picture. We were given a glossy brochure highlighting the site's eco policies and yet it didn't look as if it had been used in years. The original toilet blocks were falling down and the proper pitches were not in use. We were given a temporary patch to park on, but hey, it was right next to the sea and provided us with a perfect signal for the Euro football on Sky, so it suited us fine.

We witnessed the guard change over and then a fire engine parked up inside the site. It seemed to us crazy that guards were being paid 24/7 for one six-euro family of guests. And it got more weird. In the morning I opened the door to an array of flashing lights outside the gates: police in uniform, that fire engine, and several army uniforms all milling around. My instant fear was that we had parked on the site of an unexploded bomb or some similar nightmare, but it emerged that while we slept three army Ducks had come ashore and were awaiting police escort while they were relocated on the back of a massive transporter. All this activity took place, much to Jackson's delight, right in front of us as we ate our breakfast.

When I went to reception to pay the bill I was greeted by a very cheerful lady who informed me that our night's stay was a gift from the mayor. He invited us retrospectively to stay for nothing, because the site had only officially opened yesterday and we were its first guests.

This was our second personal encounter with a mayor on this trip. The first was in France when the local mayor was summoned from his home to come out and deliver us an electricity token. It's hard to imagine one of our mayors adding such duties to their daily schedule but it was nice to feel that we had been noticed. I wasn't surprised that we were the first guests, but what did surprise me was that it was officially open at all, because nothing about it looked that way. Anyway I thanked her politely and asked if we could fill up our water. She quoted me ten euros, over five times more than we'd paid anywhere else. I have no idea what business model these owners were working to but they seemed to have a thing or two to learn about their trade. I politely declined and we left, with her no doubt cursing how tight we were. I suspect she saw a brief opportunity to pocket the euros I had expected to pay for the pitch and hand over the balance for the water while passing on our gratitude to the mayor. I did ask about the constant presence of a fire engine and was told that they offered 24-hour cover with no less than *two* machines during the day and one at night – just as a precaution... The site was right next to the sea so precaution against what I have no idea, and even if we had paid the ten euros for water it wouldn't have covered the guard, firemen and receptionists' wages.

Geoff was more up for adventures today and, instead of taking the main road to Lisbon, I managed to talk him into retracing our steps back up the granite ridge with the breathtaking views, and with plenty of photo stops too. There was a sixteenth-century monastery at the top, which was closed, and we overtook any number of cyclists. Looking away from the sea we could see Lisbon in the distance. We discovered that this area was home to lynx, Bonelli's eagles, polecats and badgers but all we saw was a rabbit. Maybe we'd have had more chance of wildlife spotting if we had participated in the cycling or walking.

From here we headed down towards Lisbon, crossing the very impressive bridge marking the Carnation Revolution of 1974 with the massive statue of Jesus at its gateway. We had driven in Lisbon once before in a car, which had left a lasting impression in our minds. We had no appetite for repeating it in a motorhome or for getting sucked into the city by mistake, so we took the first road left along the coast and didn't stop until we got to Belém, a more manageable town close by. Lisbon is definitely a must-see city but doesn't necessarily have the same appeal when you're in the company of a four-year-old. Our memories of Lisbon were pleasurable, roaming from one bar to the next, snacking on local dishes and taking in live music, and we preferred them to stay that way and not be replaced by ones of dragging a grumpy child through a city endlessly asking about McDonald's or swing parks.

In Belém we were directed into a parking space by an old man in an area where we expected to pay a premium fee for parking, but he told us there was no charge. He seemed to be just enjoying his role and feeling a sense of responsibility, so we gave him a euro and walked off in search of a coffee, still not certain whether we were parked legally, though by now he had guided a whole row of cars in behind us so we thought it worth the risk. We returned some time later to find the van still there with no parking fine, so we were in good shape to tackle the final stretch of the journey to Sintra.

37. A MAGICAL KINGDOM

July

QUITE WHY SINTRA isn't on everyone's bucket list I do not know. It was our second visit and again it surpassed all our expectations. Since Roman times Sintra has been seen as a special place due to its location on a mountain ridge not far from Lisbon with its own microclimate, cooler, wetter and hence greener than the surrounding areas. There are no less than five castles and palaces and you could easily spend a day in each, although we met several people attempting to do everything in one day, no doubt nearly killing themselves in the process.

Our base was at the bottom of the hill below the old town, in a football stadium car park, which seemed fitting because Wales were playing Belgium in the Euros the first night. We were able to take great pleasure in watching our team's victory in the club bar. To get uphill to the various sites we could pretty much pick any mode of transport from horseback to VW Beetle, land train, bus, you name it, they had it. We had taken special note of this the previous day when we accidentally missed the entrance to our Aire and got caught in the one-way system all the way up to the top and back down, weaving our eight-metre motorhome around the horses and carts. Today we opted for an open-top Moke, which threw in two extras for the price: an improvised Moke hairstyle plus added deafness for half an hour afterwards.

We started with the National Palace of Pena, high on the hillside, home to generations of kings and queens. Looking as if it had just jumped out of the pages of a fairytale book, brightly painted in red, yellow and blue, its towers and turrets just begged us to climb and explore each and every one. From the walls, where in all directions there were magnificent views across the countryside, we found ourselves at eye level with another astounding Moorish castle across the valley. Around every corner was another weird, amazing piece of architecture, while the furniture inside was spectacularly strange. Jackson was in his element and had to see every last thing. He wanted to explore every room and tower.

To top it all off there were acres and acres of grounds, gardens and parkland surrounding the palace. We were exhausted but managed to walk down the hill via a valley containing some seven small lakes set among gorgeously planted gardens. By the time we finished we couldn't have managed another step.

As time went by on this trip we had noticed significant changes in our stamina levels and most of all with Jackson. At the start we needed to constantly encourage him to walk and not beg to be picked up. There was a point when we would set him a challenge but suggest he would never be able to do it, just trying to make his pig-headedness kick in so he would complete the task without moaning. Now, six months on, we found ourselves struggling to keep up with him. Provided his interest was captured he needed no encouragement to walk, run and climb all day and would still return to the van demanding that we get his bike out or play football with him.

I worried about how he would cope in a school environment, having to sit still for extended periods of time, and how we would deal with all his pent-up energy when he came home from school in the afternoons. On this occasion we made it back to our van just in time to flop in front of the TV for the next football match.

The next day we let Jackson choose between the Castle of the Moors, which would involve a lot of walking, or a palace with a well down which you could climb. He chose the well. We soon realised that it involved more walking than the Moorish castle, but every step was worth it. Known as the Quinta da Regaleira, it looked from the road like a formidable grey-stone Gothic-style building and was described as a place of 'hidden mysteries' – quite the understatement! The gardens were astonishing, like something from Alice in Wonderland. We tried to follow a map but found ourselves beginning on one path and immediately getting distracted by a tower to climb or an intriguing little trail leading off somewhere else. From beginning to end it felt like a real adventure, with everyone having a different one depending on their choice of path. We came across a delightful cave with stepping stones across a pond for anyone who dared, which led behind a waterfall and into a dark maze of underground tunnels, some requiring the use of phone lights to see the way or risk serious physical contact with a rock wall. It was a complete mystery when and where we would next encounter daylight but it all felt exciting and like jolly good fun. Mind you, all this time I was dreading Jackson suggesting a game of hide and seek.

Eventually we found ourselves at the bottom of the well and began to climb up the spiral staircase inside it until we were halfway up. At this point we again got distracted by yet more dark tunnels and found ourselves wandering off, returning to the well later, this time via a stone revolving door from the top, as if we were in a Harry Potter movie. All the while wonderful flute music drifted through the air from a busker somewhere out on the street.

The main house was completely open to the public. We walked right across all the beautiful old mosaic floors and from up on the roof we again had magnificent views of the Palace of Pena and the Castle of the Moors. By the time we walked back to the van my legs were in agony from all the hills and steps. We decided that for this trip we had had enough. Leave a reason to return, as we liked to say.

We moved to a family-run Aire just half an hour away, with a really nice relaxed feel about it. There was a large living room cum bar where we could sit with the owners, their kids, dogs and rabbits. They, of course, also had the football on. The final stages of the tournament were now in progress and things were hotting up nicely, with Wales still in with a chance.

We woke up the next morning to witness our British neighbours being towed away on the back of a breakdown truck. Their brakes had gone and they had been sat here waiting for parts for three days. It's a worrying time when something goes wrong and all your worldly possessions are housed in your motorhome. You don't have the option simply to leave it at a garage because, with no other mode of transport, where do you go; where do you sleep? In our experience, the larger garages tend on the whole to understand this way of life and will try to find a way around your problems. Sometimes they will attempt to set you up in a nearby site to wait until everything is ready, which helps them to move your job along quickly and get you back on the road again. At other times, where possible, they will work around you while you sit in the comfort of your van. Even so, as we set off to enjoy another day, we appreciated what a tough time this must be for the other unfortunate couple.

The other shock we had that morning was rain, our very first encounter since May. It was all over in an hour but it planted that thought in our heads that we were heading north and homeward to a land where there was plenty more of that sort of stuff. It made me feel quite depressed for the rest of the day.

These days I found myself really struggling with my emotions. On one level, after being on the road for over six months and away from family and friends, I thought I should be feeling excited at the prospect of returning and catching up on lost time. But on another level, being properly honest with myself, my overwhelming wish was to stay away, which I wanted to do more than anything else in the world. Just put down like that it does sound awful, even though it's not meant at all to be negative about the people we love. I think I speak for Geoff too when I say that we had discovered a way of living that was wildly different from what we had known before. It had opened new doors to feelings never experienced before and which may be hard to understand unless you too have experienced them.

I cannot really find the words to express the true feeling of freedom, of being free. Previously 'free' had been a phrase I played around with and imagined I would know how to feel from the outset. But I had hopelessly underestimated the true strength of the feeling. It wasn't that our relationship was in any way struggling before we left, not that we had noticed at any rate. But, by removing the everyday pressures of life – deadlines, work, chores, money, family worries – we could suddenly really see what we loved about one another. It brought everything all back and opened our eyes to the reality that for a long time neither of us had been at our best. It wasn't our love that had changed. What was different was the removal of external things that previously had pulled us in conflicting directions and made constant demands on us that wore us down.

That life had been left behind from the first night in our motorhome and since then I could honestly say we had been immeasurably happier, healthier, more sociable and generally better people. Now we understood the reality of only having one life while living in a big world that begged to be explored, and that we had barely scratched the surface of it on this trip. And yet ours was only ever intended to be a once-in-a-lifetime trip. So much time had been lost in the attempted sale of our business that our original plans had been cut short by six months. That original deadline had itself changed along the way as we selfishly opted to cast aside any good intentions to get Jackson back in time to catch the last few weeks of nursery so that he could meet his future friends before they broke for the summer, in readiness for starting his first year in school in September. Six months had been stretched into eight, and now here we were, thinking to ourselves that we really weren't supposed to like it *this* much.

As I've said before, I'm pretty sure that Geoff would have put money on me setting my expectations too high and returning home thinking that travelling was not all it was cracked up to be. If so he could not have been further from the mark. For me a seed had been sown and now my biggest fear was of how on earth to cope if I never got another chance to see it grow.

I had never dared before to have one but now I had a dream, although it was one that scared me. If only I could have had my way we would have turned the van around, made a few phone calls, booked some flights for family and friends to come out and join us periodically, factored in some regular trips back home, set up a homeschooling system for Jackson and then set about seeing the world.

I secretly questioned why Geoff was holding back, unable to decide whether he didn't share these feelings or just didn't want to admit them to me. I had a feeling that if he only had himself to consider he would jump at the chance to keep going. At the same time I knew that he had family commitments back at home. More than that, he had experienced first-hand as a child what it was like to have no real base, having to change schools and make new friends every other year, catching up on his education in different countries and always being the new boy in town. Much as he had memories that might sound magical to you and me, he had also been through experiences about which he really didn't like to talk. He knew he did not want Jackson's life to be like that, and I knew I should respect him for that selfless way of thinking.

It was an inescapable fact that we were heading home and, of course, I knew I would be excited once I got there. I missed everyone, but I also shed a tear for what we would be giving up here. I was under no illusion that once we were home, even though this experience would have changed us forever, we would not be able to escape the financial, educational and emotional restrictions imposed on us when we got back. Before we knew it we would be back on the mundane supermarket or school run, watching the clock, counting the pennies and arguing over someone else's problems or whose turn it was to put the bins out.

I hope this goes some way to explain my feelings of guilt when, immediately after telling my family down the phone that I couldn't wait to see them, I hid myself at the back of the van, welling up with tears as I realised that what I had just done had hastened the closure of this whole wonderful experience.

38. SICKENED BY SARDINES

WITH ACHING LEGS our lasting reminder of Sintra, we set off in search of surf and sun, heading for a stretch of Atlantic coastline where there was no shortage of famous surf breaks. Any of my friends who have had the pleasure of surfing in Geoff's company when he is presented with a choice of beaches will fully understand the following scenario, and I'm sure it will be familiar to many others.

When he is not at home he never ever simply drives to a beach and surfs. Oh no! – he requires a good hour or more to complete the process. First off he has to look at and compare a minimum of two beaches. Next he has to study the waves over a coffee. Then he has to decide if it's now approaching lunchtime: maybe he should eat now and surf later? Or will the tide turn, the wind drop or the swell pick up?

So already you can imagine how my day went. The weather was awful, cold, windy and grey with a thick sea mist, and I wasn't particularly enamoured by the thought of sitting on a beach. I soon concluded, though, that I would far prefer to do that than drive backwards and forwards for hours while he made up his mind. Already into July it felt to me like every moment wasted was one too many.

At the first beach the waves were, in my husband's own words, too big and lumpy, which I presume is official surf talk. In the next town, Ericeira, the streets were so narrow that we got in a right mess and actually ended up in a boatyard practically out in the sea, eventually having to utilise the full length of the slipway in order to turn round, get out and find somewhere for that coffee I mentioned earlier. A local surf shop with a live webcam of three nearby beaches and a very helpful assistant told Geoff that only one was working today in the current wind conditions. So, yippee, we went there. But no, he didn't fancy it. Naturally I couldn't resist giving him a bit of a ribbing, even though I was secretly glad because although there were a few surfers in, it looked really unsafe to me.

Well, of course, the obvious thing to do now was to go to the beaches he had just been told were not surfable today. Coxos was next and, referring to Geoff's diary for his description, these are his own words: *There was no-one in and it was not easy* – which is the absolute understatement of the century… There was a lifeguard on a deserted beach but it was so rough that if I were him, on the off-chance that anyone took leave of their senses and decided to take a dip, I'd have run away. Geoff's written musings then continue: *Went to a few more and stopped at St Lorenzo* [São Lourenço].

Now are you getting the gist of the process? On this particular day I lost count of how many times we stopped.

São Lourenço was actually a very nice beach and there were a handful of vans parked up, obviously staying the night more or less right on the sand under a cliff. That dream lasted for fifteen minutes, at which point the police came along and advised (or, to put it another way, ordered) us to move immediately for fear of falling rocks. We retreated to a large public car park behind, where there was no view of the sea, along with a German van. Not one of the Portuguese vans took the slightest notice of this instruction in spite of a further police visit in the early evening, by which time the lovely camp under the cliffs was jam-packed. Five minutes later we observed the police departing for good and for the rest of the night we and the Germans remained the only two vans in the oversized and deserted car park. Personally I think they just wanted us foreigners out of their space although, having had the rather large overhanging lump of rock brought to our attention, we'd have been happy enough to oblige.

Anyway, back to the surfing, which still hadn't taken place. This beach was another mess due to the wind. A massive party of school kids was on the beach. The closest they could get to the water without drowning was for all the teachers to line up in ankle-deep water and throw buckets of water all over the kids, not with the intention of cooling anyone down, because it was totally freezing without any of that, but purely to escalate the excitement level to a nonstop screaming pitch.

We had another cup of tea in yet another café where we watched two bodyboarders being hammered by the waves. Finally, at about 5 p.m., came the great man's announcement: *I think I'll surf tomorrow instead and give my back another day to recover!* I replied, with icy politeness: *Very sensible!* And then I made him cook tea for the sin of dragging me from pillar to post all day for nothing.

We both felt a little vulnerable in this spot with all the other vans hidden around the corner, so we slept with the seat belts threaded through the front door handles and the bar across the main door for extra security. We awoke to a sea mist and messy surf again and decided to push on farther along the coast. Ending up in Santa Cruz, we instantly thought it had an inviting feel with its pretty beach and waves that actually inspired Geoff to put his wetsuit on and get in, although he was out again after half an hour having caught just the one wave. He then took Jackson in bodyboarding, giving me a well-earned rest from the mammoth sand castle I had been commanded to build.

There was a fabulous café here with a classy, chic, modern yet very beachy appeal. Formal seating was replaced by multicoloured bean bags, hammocks and swing chairs, and fancy micro salads served in glass jars was a sign of high standards. But everyone can go one step too far and the glass toilet doors here represented exactly that tendency. The men's faced the women's with a communal sink directly in between the two. I don't know what I looked like because it was me who went in, but I immediately realised that if I could see the sink through the wall I'd be able to see someone washing their hands – which presumably meant they could see me sitting on the loo. I came back out again just to check. I put just one arm in the other loo while I stood outside and sure enough my suspicions were confirmed: the walls *were* pretty much see-through. Modern it might be but what a waste of money. They might just as well have stuck a bucket in the middle of the café and done away with the walls altogether.

Recently we had wild camped as much as possible, partly to save money but mainly because it was so easy to do here. The only drawback was not having many opportunities to empty and refill our water. We often took advantage of beach showers where we were not permitted to use soap. In Santa Cruz we all showered the salt off in the beach shower, then filled sand buckets with fresh water and beat a hasty retreat to the van just up the road, where I proceeded to shampoo my hair on the grass verge and rinse it from the sand buckets. By now I had learned to find more pleasure in this approach to life than being parked up in a luxury campsite.

Fresh and clean, off we went on the road again to world-famous Peniche, a beach with huge waves known as 'super tubes'. Except that today it was almost flat, at least by its usual standards. Peniche is located on a narrow peninsula opposite Baleal, a little village on the end of a smaller peninsula at the other side of a bay. At one point the strip of land is just the width of the road with a narrow beach on either side so you can surf on either one. On this particular day both beaches had a wave, on one side very small and ideal for beginners, the other side a bit bigger and more fun, though by no means the world-class standard I had seen here before. Geoff and Jackson both went in and Jackson later beamed from ear to ear when he told someone he had surfed a famous wave.

For camping we moved back into town off this strip, because although the car parks were full of vans we had the distinct impression that at night this spot would be very young, surfer-orientated and noisily raucous. Someone pointed us in the direction of the Fort of Peniche, an easy walk from town but a much quieter location although equally popular with motorhomers.

Again it was a free site, designated officially but not offering any facilities. It was located across the moat from the fort, and this brings me to the other industry for which Peniche is famed, namely sardines. The town is home to a massive sardine factory and I can promise you that if you find yourself downwind of it you will never eat another sardine again. The only thing to rival its stench had been a paper factory we stumbled upon accidentally during this trip, but as you never expected to eat paper later in your life the stench of it was psychologically easier to deal with. Although we loved this place and stayed for two nights the downside was spending the whole time accusing each other of farting or spraying perfume around the van. I think the smell was a combination of sardines, stagnant water in the moat and grey water stored in the tanks of fifty parked vans in the heat of the sun. Oh, and don't ever make the mistake of thinking you can purchase a fish from the local market and get it back to your van in one piece. We witnessed, initially with much laughter but then with mounting concern, one gentleman attempting this. Clearly, being armed with a very large leafy branch he was not a first-time amateur. This was what initially caught our attention as he waved it wildly above his head while trying to run the gauntlet with seagulls viciously swooping and attacking his head in a bid to win the fish, which they eventually did.

Despite these minor drawbacks we remained here the following day and enjoyed another very pleasant time on the beach before walking into town for some shopping. There was a fruit and veg market where, as we passed an old lady with all of two teeth in her mouth, she came rushing across to Jackson and planted a huge kiss on his head. She kept pointing to his blonde hair and then she kissed both his hands. The look on his face was pure disgust. I can't say I blamed him, but I whispered: *Don't worry, I have wet wipes.* She proceeded to fill a small bag with tomatoes and tiny inedible looking apples for him. Of course we were going to buy something from her anyway by this point but she made sure she had sealed the deal by telling us that she had no money. We picked and handed her a bag of potatoes for which she asked two euros for that plus the gift she had just given Jackson. Still we hadn't finished and, peaches, onions and beans later, she put all these different things together on the weighing scales, studied them and asked for two euros for everything. We gave her four and still got a bargain, though at the cost of an extra kiss for Jackson and one for myself.

We had booked a table in a small *tapas* bar, having applied some care into selecting it as we were about to watch Wales take on Portugal in the semifinal of Euro 2016. Obviously we were the only Welsh supporters but we received a lovely welcome with a round of applause and a commiserating drink on the house when we lost. Although it was not the result we had hoped for the impromptu street party that followed made it all worthwhile. We walked out into complete mayhem. The roads had disappeared beneath crowds of people climbing all over and hanging off every moving vehicle. Trucks full of people with flags, horns and drums did circuits of the town. A dustbin lorry had somehow got snarled up in all this and, although from the front it seemed the only vehicle trying to detach itself from the madness, to the amusement of the crowds as it passed by could be seen a very drunk, flag-laden lady hanging off its back, unbeknown to the driver. We felt quite moved to witness the sheer joy of the locals. Throughout the evening not a single policeman was spotted and there was never a scrap of trouble. For us from now on Peniche will bring back memories that are more than the stink of sardines.

The following day began with a drive inland through vast pine forests and across country until we rejoined the coast at Nazaré, another world-famous surf spot, which holds the record for the biggest wave ever surfed anywhere in the world. Of course we're talking winter surf there. On this day the sea was calm but the wind was a cold strong northerly and soon we were all reaching for an extra layer. We parked high up on the cliffs and followed the road out to the lighthouse, walking through a large arch with a sign welcoming us to the home of the world's biggest waves. There were a couple of mobile souvenir shops selling all manner of wares adorned with pictures of crazy seas. Linked to the lighthouse was a gallery exhibiting surf art, sculpture and photography, excellently designed to capture the equal interest of surfers and those who, like me, simply think they are mad. Anyone who rides this wave has got to have a death wish. I experienced vertigo standing on the cliff just watching the fishermen doing their work in what seemed to be the most precarious positions right on the edge of a sheer drop of scary proportions, and yet there were some photographs showing bigger waves even than that crashing over these very cliffs. Anyone crazy enough to choose to stand on a small piece of plastic on the face of one of those monsters would be up at the same height as me, looking straight down a wall of water with a genuine prospect of death at the bottom if they made the slightest error of judgement. The spectator in me hoped to return some day to witness someone attempting this feat.

Waves apart, the views were breathtaking and revealed a very attractive looking beach in front of the town below us. Down there we found a colourful scene of brightly painted wooden boats and an exhibition of historical fishing boats and lifeboats. All kinds of fish from sardines to octopus were opened out and pegged up on large stretched-out nets drying in the sun, the whole thing looking like a vast art display.

A little farther along, in complete contrast to all this tradition, there was a whole world of bouncy castles. Partly as a bribe to drag him off one of them and partly because we no longer had to worry about being Welsh traitors, we finally gave in and allowed Jackson to have a Portugal football kit in readiness for the Euro final. Not at the seventy euros we'd previously been quoted, I hasten to add: this was a very fine copy from a market stall, such a bargain, in fact, that we bought souvenir kits for his friends too.

Moving on from Nazaré in search of somewhere to sleep before continuing our journey to Lavos the following day, we found ourselves in a small residential area where, by chance, we spotted another motorhome parked up opposite a row of houses. Enquiries revealed that it belonged to people visiting one of the houses opposite and that we were welcome to settle in for the night directly behind their van. Not for the first time I woke up in the darkness of the van racking my brain to remember where we had parked and what our view would be when we opened the blinds, a feeling that often caught us out on this trip. So unlike our old routine of opening the curtains to our familiar garden and street, we now had the privilege of a different view every day. Today's view, though, was nothing to write home about, with the rear end of a motorhome directly in front of us, houses to our left and a bit of wasteland to our right, and after a quick breakfast we were on the road again.

Aires, as we had discovered, came in every imaginable variety, and in Lavos we managed to check into the most impractical one we'd encountered to date. It was a sandy car park with bays marked out by wooden poles resembling goalposts. We guessed that way in the past there may have been some sort of cover to provide shade, supported by these poles. If so that was long gone and now the poles served no purpose other than causing mayhem because, apart from a handful of small campervans, everyone else was too high to fit underneath them into their space, resulting in a chaotic scene of vans parked sideways, diagonally, any way except the intended way. Here we met a lovely British couple who immediately made me jealous when we found out they had been travelling continuously for three years – and counting. They never used campsites so mostly their expenses were just food and petrol. Like us, they were planning to head north where they would spend the summer in the slightly cooler climate of northern Spain. Unlike us, who would be heading home as our trip drew to an end, they would then turn round and head south again to over-winter in the warmth of southern Spain; and on and on their cycle went. Like so many other people we were now meeting, they had no plans to return to the UK. In fact they had no plan at all, and hardly felt they needed one, which, if you are that way inclined, can be the beauty of this way of life. Whenever they fancied seeing something different they simply pointed the van in that direction and set off on another adventure.

We were situated right next to a beach, separated from it only by sand dunes. Noticing excessive seagull activity, curiosity overcame us and led us to the water's edge where we found a group of fishermen hard at work in a form I had previously only witnessed in Sri Lanka. Standing in two lines at a fairly large distance apart on the beach, each team worked more or less in unison. It looked like a giant tug-of-war match with maybe seven men on each rope, but they were not competing with each other but with an immense net they slowly and systematically were dragging in with all their strength from the choppy sea. Each team took control of their end of the net, partly assisted by winches on the beach. As the net came ever closer, the spare rope accumulated as it passed between the men's hands was carefully and neatly wound up by a man at each end. Simultaneously others loaded empty nets from a trailer onto a wooden boat, while one man made hurried repairs to any large holes as each net was folded into the boat. The timing was precise so that the moment one net was loaded off the trailer onto the boat, the full net was finally exiting the water and being dragged onto the sand by the exhausted fishermen. Then while they set about collecting the fish, the now loaded wooden fishing boat took again to the water in readiness to set the fresh net. The whole operation involved some twenty men, a tractor and two winches, plus a boat, of course, and I could only wonder how much profit would be left after paying for all these people and capital costs.

At any rate, when the net was landed there was great excitement not only from a beach full of onlookers but also from a sky full of birds.

The net itself was full of thousands of sardines. We all rushed up with our cameras to get close-up shots of the net, which was alive with frantically flapping fish. Some of the smallest ones escaped onto the sand, where Jackson and other kids ran around gathering them up and throwing them back into the sea, causing even more frenzy among the seagulls. We ended up drenched with spray from the net.

After watching the entire process right through to the fish being sold on a table at the top of the beach, we started to walk back to the van. Noticing that Jackson was glistening as if doused in glitter, it dawned on us that the spray covering us was mostly made up of fish scales and that we looked like three mermaids walking up the street, with even our sunglasses plastered in the stuff. As if the sardine factory in Peniche hadn't already put me off sardines for life, this had definitely sealed the deal. Now we had to brave the freezing sea and then an outdoor shower before we could even set foot back in the van.

That evening we had the pleasure of a vanload of British artists as our neighbours. One was a guitarist and singer who had just played at Glastonbury and was heading to the Algarve with his mates in search of work. Their van was loaded with paint in the hope they would pick up a commission for some large-scale artwork on a building somewhere. This bunch of lads provided us with priceless breakfast entertainment and had me rolling about our van in hysterical laughter as they struggled to pack up and leave. All they needed was a solitary woman to co-ordinate the procedure. One lad would be working hard to pack a bag and load it, while meanwhile the others would just sit around staring distractedly at the mess. Then one would get up and go in search of a toothbrush or dish or something, which of course would just have been packed away. Whereupon the bag would have to be removed, opened and its contents emptied and strewn over the grass so that its owner could set about making his breakfast. While he was busy doing that, his chair would be loaded into the van as soon as he removed his backside from it. Words would be exchanged, the chair would be unloaded again, and so on and on it went for well over an hour. I gave them all names: Mr Lazy, Mr Organised, Mr Clueless... It seemed a mystery that they had ever got this far travelling together.

As a parting gesture they gave us a CD of their music and, whatever they might have lacked in logistical skills, I could not fault their creative talent. It accompanied us during much of the rest of our journey.

39. THE VENICE OF THE WEST

O N LEAVING LAVOS we used the motorway for the first time in Portugal and immediately managed to screw it up, possibly resulting in a fine when we got back to Wales. When you cross the border into Portugal every vehicle is photographed, recording its number plate, and you are required to enter your credit card details. We didn't understand why but complied nonetheless. On entering our first motorway we chose the lane where you take a ticket and on exiting took the automatic payment lane, thinking it would just be charged to our credit card. We soon realised that by mixing up two different payment methods we had got ourselves a ticket to enter the motorway but none to record where we left it. Would we consequently be charged for the entire length of the motorway? Finding no manned ticket booths the only option was to keep the ticket and a written record of our mistake, the time, date and junction number and hope for the best. As it turned out we never heard any more about it. We had probably completely confused the system.

We arrived at Aveiro around lunchtime and were directed into a space in a car park by two women who we assumed were parking attendants. There seemed to be a charge of five euros for the day, which we handed over – and then the second lady stuck her hand out for the same. We'd been had! They were just two scammers who were no doubt making a fortune. We looked on the bright side: if nothing else, while they were busy earning they provided a presence in the car park, hopefully deterring any would-be thieves. But no, we were proved wrong again when later in town we were approached by the same two ladies carrying a begging board.

That aside, Aveiro was a beautiful town built around a series of canals formerly used for transporting salt. It felt like a very small, calm Venice. The old wooden fishing boats and salt boats, as brightly painted as any gondola, were now used to ferry tourists around on a 45-minute trip at a twentieth the price of a gondola trip in Venice. It was fun and informative and there was a lot of banter between boats, with the captain of each trying to upstage the others with their special horns used for narrow canals only wide enough for one boat. Each did their best to encourage their passengers to be louder than the next. We passed one boat where some six tourists were stood up dancing, no doubt only until one or other of them fell in or banged their head on a low bridge. It was a really vibrant place, with a big choice of outdoor eating, a bandstand providing continuous entertainment, and a big street market selling wonderful foods for snacking on as you walked.

A few hours later we drove on to Torreira, across the estuary. We planned to swim because it had got quite hot but arrived to see red flags up. With a sloping beach and currents that were clearly visible, swimming was clearly out of the question. As yet we didn't know where we would sleep that night, and not having water to waste we decided to use a beach shower on the opposite side of the road. It was early evening and most people were walking around dressed to go to the restaurants but we, completely shameless these days, stood there on the pavement in our swimming costumes showering in cold water. I even washed and conditioned my hair. I wouldn't have dreamed of behaving like this a few months before, but how quickly you adapt when you live in a motorhome.

Mission accomplished, we relocated to a quieter car park nearby, overlooking the estuary with its colourful array of traditional little fishing boats. There were storks nesting everywhere. The traffic lights hung out over the roads and each set was home to three or four nests. They adorned every church, lamp post and chimney with gangs of inquisitive heads popping out everywhere. It was a lovely tranquil scene to wake up to in readiness to attempt the roads around Porto. With time so limited for us now we decided this would be another city that had to be relegated to our 'must return another time' list. We've since been told that Porto is a big city with attractions that are spread out, meriting at least a few days to do it any justice.

It was now approaching mid-July and we were in northern Portugal. Of course, we couldn't leave without watching the Euro football final this very evening. Having witnessed the wild impromptu street parties that erupted when Portugal beat Wales to make it to the final, our priority was to get the van far enough away to be out of harm's way in case they actually won the tournament. We skirted Porto and headed north to a fairly upmarket beach resort called Vila do Conde. The place was buzzing and when we found ourselves caught up in endless traffic jams in the heat, we concluded that in the unlikely event of even finding somewhere to park up there was little expectation of getting any sleep.

About half an hour farther on we seemed to leave the madness and crowds behind us. Soon we pulled up in a quiet dead-end road adjacent to a beach and, most importantly, right opposite a bar showing the match that night. I make that sound like finding somewhere showing the match was lucky when in fact there can't have been a single public building not showing it anywhere. Even the ice-cream parlours had TV screens up. We asked in the bar if there was anywhere nearby where we could park and sleep in the van and were assured that nobody would mind us staying right where we were. The next move definitely was to get onto the beach and cool down.

Fat chance! For the past few hours stuck in traffic we'd almost died of heat stroke. We'd arrived here under blue skies, packed our beach bag and walked all of five minutes to the sea only to find we had been beaten to it by a sea mist that had been following us for days. Within minutes we couldn't even see the water. At least it made for a highly atmospheric walk among sunbathers who remained flat on their towels appearing not to notice that the sun had long departed.

That evening Jackson wore his full Portugal kit and we were greeted with open arms as the only foreigners in the bar. Revealing that we were Welsh and so, obviously, now supporting Portugal, we were treated as honorary locals and wholeheartedly included in all the banter, while Jackson was treated like their personal mascot. I'm not sure we'd have had the same welcome if we had beaten them in the semifinal, mind you. Ronaldo was stretchered off injured, which was a massive blow to them, and as the cameras closed in for a shot of his pained face they revealed, of all things, a moth, weirdly just sitting on his face. By now Jackson had lost interest and was crawling around the floor under the pool table playing with his toy cars. Would you believe it, he emerged, grinning from ear to ear and displaying a dead butterfly in his cupped hands for everyone to see. The place erupted with cheers and screams of *Ronaldo! Ronaldo!* as they hugged him and pointed at the butterfly. Poor Jackson hadn't a clue until hours later why everyone found a dead insect even more exciting than he did. It was certainly seen as a good omen and not long after, when the final whistle went, Portugal had won against France and were holding the cup aloft, Jackson was showered with kisses and hugs and adorned with a gift of the Portugal football scarf. The entire crowd in the bar, us included, were plied with free drinks in celebration. It was a night to remember and in this quiet village the only thing we missed out on were the street parties, although it was easy to imagine what they must be like.

The following day we stopped at Cabedelo Beach opposite Viana do Castelo. It is predominantly a kitesurfing beach and the wind was in its favour today. We sat huddled behind our windbreaker and watched a crazy display of kites and windsurfers. Jackson insisted on joining them with his bodyboard so with gritted teeth I braved the freezing waters for all of five minutes. Across the river we could see the basilica of Viana do Castelo high on a hill overlooking the bay. That was our next destination.

We caught a small water taxi across, followed by a funicular to the top of the hill. Then we took a lift to the bottom of the dome, after which it got interesting. There was a dark, spiralling stone staircase so narrow that you had to squeeze and contort yourself around it, with a traffic-light system ensuring that there was no passing anywhere on the stairs. Emerging outside at the top of the dome into an incredibly strong wind, I found that, magnificent though the view was, fear was winning over spectacle. We felt like spare parts during a wedding proposal taking place on the other side of the walkway: not something you experience every day. She must have said yes because an abundant display of public affection ensued. To give them some privacy we beat a hasty retreat as soon as the traffic light turned green.

Our final farewell to Portugal took in some chores such as a supermarket stop for copious amounts of port. It had become a habit of ours to leave all purchasing of souvenirs until the last possible moment, always suspecting that we might see something nicer farther along and invariably resulting in a last-ditch dash to a supermarket practically on the border. Now we remembered that we had postcards written with stamps on them that needed posting on this side of the border, so we took a detour to find a post box in the last town on the map before we crossed into Spain.

And boy, did we find a whole lot more than a post box. The village of Vila Nova de Cerveira was literally dressed in knitting from chimney top to doorstep. The lamp posts, street signs, trees and shop fronts were all covered in brightly coloured knitted designs. One house was covered from top to bottom with beautiful white crochet work. We never got to grips with who did it or why but all the same it was an amazing sight, which we would have missed if we hadn't been so absent-minded about our postcards.

We encountered a lovely lady who told us she was originally from this town but had lived for a long time in New York. She was completely Americanised in the sense that she spontaneously handed out her address as if on the off chance that we might ever find ourselves in the Big Apple. She went on to tell us all about her husbands, or by now ex-husbands, the many affairs and messy divorces and their business empires of many hundreds of staff. Then she offered us some lasting advice. Being alone was no fun, she told us, and travelling was more enjoyable with a partner to share it with. *So if something can be fixed, just fix it, no matter what it takes – it's always unquestionably worth it.* I felt so sad for her and wanted to invite her to travel with us for a bit, though I bet she'd have changed her mind pretty fast!

She urged us to take the van high up onto the hillside overlooking this village, where deer roamed freely, picnic spots overlooked the most beautiful views and you could explore for miles. She had grown up here and was passionate about passing on her knowledge. There's no doubt that a few months back we would have done exactly what she advised us to do. It's in places like this that you can lose yourself for a few days, walking in the countryside, taking coffee in local bars, meeting people like her and learning about your surroundings. We felt annoyed that we simply couldn't just follow our hearts unless we were prepared to compensate farther on by missing out some other area. Somehow our journey had become less about the *now* and more about the *what awaited us farther along* – not necessarily a good thing and a sure sign that once again we were in the grip of time constraints.

So it was that with colourful memories and sound advice ringing in our ears we said goodbye to Portugal and hello once again to Spain, all with a slight air of sadness.

40. A DIFFERENT SIDE TO SPAIN

W E HAD NEVER been to Galicia before. From the moment we crossed the border it struck us that this was nothing like the Spain we knew. And in fact it was markedly different to anywhere we had been in recent months. In general it had a prosperous feel, with smart houses on large plots. We were back in wine territory once again with vineyards aplenty. The scenery most closely resembled Croatia but with a far more laid back, less rule-bound appeal to it, enticing and tempting us down winding dead-end roads to deserted coves or spectacular secret clifftop views. We felt welcome to park up and sleep in almost any available car park, making it easy to wake up to a free and uninterrupted sea view.

Perhaps you have noticed how our confidence levels had changed since we started this journey. Now we weren't in the least bothered by the possibility of a thirty-point turn awaiting us at the end of some obscure track. Our attitude was: explore first, ask questions later. Beware, though: confidence like this can be dangerous. Sooner or later you'll find yourself up to your ears in a mess somewhere, and all your boundless confidence won't make the van any shorter or the turning area any wider.

Our first proper stop was Baiona's crescent beach on a turquoise sea with barely a ripple on it. It verged on estuary and we found ourselves sinking in mud long before we were able to wade out deep enough to swim. It felt as if we were wading for miles and yet we were still only up to our knees in the water. This made it a safe haven for children and families, and today, in glorious sunshine, was no exception. The sand was like nothing I had ever seen before, glittering bronze in colour and feeling like you were walking barefoot on a really plush, expensive carpet. Every little wave sparkled with silver and gold flecks and the water was so clear I could see all the glitter on the seabed. It was teaming with fish and, as we paddled right round to the other side – oh horror!

crabs in their hundreds all around our feet in the water. Mobs of kids with buckets were catching them, Jackson among them, while I retreated to the safety of dry land well above the crab line. We found it too easy to lose track of time here, as we found out when we got back to the van with thoughts of tea, only to realise it was way past a sensible bedtime for a four-year-old who would soon be needing to get into a school routine.

We slept farther along the coast on the approach to Vigo, a very big port and industrial city. We found a car park just across the road from another beautiful sandy beach occupied by plenty of motorhomes. As by now it was 10 p.m., we simply parked up without a second thought, tucking ourselves out of the way at the back of the car park. After a good night's sleep we opened our blinds to see an official in a yellow vest collecting money. He asked us to move to a different space and pay him all of two euros for twenty-four hours – a bargain. We moved without even taking the kettle off the stove or shutting the cupboard doors, all the while feeling sure we had been less in the way where we already were, but complying like good children.

As we left for the beach we noticed that a drunk person was laid out cold directly behind the van. As the parking official had disappeared, we made a mental note to check later before we attempted to reverse, and then off we went. We came to a handsome promenade with a vibrant African market in full swing, three large, waist-deep paddling pools for kids, with two lifeguards on each pool, a skate ramp and a rollerskating pitch. There was live music at two cafés and everything from ice-cream shops to very up-beat and expensive wine bars. One side of the prom was lined by pine woods full of shaded picnic benches and barbeques for anyone to use freely, while on the other was the white-sand beach. I had never before seen a beach front that catered so well for so many different tastes while still managing to feel unspoiled. What's more, pretty much everything was free, from all the pools and activities to most of the car parking. Not surprisingly, and bearing in mind this was a weekend, there were countless thousands of people sharing the beach. Normally that scenario would be my worst nightmare but for some reason it seemed fine and fitting here.

Galicia, the northwest region of Spain, tends to escape the attention of most tourists who leave its wild and natural beauty unspoiled and flock unthinkingly to Barcelona or farther south. Its coastline is rugged, consisting of a succession of peninsulas, each one small enough to drive around in a day. Off these peninsulas lie a series of small islands, most of them uninhabited but reachable by boat and with some very attractive-looking coves. Just from where we were sitting on the sand we counted eighteen different beaches spread out in almost a full circle around us, covering every possible wind direction. All this made the region a very attractive destination in which we could happily have spent a few weeks.

Jackson wore himself to a frazzle trying every available activity. We joined him in swimming, snorkelling and building sandcastles. When we got back to the van we encountered three drunks who were taking it in turns to guide cars and motorhomes into what at that time of day were nonexistent spaces. It was bedlam. One of them was on the entrance beckoning in more vehicles while the other two were in no fit state to judge if there was any room left. There was no escape for us as we were doubly blocked in, and we saw one van being bumped by another as they both got completely gridlocked. One of the 'attendants' was holding himself up by a wing mirror while trying to instruct a motorhome driver whose patience was fast disappearing. We realised that the 'official' we had paid in the morning was simply the smart one who had got up early, put on a bright shirt and collected his beer money for the day. Once that penny had dropped, we decided, while we sat there waiting for our van to be hit, that we would look for alternative sleeping arrangements as soon as we could get out.

Some hours later when the mess was finally cleared we got back on the road again. Although it was late we took advantage of the now quieter roads to get to the other side of Vigo before finding an official Aire, which was in a small harbour and free of charge. Once again it was 10 p.m. by the time I had prepared our meal, and at 11 p.m. Jackson was still in the swing park in over 20 degrees.

The next day we awoke to an astounding view across a mirror-like estuary bustling with boats and fishermen. Having watched them working while we enjoyed a leisurely breakfast, we decided to drive on and look for our next beach. We had the option of taking the motorway north and skipping all of these peninsulas. But we had intentionally come to this region to explore its coastline and see what we would find there and so far it had certainly not disappointed us.

We stopped for a lunchtime swim at Bueu, a small fishing town with an attractive sandy cove with rocks at either end. We snorkelled away happily before sampling *empanada*, a local seafood dish of savoury pastry stuffed with spicy fish. From here we rounded the coast to get onto the next peninsula where, following a free guide to local surf spots that Geoff had picked up in one of the surf shops, we made our way to Playa de la Lanzada, one of the more exposed beaches.

Lanzada lies at the tip of a peninsula along the length of a very narrow strip of land connected to O Grove, a sort of semi-detached peninsula which otherwise would be a small island. Nosey to the end, we of course had to drive the full length of the road to check it all out before deciding where to park and spend the night. I nagged and nagged Geoff into completing the full circuit around the would-be island for fear of missing something. Apparently O Grove had twenty-four beaches, though many of them would probably have been unreachable by Dotty. We were tempted by one place that reminded us of Sri Lanka, where nature had strategically placed large smooth boulders along the sand to create maximum eye appeal. We took a little picnic there but soon realised that we were on the only dog-friendly beach in the area. Much like at home at this time of year, most beaches were barred to dogs, and yet here we were on the only one that wasn't, the only idiots without a dog but in possession of food. We now had the undivided attention of every four-legged, wet, sandy, saliva-dripping creature on the beach. I found myself giggling at how this daily activity was carried out by most of the owners in the barest minimum of clothing. I wondered how I would have felt when I was dog-walking for a living if I had bumped into customers, as I often did, and recognised them as much by their breasts as by their pet.

Having completed the full circuit of the headland, we backtracked a short distance to a large car park we had passed earlier. Views of the beach were concealed by sand dunes but an investigative short walk revealed that the surf wasn't in working order. But the first thing that caught my attention was the sight of two men with their feet in buckets at the lifeguard hut, and others who were receiving treatment. Geoff asked at the surf hut if they knew when the surf might pick up, followed by me asking casually: *What happened to them?* The response, very matter of fact, was: *Oh, just weeverfish.* For me there's no such thing as 'just weeverfish' and I instantly developed a dislike for this beach. For once the lack of waves worked in my favour and I convinced Geoff that we should move. What the heck, by now we were quite used to arriving in Aires at 10 p.m.

For a while we reverted to the motorway and drove directly to Boiro on the next peninsula, arriving at a grassy Aire with a swing park, right opposite a lovely beach. I assumed there would be weeverfish, but out of sight out of mind... Yet again it was 10 p.m. on the dot again and two policemen, well, even if they weren't true policemen at least they seemed sober, were collecting a fee of six euros per van. At Aires we had come across all kinds of official money collectors, from nearby campsite workers to farmers. But police doing the job was a first for us, although the Aires guide had actually alerted us that this would be the case here. It is quite a challenge for them to keep track of everyone's comings and goings and it is perfectly normal to get a knock on your door as late as 10 p.m. or as early as 7 a.m. as they try to catch everyone before they sneak in and out under the cover of darkness.

Each day brought slightly higher temperatures and we spent longer and longer snorkelling to cool off. Across the bay were platforms, presumably used for growing mussels, which is an important industry in Boiro. Our attention was intermittently drawn to them by a regular series of loud bangs followed by a puff of smoke in the sky. As clearly they were not caused by flares or fireworks, we thought they must be some form of bird deterrent – maybe something to do with fish farms. Until, that is, about a hundred of them went off at the same time, accompanied by a great racket of boat horns, whereupon, with the sky full of smoke and noise, a whole flotilla of fishing boats, speed boats and jet skis set off from both shores, all of them laden with bunting and overloaded with people. Here we were yet again, completely by chance, witnessing a local annual festival paying respects to the sea for keeping the town's fishermen safe.

In the late afternoon, just as we were about to leave, a British couple pulled into the Aire. In a very British attempt to think ahead and make space for one more van, instead of spreading themselves out and hogging the last space they parked a little closer than you might ordinarily expect to the Spanish motorhome next to them. I don't think they had even turned the engine off before the woman was out gesturing at them to move away. Even though in the motorhome world this was a rare instance of animosity, it was a reminder of the basic unwritten rules that we had picked up as we went along. Everyone's view is different and more often than not it boils down to individual interpretation of camping etiquette. In many Aires marked spaces alleviate any issues. But these can range from very generous spaces around each van to some where there is just enough room to open your door. Where you're free to park anywhere, as was the case here, it is considered polite to leave a motorhome's width between yours and the next vehicle. However, that said, I have also read advice that these Aires are there to be shared between as many fellow motorhomes as possible and that if space becomes limited you should, where possible, move closer to your neighbour so as to make room for another vehicle. As is the custom, you should park with your door facing away from your neighbour. This is not always possible and we had found ourselves in much more cramped situations in some expensive campsites than in most of the Aires. There is no definitive right or wrong and our policy became simply to try to keep the peace. On this occasion the newcomers moved their van a few feet further away, which seemed to make all the difference as far as the Spanish lady was concerned. We all had a little smirk to ourselves and that was how we got to meet Karen and David, with whom we remain in touch to this day.

We promised to share a beer with them when we returned later that night after Geoff had been surfing farther up the coast. When we arrived at Furnas we found it was much wilder, with significant waves, rock pools and coves. In the dusty car park there was one space left. It all felt remoter and more natural than the site at Boiro and seemed far too nice to leave. We decided to email Karen and David to postpone that beer and invite them to join us here the following day instead.

A very jolly beach café owner assured us we could sleep anywhere here and that, being a Sunday, the car park would empty out by dusk and we would be alone. There was even a Portaloo provided. Jackson and I walked across to investigate it. It was massive, with enough room for three wheel chairs in the cubicle, but there was no water supply. In effect it was a humongous chemical toilet with no flush and no sink. I was just about to lock the door when Jackson let out a frantically loud scream and I jumped out of my skin, thinking spiders or snakes. I couldn't decide whether to laugh or retch when I got to Jackson who was holding the lid open to reveal a wide-open hole with a bathload of poo in it in full view ready for any brave person prepared to risk the splash back. It wasn't for us, thank you very much, although a lorry did come along and empty it the following day.

Again we tried every beach activity available and Geoff even joined in the cliff diving. While he surfed for hours Jackson and I found three bouncy castles and a human version of table football in which you hung by your hands underneath a swinging bar and aimed to kick the ball into the goal, thus taking the place of those little plastic men and rendering your audience weak with laughter. Armed with lollies and free balloons, a very happy child left with me at 9 p.m. There was no charge for any of this. We sat on a clifftop watching a magnificent sunset that seemed to last for hours and then moved to the open-air café for some beers, using the excuse that the van was too hot. I remarked to the owner how lucky he was to live in such a beautiful spot and was shocked when he said that this wonderful weather was not the norm. Apparently it was set to last five days here before the temperature was expected to fall by about ten degrees, with rain due to return. So that explained why this region was so green. I should have known, because it's much the same in Wales, but to be honest I was disappointed. I had been all geared up to enjoy a final month of 35-degree wall-to-wall sunshine.

This proved to be one of those spots that capture you and won't let you go no matter what plans you might have had. It wasn't highlighted on any map, so if it hadn't been for Geoff's little free fold-out surf guide we would never have known to detour from the main road or that it even existed. There was nothing there but a little shack that doubled up as a café and small restaurant, and yet we filled three whole days with ease and loved every single minute. More importantly, at no point did we ever feel that we might regret our extended stay here when farther along the road we might have to bypass somewhere else to make up for lost time. We realised how often we had been caught out by the simplicity of the few places that just would not take no for an answer, as against some of the important places we had chosen to miss due to lack of time.

Every day as the tide pushed in it formed a very deep rock pool where crowds gathered to watch or join in the cliff diving. The pool was a vivid sapphire blue, sparkling in the sunlight. Having watched Geoff dive in and swim beneath us, it was too good an opportunity to miss out on, and Jackson and I crawled all the way down the rocks in a most unsightly manner just to access the water without risking a belly flop.

Seeing my baby, four years old and swimming unaided by my side, looking at the bottom some twenty feet beneath him and commenting on the various forms of life with which we shared this pool, I felt an overwhelming sense of pride. Of course, even in the sea, the questions kept on flowing: were there any octopus here? Or sharks, maybe? He was fearless and I was struck by how much he had matured since we set off seven months ago. He never turned down any opportunity to try his hand at all kinds of sporting activities, regardless of the weather and how much or little time we could afford to give him during these increasingly time-scarce days. He was indefatigably inquisitive. He had seen things in the flesh that I had learned about only from books much later in my school life. He was eternally curious and wanted to know what made everything tick. Looking at him now in this pool at this very moment convinced me that nobody would ever be able to tell me we had done the wrong thing by not putting him in nursery this past year. Everything he had gained in life experiences and learned about different countries, their cultures, cuisines and languages, would stay with him forever and feed into his future understanding of the world.

Inevitably these insights sparked another round of the conversation with Geoff that I knew he had come to dread. The conversation popped up under various guises but generally it followed this pattern:

Geoff, can you just give me one reason why we are going home to the pouring rain and cold, miserable grey skies? You won't be able to surf in board shorts and Jackson is too little to start school. We'll all be stressed out again. And it doesn't make any sense to go home when we are actually making money by living here. We could just turn round now and keep going, just for another year please, please, PLEASE...

He didn't really have any answers and I always felt a pang of guilt afterwards for putting him on the spot in front of Jackson. The reason for my guilt was that although I was pretty sure he agreed with me I also knew he believed that someone had to wear the sensible hat. These days I would often retreat to the back of the van where I would desperately attempt to breathe away the tears every time I thought of the prospect of sending Jackson to school. Instead of breaking ourselves in gently with 2½ hours a day of nursery, both Jackson and I had done completely the opposite thing and spent 24 hours a day side by side for the past seven months, and it had all been just perfect. It wasn't that I doubted his confidence, having seen at first hand how easily he made new friends throughout this trip. No, it wasn't him: it was me for whom I feared. Everything would change... he wouldn't need me so much... he would grow up too fast.

Of course I never allowed Jackson to see my emotions. If he ever asked what school would be like, I would put on my most positive face and say: *Well, you have had so much experience now, all you'll need to do is treat it like a campsite. You'll just walk in and say: Hello, I'm Jackson. Would you like to play with me? Before you know it you'll have a whole new group of friends.*

Karen and David arrived in the evening and we joined them at a different beach bar for food. There we learned about the genius idea that had brought them here into our lives. They jointly went by the name of 'The Grey Gappers'. Their year-long trip had come about after David wrote seven letters to motorhome companies, offering to trial a van and promote the brand while journeying through Spain. Putting this into no-nonsense-speak, they'd fancied a gap year and a year in sunny Spain appealed, so they put all this together and thought: now how can we get someone to pay us to do this? And why not? I only wish I had thought of it first. Only two companies replied. One politely told them to bugger off. The other lent them a brand-new top-of-the-range motorhome and even threw in the insurance for a year, all for nothing. Their target audience was supposed to be the over-fifties but they had turned out to be so good at what they did that they managed to draw in over 8,000 followers. They would blog at least once a week, not just about the performance of that particular vehicle but with their latest tales of hilarity, reviews of campsites and Aires, helpful co-ordinates and even cookery tips. I believe they had sampled just about every local Spanish delicacy and blogged about it. They had faithfully promised the sponsoring company that if by the end of the year they had found no fault with the motorhome, their followers and readers would be assured about its quality. It really was a no-brainer because with that many followers a few sales were bound to occur, which would more than cover the company's costs in loaning them a new vehicle for twelve months. I felt so envious, because while our trip was drawing to a close, they still had six months ahead of them and had already planned their Christmas in a motorhome. That night I couldn't sleep as I tried to think of some good reason that would allow me to travel the world testing something nice – maybe spas?!

Karen and David continued on their way the following day, but for us the waves were still good and we stayed for an extra night. In the afternoon we walked to two lakes. Just as we were approaching the first one our old friend the sea mist rolled back in, just in time to obliterate two bare backsides we had been fast catching up with. We were walking along a nudist beach, which wasn't a problem as far as I was concerned, although Jackson wasn't exactly subtle in his comments!

The mist lingered for the rest of the evening. At one point as we were sitting in the van we heard a very unusual noise. Puzzled, we looked at each other, then we suddenly all shouted: *Rain!* It was only a few spots, but we hadn't had rain for so long that our reaction was quite extreme. Just imagine how I might slip into a full-scale panic attack if we crossed the Severn Bridge on the way back to Wales running into a storm.

We left the next morning and the weather was still a bit dull, as had been predicted. This put all of us into a bad mood. Geoff instructed me to get the van ready ASAP. I was rushing around clearing three days' worth of three people's clutter back into cupboards, washing up and serving him round two of his breakfast because he had still been asleep when Jackson and I ate. Now his lordship was sitting in the middle of my labours writing in his diary.

Finally he took his life in his hands by asking: *Are we having a cup of tea, or what?* That set me off at the deep end. He and Jackson fled the scene for a walk. When they got back I opened the door to a now grumpy Jackson, who had been given a row about something. I was greeted with the unforgettable, well, it's unforgettable when you hear it from your four-year-old: *I f***ing hate this van!* In total disbelief I ridiculously asked him to repeat himself, which he obligingly did, quite innocently. I was floored. I had no idea whether it was me who had said it, or if Geoff had been moaning about me when they both stormed off. Anyway, I gave the poor boy a row and silently prayed he wouldn't find any reason to say something like this again when he started school. It had the effect of snapping Geoff and me out of our little war and shortly we all set off as friends again.

We only ventured about an hour away to the next peninsula, to a small village called Muros. Our destination, for one night only, was a proper campsite. There comes a time when you just crave the mod con of a washing machine. When we got there we stripped the van to its bare bones. Every towel, all our bedding, all the beach stuff now stiff with salt and sand and almost all our clothing filled three machines, and afterwards we hogged four washing lines in the sun. Every electrical item was plugged in so that we could barely walk inside the van without clambering over wires.

Then it became a competition to see who could spend the longest in the first hot shower in weeks in which we didn't have to limit the water. Jackson won that one hands down. By the time we had put everything back together again we were completely worn out, although it felt like the most therapeutic washing day we'd ever known.

Living without mains electricity and on limited water for weeks on end now made me see these things, which I had always taken for granted, as quite a luxury. And yet we never really wanted that luxury to last for too long. At heart we had evolved into wild campers and after one day of mod cons what we really craved was to get back to rugged nature.

41. COASTLINE, CULTURE, COLOURFUL LANGUAGE

BRIEFLY WE LEFT the beautiful coastline behind for our next destination, Santiago de Compostela, capital of the Galicia region. It was a place about which Geoff had read a lot while en route, so much so that when we were roughly highlighting a route through this region we both thought we should make it a priority destination.

Santiago de Compostela marks the end of the famous Way of St James annual pilgrimage route, which originated in the 9th century and begins in the French Pyrenees. According to medieval legend it is the burial site of the Apostle James, whose remains are said to lie within the cathedral inside the medieval walls of the old town. Pilgrims walk this route, or sections of it, throughout the year, and a special festival celebrating St James is held annually starting on 25th July. If that date happens to coincide with a Sunday, its popularity increases twofold. Presumably many pilgrims set off weeks or even months before with little certainty whether they will make it to Santiago by that particular day, and yet, come July, the pressure must surely be on every single pilgrim to time their arrival perfectly to hit the celebrations when they are in full swing.

Karen and David arrived on 21st July, having planned their visit well ahead and booked a campsite here for the full three days of the festivities, which would begin in just four days' time. Unfortunately we couldn't afford to stay that long and realised we would to have to settle for their account of it. Already the amount of preparation and security measures being organised were plain for everyone to see.

The town itself was reasonably attractive, despite coming close to being spoiled by the insane number of tourist shops selling tat, for want of a better word. Among them were a few unique arty shops with very attractive displays, but otherwise most of the shops dedicated a whole section to feet, everything from plasters and bandages to specialist shoes, with consultants on hand in some of them to offer advice to anyone whose feet needed repair. As we approached the old centre the famous cathedral loomed up, its clock tower visible from most of the narrow streets and, in case we weren't looking up, bronze scallop shells set in the paving stones led the way. They are the symbol of the pilgrimage and could be seen marking the route all over the region.

The cathedral itself, one of the largest in Europe, was undergoing a clean-up and all but one section was hidden under scaffolding. As we entered we were immediately struck by the immense bright gold altar, and indeed every part of the building seemed to us exceptionally grand. Various traditions are associated with its statues. If you headbutt three times the statue of the architect who designed the building you will be granted a portion of his genius. This one had been closed off after excessive headbutting left a dent in it. Another invites pilgrims to touch its left foot to signify the completion of their journey. Same thing again: following the constant laying of hands on the same spot, a groove had been worn in the stonework. Completing the tour, we joined a long queue to walk in silence behind the altar and, one by one, hug the bronze statue of St James. The bronze was smoothed and tarnished from hundreds and hundreds of years of hugging. All this was a little too weird for Jackson who announced that we were all mad. Fair comment, really! The last point of interest was the tomb itself, again with quite a queue.

Back outside more pilgrims had arrived. Unlike us mere tourists, they tended to lie around on the ground looking dishevelled and exhausted, or limped about on sore feet. But you could sense their elation at what they had achieved and actually it was quite moving. I had followed a pilgrimage route many years ago in Sri Lanka, much shorter than this one. We set off in the middle of the night to climb no less than 5,500 very uneven steps to reach the summit of Adam's Peak by sunrise. Memories of the route, the change of temperature between the bottom and top of the mountain, the feeling of total exhaustion that I never thought I would be capable of battling through and the excruciating pain that I lived with for days afterwards – so much so that three days later I couldn't even step off a kerb without wincing – will stay with me forever. But way stronger than this memory is that of the true pilgrims we met and talked to along the way. Not the ones that arrived like us in an air-conditioned car and slept in a nice bed before setting off, but those who had travelled for a day or more in a hot cramped bus with standing room only. Some of them were elderly, by which I mean some of them were in their eighties or even older. As we were on our way back down I saw one man nearing the top who had no legs. Somehow he had pushed himself on his hands all the way up this gruelling route. So now, seeing the faces of the people here in Santiago took me back. I tried to imagine the sights they had seen, the conversations they had along the way and the memories they would now hold forever – and how hard they would probably be partying in the coming days.

We stayed in the city until 8 p.m. and then, on getting back to our rather unattractive car park full of motorhomes, we made one of those late-in-the-day decisions to start driving again in the hope of finding somewhere nicer to wake up in. I laugh now to think how, before this trip, I would have had my pyjamas on by 5 p.m. and if anyone had suggested I get in a car and go for a drive I would have asked if they were feeling alright. Now I considered it perfectly acceptable to drive till anything up to 10 p.m. before deciding where we should sleep for the night.

Not, it has to be said, that we always made our best-informed decisions at that time of night. On this occasion a brief reference to our Aires book suggested one right next to a series of trout-fishing lakes somewhere in the countryside, described as 'slightly tricky to get to' but, the book said, 'well worth the effort'. We had long since learned to read between the lines in this book and identify any hidden messages. In this case two words should have struck us had we not been quite so tired: 'tricky' and 'effort'. After a difficult attempt to negotiate narrow lanes in the pitch dark, relying totally on the grid reference we'd put into the sat nav, we arrived, unable to see a thing in this unlit Aire, and parked up behind the only other motorhome there. Moments earlier the thought had struck me that perhaps we had set off too late in the day to get a place in this obviously popular Aire. Clearly I needn't have worried.

All seemed well until Geoff woke me up at 3 a.m. and put all the lights on to hunt down a mosquito that had bitten his foot. That was the last time any of us shut our eyes before daylight! Dogs in every direction seemed to be conversing with one another constantly and mosquitos were multiplying everywhere. It became an endless battle with them. We realised that they were getting in from somewhere rather than having hidden in there all day. But where from? All the mosquito nets were closed, so it must either be through the air vents or through the garage and then up underneath our mattress. Either way we were in a no-win situation. There's nothing worse than lying in bed listening for that high pitched *zzzeeeee* in your ear, knowing that hearing it will force you to put the lights on again to kill it, which is like turning on a neon sign inviting all the mosquitos in the area to join in this tasty banquet of human blood.

I got up at 9 a.m. after finally dozing off about an hour before. A kids' sports day was in full swing right outside the van and I cannot imagine how Geoff and Jackson managed to sleep on through all that noise for another two hours. By then I had walked the full circuit of the lake and tried but still failed to see that it was 'worth the effort' unless you were a trout fisherman. I immediately messaged a couple we knew who were heading in this direction to say don't be tempted by this one.

Because of time constraints we had to miss the far northwestern corner of Spain and cut across to the northern coast of Galicia. A passing traveller had advised us that under no circumstances should we miss a beach called Praia das Catedrais, or Cathedral Beach, which has some very unusual rock formations. It had been declared one of the best beaches in the world and he insisted it would be madness to end a trip like this without seeing it. Madness, indeed! What he failed to elaborate on was how many hoops you have to leap through to get onto the sand.

Finding the place was easy enough. It was late in the day so parking was easy and, as we approached the steps to the beach, the access was clear but because the tide was in there was nothing to see. After an expensive coffee in a clifftop restaurant we found a small information hut where we were given the following instructions:

1. You have to visit at low tide.

2. You have to get a permit, which is free. This can only be done via the internet. But there is no Wi-Fi signal unless you drive two kilometres farther down the road.

3. Otherwise you have to go to a village eight kilometres away and book into a hotel for the night, which will entitle you to a permit.

4. Failing all of that, you can just drive to that same village, find a car park and queue for a bus to get back to the beach. *Get there early*, she advised, *numbers are limited to 5,000 per day.*

OK, we thought, if 5,000 people a day think it's worth visiting, it must be worth waiting until low tide tomorrow. We drove along the coast until we found a signal. I then proceeded to wind myself up for the next hour while Geoff and Jackson went to the beach. I tried the link the tourist office had provided but it wouldn't open. I went through TripAdvisor, Spanish tourist information and heaven knows what else. I took it so far that warnings of unsafe websites were being flashed at me but, frankly, I couldn't care less, I just wanted to get it done, but still I could find no way to get this permit. When Geoff returned I practically threw the phone at him. He took over, went through it all again and got nowhere.

The next morning we thought about driving in the opposite direction to that village for the bus. But then we decided, no, we would blag our way in somehow. Would we hell?! This time, with the tide at optimum point, the parking was a whole new ball game. When we had played that, the next game was getting actual tickets. We, and hundreds of others, were turned away and directed to a board with the very same website on it... Randomly a few achieved their goal while others, and lots of them, failed to open up a link. I was stood there holding our EE 3G Mi-Fi up in the air and, turning slowly in circles trying to maintain a very weak signal while Geoff attempted to access the link. Foiled again!

By now he was in a really, really bad mood. We marched back to the same woman and Geoff advised her that I was writing a book about my experiences in Spain and all this nonsense was being noted. That failed to sway her one bit, but she did hand over her personal iPad, connect it to the link and, following yet another plea from us, eventually convert it to English for us. Now all we had to do was complete a form requiring our passport numbers and even our bank card details, for security. Security? For what? We just wanted to look at some rocks! Of course we had none of these documents to hand so Geoff put his UK

National Insurance number in place of the passport number and completely made up a bank card number. It fooled her, but when she said: *Good, now do it again for your wife*, I honestly thought Geoff might smash her iPad. After at least half an hour she announced: *Thank you, now you can go to the beach*, just as if this was completely normal behaviour.

Happily we immediately came to the conclusion that it had all been worth it. It was a kids' paradise with pools to splash in, caves to explore and wide expanses of sand to run on. For the hoards of photographers, on the other hand, it was a complete nightmare, because with 5,000 people down there, there was more chance of winning the lottery than of taking a decent photograph. I should elaborate: the attraction of this beach is its astounding rock formations, which were created completely naturally by the power of the sea. They stand about thirty feet high and form a series of arches, towers and caves. The effect is both beautiful and magical – and then it all disappears when the tide comes in.

We got back to the top of the cliff several hours later. By now my dear husband had calmed down but still had a bee flying around in his bonnet. He was determined to go to the tourist hut and tell the woman exactly what he thought about the fiasco. He managed to remain icily polite but I was so embarrassed that I decided to leave him to it.

From there we decided to drive the eight kilometres to the next town and look around. It seemed an extremely strange place with many derelict buildings, including one in the centre that was so beautiful it seemed criminal that it had not been restored. By this point we had clocked up 10,000 miles in poor Dotty and had only tried once, unsuccessfully, to locate a garage big enough to house her for a service, so we decided to call in at the local tourist information for advice about local garages. We might have got further than we did had it not been staffed by the very woman whom Geoff had offended earlier. Need I say she was no help at all? Actually she was rather rude and I almost understood the Spanish insults that pursued us as we headed out of the door.

42. THE VIEW FROM THE PICOS

T HE WELSH GIRL in me had been missing the mountains of late and I insisted that we couldn't leave Spain without at least a fleeting glimpse of the Picos de Europa range of mountains. Geoff, having spent so long driving along coastal roads, admitted to slight trepidation about this, and I had to admit I understood him. Mountains equalled hairpins and steep, slow climbs for Dotty, who was carrying a ridiculous and ever-increasing amount of weight from memorabilia picked up along the way, often in the form of rocks courtesy of Jackson. But Geoff consented and we left Galicia behind and headed into Asturias.

As we entered the foothills, looking for a viewpoint, we were lucky enough to catch a village *fiesta*. Across water or on land, most nights during the past few weeks we had heard fireworks all over this part of Spain – a sure sign that *fiestas* were going on here, there and everywhere. This was only a tiny mountain village we were passing through and it seemed to me that everyone who lived in it was taking part in this particular procession on foot, all in national costume walking behind a series of beautifully decorated tractors and carts. We pulled over to watch as they passed, Jackson waving to all the children and straining to join in the fun. By now we had travelled hundreds of miles from Santiago de Compostela, yet even here we were still crossing back and forth over the pilgrim route and encountering hundreds of walkers on their way to the big festival starting in a day or two. Before visiting Santiago we would have passed all these walkers and been completely unaware of where they were all heading.

In the limited time we could spend here it was hard to decide what we should try to see. The first viewpoint was hidden in the clouds so we moved on farther to the village of Arriondas. The sun there was shining and, as we drove over a bridge, we noticed hundreds of kayaks on the river down below. It looked like fun and we stopped to ask if we could join in. But Jackson was too young to be covered by their insurance. We thought about using our own kayak, but the river looked a bit serious in places. Not, in any case, that we'd have had a cat in hell's chance at this point in our journey of extracting our kayak from the garage...

Instead we settled for a walk around the village, and what an amazing place it turned out to be. On offer in the vicinity was every outdoor activity you could think of, from river sports of every kind to quad biking, paintballing, photography and foraging. It was quite plainly a mecca for stag and hen parties, with streams of them paddling down the river in fancy dress. From here you could paddle sixteen kilometres all the way to the coast. The following weekend the annual kayak marathon would be starting here, when more than a thousand canoes would leave the banks simultaneously in a race to the sea. Postcards illustrated the complete madness that descended on the town each year, and we wished we had timed our visit to be here to witness it.

Taking advice from tourist information, we parked for the night next to the bus station and caught a bus for a fifty-minute journey up hairpin after hairpin into the National Park, me sitting armed with a carrier bag at the ready for Jackson. The lower section along the river looked very much like a greener version of Betws-y-Coed in North Wales, with that same young, vibrant mix of outdoor sports shops and pavement cafés filled with bikers and walkers. Within the park the upper section of the road was only for buses, thank goodness because on the narrow sections they seemed to avoid meeting via their own private code of communication. Had a few oblivious cars or motorhomes been thrown into the mix it might have been carnage. As we climbed ever higher the scenery became more and more rugged. We could still see the sea, which helped us appreciate the vast scale of this mountain range.

At the top we found two choices, either a five-kilometre route with waymarkers, estimated to take 2½ hrs, or an easy three-kilometre walk on a stone path around two lakes. The bus back would leave in three hours, so not wanting to risk it we opted for the easy walk. We stopped at a little mining museum and then at the first lake. Beautiful yellow flowers covered the grass, cows with big bells wandered around almost lulling us to sleep with their wind-chime-like sound, and it all made a perfect chocolate-box picture.

We were enjoying a picnic beside the water when everything changed. By the time we finished a cloud had dropped on us out of nowhere and we could barely find our way back onto the stone path. Ten minutes earlier people had been wandering off all over the place, so I bet a few rescues were needed up there on that day. By the time we reached a viewpoint from where we were supposed to see both lakes I couldn't even see my hand in front of my face, never mind a lake. We sat it out for a while in case it lifted but with no sign that it would, we decided to make our way back to the bus.

Perhaps on the way up if I had paid less attention to the wonderful scenery and the ridiculous drops off the side of the road, not to mention all the cows that chose to cross right in front of the bus, I might not have needed to spend the next hour all the way down in fear of my life. I swear the wheels on my side were hanging over the cliff several times and still I could see the driver managing to unwrap a chewing gum. Obviously we made it back in one piece and despite not having all the nonstop views we set out for we had still seen plenty enough to draw us back here for a longer stay some day.

On our walk Jackson and I had collected, probably illegally, flowers in every colour of the rainbow. I asked Geoff to help Jackson stick them in strips onto a piece of paper to show him the colour order. In my mind's eye I visualised a beautiful A4-sized rainbow made up of all our flowers – my idea of schooling on this trip. I turned my back for two minutes, turned back round and it was all done, all of five centimetres long, if even that. He hadn't bothered with red at all, apparently blue was too 'spiky', and he had taken two or three petals off for each colour. I'm talking about Geoff here, who then sighed as if he was utterly exhausted by it all and said: *Put it somewhere safe for him to keep it.* Heck, the poor boy would need a magnifying glass to ever find it again! All the rest of the flowers went straight into the bin. I had to take a photo and resolved never again to let Geoff help Jackson with his art homework.

That night we were woken up once more by fireworks. Opening our blinds, we were treated to one of the best firework displays we had ever seen, all for free while lying in the comfort of our bed. Jackson slept like a log through all of it.

Next on the itinerary, after our day in the mountains, was supposed to be a day on the beach searching for dinosaur footprints in San Vicente de la Barquera, which is reputed to showcase one of the best collections in the world. Jackson was agog, hardly able to contain his excitement at the idea of finding a footprint all by himself though a little fearful of seeing live dinosaurs. It took a fair amount to convince him that this wasn't very likely. Rather stupidly I expected it to be very easy: we'd drive to the beach, park the van, look no further than the end of our collective nose, find a footprint and we'd all go away happy. Er, no! Driving to the beach happened. Parking did not. After that the one-way system forced us through the centre of a tiny village where I think I held my breath until I nearly died, because the whole way we were millimetres from parked cars and buildings. It just kept getting narrower and narrower and, with traffic building up behind us, there was nothing we could do about it. This was exactly the situation Geoff had tried to warn me about many months ago when I suggested having a go at driving the van. What he'd said was: *The trouble is, you never know what's around the next corner*, and by now I had seen enough to understand what he meant. I also realised that any time I found myself in this situation, all I would do was get out and force him to take over, and getting yourself out of a self-made mess is one thing but being expected to get out of someone else's mess I imagine takes it to a whole other level. So I certainly understood why there were times he was nervous about what might lie ahead down the road, and I felt pretty sure I would have put us into this situation much more often than he did.

We did finally get out in one piece and drove miles around to get back to where we had started, this time on a wider road. We thought we'd better not try to go anywhere near the beach but instead park in the bigger town farther along, where we spotted a motorhome in a car park below us. By chance, as we indicated to turn in, there was a policeman standing on the pavement who held up the traffic in all directions and gave us the extra room we needed to negotiate the tight corner.

We took the opportunity to wander around a local craft market where there was extra entertainment laid on for kids, such as face-painting and entertainers. Geoff drew some unwanted attention when a man dressed as a washerwoman and carrying a laundry basket waved some red knickers under his nose for him to sniff. This was a clue that it was more than just your average craft market, and that certainly woke Geoff up after his nerve-racking drive.

Discovering that there was a dinosaur museum a few kilometres away, we chose that as a logical starting point. The museum turned out to be really well done and Jackson was totally enthralled. There were models made from moulds of dinosaur footprints on the beach next to photographs taken on the beach showing the imprints in the rocks as they now looked today. To me they just seemed to be bumpy rocks and I honestly would have walked right over them without noticing anything if we had ever made it to the beach. After the excitement of seeing full-sized dinosaurs we'd have seriously struggled to match it with a trip to the actual beach. We managed to convince Jackson that we had seen the best the area had to offer and, as far as dinosaurs were concerned, decided to call it a day.

Looking for a place to stop for the night, we turned into a road signposted to a beach. The driver of a motorhome just coming out of the junction waved at us not to go down. We pulled into a very convenient lay-by with enough room to turn around and were sitting there thinking up Plan B when Geoff decided, sod it, he was going to try it regardless. Having spent seven months literally right by his side in Dotty, I still can't figure out the man's logic. Sometimes he'd be over-cautious, sitting there thinking through a whole situation and ignoring a queue of cars behind. At other times, when he was in no one's way and could easily avoid trouble, he'd charge headlong into it instead. Somehow, whichever he chose, it was me who seemed to end up in the firing line. On this occasion, yup, we got into a proper mess again. We started by nearly adding another storey to our sleeping quarters by almost taking a hay barn with a low overhanging roof with us.

And when we actually made it to the car park, the attendant charged us five euros and waved us into ...

... Hell: a series of fields with wooden fencing segregating different areas, all so busy it was impossible to make out whether there was a free space in any of them. If you dared to enter one of these fenced areas and found it was full there was no way to turn around. We judged the first two to be full because we could see cars double-parked. The third had an entrance far too narrow for us – and then we hit a dead end. Cue: a long reverse along a track just wide enough for us, 'guided' by me, red-faced, from behind the vehicle; a few wheelspins in deep sand; a queue of cars behind us also being forced to reverse; and a quite annoying Spanish bloke in my ear advising me: *You are too big*, like I didn't know already and I hadn't just been trying to tell my husband exactly that before we ever landed ourselves here. It made for a very stressful ten minutes. And then, hey presto, I accidentally tripped over some fence posts, they accidentally fell down, and what should be accidentally revealed but a nice tidy space made just for us.

After all this drama the beach turned out to be lovely and there was even some nice surf for Geoff. We slept the night here along with about twenty fellow vans, surrounded by signs that very clearly said 'No overnight camping'. A local person let us in on the secret. The ground was privately owned and the police could do nothing about it, but we should expect a visit at 10 a.m. sharp by the owner to collect another five euros for sleeping there. He also mentioned that tomorrow was a public holiday, which explained the crowds who were thronging in today. To avoid being hemmed in until midnight we turned the van around while the field was still empty, which enabled us to slip away by 9 a.m. the following morning without even having breakfast and without parting with another euro.

We enjoyed a really scenic drive with the Picos mountains to our right, the sea to our left and blue skies all round. Stopping for breakfast in a small inn with a terrace overlooking a valley winding its way down from the mountains, we sat outside watching birds of prey and listening to birdsong while attempting to order breakfast from an establishment that felt like a five-star hotel but was oddly full of pilgrims on their way to Santiago de Compostela. This was a challenge, with no menu, hence no prices, and owners who spoke no English. But at least it was entertaining, as was the breakfast. Our 'egg on toast' turned out to be a fried egg on a plate accompanied by a basket of French bread. Then Jackson wanted 'jam on toast' and got a plate of cured ham and some now toasted French bread. But at least we were fed, and the next leg of our journey would take us along the coast to Bilbao.

43. PERPLEXED BY THE BASQUE COUNTRY

NOW WE WERE in the Basque Country and it instantly felt quite different from the rest of Spain. We opted for a paid Aire with the added security it offered of being so close to a major city. Perched high on a hillside, the view overlooking the whole of Bilbao was astounding. We parked right in the front row and spent most of the evening with the blinds open admiring the view below us, as if we were on a plane. And it just got better and better as darkness fell and the city lit up. Part of our evening's entertainment was trying to identify Bilbao's various landmarks.

As I've noted before, we struggled to think of the best way to tackle a city with a young child. Our general approach was to do little, if any, forward planning and instead to see where our noses led us. Aiming just to get a feel for a place and see some of its main sights, we felt happiest wandering around and enjoying light-hearted activities such as parks or pavement cafés. In this case the Guggenheim Museum was the only must-see on our agenda. Otherwise we stayed true to form, catching a bus from directly opposite the Aire down to the old cathedral, from where we walked all along the river. We had a map but it took a while to work out how far we had gone. Then we realised that the best method was to count the many, many bridges and match their appearance to the diagrams on the map.

My first impressions of Bilbao were of physical darkness and an oppressive feel about the place. I felt surrounded by nine-storey buildings, which all lacked colour and blocked out much of the light. What struck both of us most of all was the quietness. It was a Sunday, which in Spain we associated with hoards of people and particularly families milling around, picnicking, kids playing, background music from cafés, bars spilling out onto the street... But here, for some reason, all of this was lacking. Even the river was empty: all we saw was just one boat. These last few months we had passed through so many towns and cities – in Spain and elsewhere – where pretty much universally any of those that featured any river or other body of water had made it their focal point and a hive of activity and colour. But the riverside in Bilbao almost felt as if we had accidentally walked into an area where we weren't supposed to be.

We found somewhere to have lunch beside the river and looked on with surprise from our table as the waiters cleared plates and threw the food remains straight over the wall into the water. Jackson chose a suitably inappropriate topic for his day's list of questions, which were about fish and delivered at a volume high enough for all our fellow diners to hear. *How do fish wee and poo? Do they have a bum? Do they have a winky? Do they wee out of their bum?* On and on he went in his very determined manner all through lunch, demanding answers to what he clearly thought were perfectly reasonable questions.

Feeling a bit more relaxed and at our ease, we continued on the final leg of our walk towards the Guggenheim. Rounding a corner, suddenly there it was, Frank Gehry's famous masterpiece, like entering a different world. The more I looked at the architecture the less plausible it seemed. There stood the unmistakable giant spider by Louise Bourgeois on the riverside plaza and Anish Kapoor's tower of hugely oversized and precariously balanced silver ball bearings. Steam poured through the neighbouring La Salve bridge, shrouding the river in a mysteriously atmospheric fog. The inside was every bit as amazing. Even the lift was like nothing I had seen before.

Here I have to confess to being poorly educated in the world of art, which makes me an impatient viewer. I'm prone to make an instant decision and admit no middle ground, either loving or hating whatever is in front of me, so I'm sorry to say I disliked nearly everything in the Guggenheim collection. One significant exception was Richard Serra's enormous walk-through metal sculpture, a towering series of rusted metal sheets bent and arranged to form high-sided, almost maze-like walkways. I enjoyed standing on the viewing gallery above, from where I could watch people walking between the sheets and study the extreme simplicity of Serra's design. Returning to ground level I noticed how he had cleverly and subtly twisted and inclined the walls to give the illusion

that they were closing in or opening out, and other similarly disorien-
tating experiences. I wasn't alone in finding myself walking through
them with my arms outstretched as if in a futile attempt to push the walls
back out, or hastening my speed as these illusions somehow forced me
to perceive myself becoming trapped, then relaxing and slowing down
as they seemed to open up again. When we exited the museum on a
different side of the building we found ourselves facing a huge sculpture
of a cat made entirely out of living flowers. By then my overall opinion
of the museum had turned around. Jackson too had surprisingly enjoyed
the whole experience.

On our walk back I felt my mind starting to change about the city
too. Now somehow it all felt very different. I don't know whether I was
seeing things in a new light or just that it was evening time and there
were more people about to liven the place up. Perhaps Bilbao was more
a town of nightlife than a vibrant place during the daytime. At any rate
it now presented a brighter and happier side than before.

Back at the Aire the receptionist kindly went beyond her duties by
phoning a local garage to book us in for a service and writing down the
co-ordinates for us. Relying solely on our sat nav, we headed off first
thing the next morning right into Bilbao, something that normally we'd
have tried to avoid at any cost. All seemed to be going well until the
road we needed was blocked by temporary road works. In that situation
we knew it was futile simply to assume that in a vehicle of our size we
should safely follow the diversion signs. The sat nav, with its long-
established reputation for being untrustworthy, was taking an age to
update its suggested route. Cutting a long story short, having criss-
crossed the city centre every which way, we eventually approached our
target from the opposite direction, with a further half an hour stolen
from our day and the sat nav triumphantly highlighting our final
destination on its screen. In the real world it was plain to see from the
end of the road that we were heading towards nothing more than a tiny
town garage, barely big enough to turn a car into. Once again we gave
up and, feeling even less affection for Bilbao than when we'd first
entered its outskirts, we left the city behind us and drove towards the
coast. By sheer chance, as we passed right through the middle of an

industrial zone, indicating that yet again we were lost, we spotted another garage with the same name as the one we'd just dismissed. It turned out we'd been given co-ordinates for the wrong section of the garage. In contrast, this garage was easily able to accommodate Dotty, and although we had missed our slot they kindly gave us a new booking for a few hours later. Left with time on our hands in the middle of a maze of workshops and warehouses in a vast industrial area, we sought entertainment and refreshment in the nearby streets.

We managed to find one coffee shop open in what was otherwise a ghost town, although the waitress wasn't at all welcoming. This was our first encounter with *pintxos*, a typical Basque tradition. Along similar lines to the *tapas* theme that Spain does so well, in the Basque region the bite-sized snacks that so often accompany an alcoholic beverage go by the name *pintxos*, meaning 'thorn'. A little unnerving it might be to connect thorns to food, but in this case it alludes to the spike, usually in the form of a cocktail stick that spears a mouthful of fish, meat or whatever they have available to a piece of bread. The idea is to make drinking a more sociable experience without the need to sit down for a formal meal. On this occasion I don't think we chose the best establishment to inspire us to rush out and partake in the tradition any time soon. All the plates were uncovered and alive with flies, and we were sweating in 30 degrees in an empty café, which suggested that they may have been sat there since the night before.

These observations and a swing park were sufficient to pass the time until the garage was ready for us, and before long Dotty emerged with a clean bill of health. The mechanics were lovely, apart from the moment when one mechanic had his head under the bonnet and out of the blue Jackson took an almighty leap off the seat in the van. We were promptly but politely directed to the waiting room where the boss plied Jackson with free gifts of key rings, magnets and a bag. As we left, even after a particularly boring morning for a four-year-old, he managed to produce a winning smile.

From here we took the scenic coastal road rather than the much faster option. But it proved to be a waste of time. After endless hairpins through heavily forested areas with no views anywhere we only actually caught two brief glimpses of the sea. One was mostly filled with a nuclear power plant. The other view revealed a small island connected to the mainland by a walkway, with about a hundred steps leading to a church on the top. We could see cars and people all around it but the information board merely translated to a model of some saint or other being built and placed underwater here to commemorate everyone lost at sea. Clearly you could dive or snorkel here but it didn't seem to justify attracting so many people unless we had missed something.

We were heading for Mundaka, which for decades had featured on Geoff's must-see list. Of all the waves in all the surf books on our bookshelf back at home, this was one of the most iconic and the one he was most excited to see. It's famed for having the longest wave in Europe and I'm sure he had many a time envisaged himself inside its barrel for minutes – no, let's make that hours. Never before had I witnessed such disappointment on someone's face. We drove right through the centre of the village, only realising the next day that we'd missed a sign barring all traffic. Maybe all eight metres of us slipped through unnoticed. Or maybe not. In the blink of an eye we were out the other side.

Once again everything felt dark and uninviting, with no sign of any beach. We looked for somewhere to park but before we knew it we were a mile up river with nothing so far having even mildly attracted us. The day was fast disappearing and Geoff was getting tired. We parked up and took in some fresh air while planning our next move. It seemed clear that we were in no-man's land too far away from both beach and town.

We took a walk along the pretty river bank. The tide was coming in at a fair lick and we made good use of this opportunity to teach Jackson about the dangers of being cut off with an incoming tide. In the scant minute or two we talked to him while he drew in the sand with a stick, we were able to show him that he was technically now standing on an island, the water having come up from both sides and surrounded him. He was properly freaked out, and although it was still less than toe deep he ran all the way back to the top of the beach without stopping. Lesson learned!

As for what to do next, we just couldn't be bothered to move and, hoping we might catch Mundaka in a better light in the morning, we slept there in a picnic area surrounded by lots of other campers, many with young children. Despite the multitude of midges, kids' football went on well into the evening, each van taking on a share of the childminding from their windows.

In the morning, after failing the previous day to find the beach, never mind its famous wave, we headed back to town and this time spotted the sign banning vehicles from the very road we had sailed along yesterday. We took a higher road and, as luck would have it, found a parking space in a car park right above the beach we were looking out for. We needed to park sideways across three spaces to avoid sticking out too far but, in an otherwise quiet car park and with no signs prohibiting motorhome parking, there seemed to be no issue. We had no other choice. The only other car park in town, a very large one right by the beach down below us, had height barriers prohibiting all motorhomes. I'll elaborate later but no prize for guessing: we came back to a notice on our windscreen.

We had a decent day on the beach. Saying that, of all the images I've ever built in my mind before seeing a place, this has to be the one I got most spectacularly wrong. Bearing in mind the World Surf league championships are hosted here and it features in just about every surf book or magazine I had ever looked at, the very least I'd expected were surf cafés, modern bars, wall-to-wall surf shops and tourist signs with pictures of the big wave, much like Nazaré. But no, there was absolutely none of that. In fact if you didn't know about the surf you could walk right past and be none the wiser and probably feel a lot less betrayed than my husband felt right now. The town itself had no appeal worth mentioning, with no coherent theme or sense of any design or planning control. The buildings gave it a dark and cramped feel and it seemed clear they were not looking for tourists. The local people weren't exactly rude but nor did they go out of their way to welcome you.

There was no real sign of any wave but the beach looked ideal for Jackson, very shallow even a long way out and with a rope sectioning off a swimming area where you were only waist deep even at its furthest point. But then, as the tide retreated, the surf schools descended in their dozens and the underlying dangers of this beach were revealed in their full glory. In its set-up Mundaka is not your average beach, being essentially a river mouth. At high tide it's all filled in, leaving only our little sandy beach with a similar one directly opposite. But as the tide retreats, this safe swimming area becomes dry sand and various sand banks are exposed. Now we could see that to our left, around the corner from our beach and protected by a jetty and some rocks, was where the surfers caught the waves, riding in at 90 degrees to where we were facing, while directly opposite us people were still paddling and facing us.

A large sand bank meant that even the surfers were only up to their waists in the sea, adding even more confusion to the equation. Unknown to many who didn't look properly at their surroundings, between us and the people paddling opposite was a deep river channel with a deadly current. Boats regularly went up and down and yet astonishingly many people just didn't notice them and assumed they could simply wade across to our beach. From anywhere on the beach you could see a clear line on the surface of the water where it switched from flat to turbulent as the water raced out to sea, yet countless people seemed blissfully unaware of the whereabouts of their children as they floated innocently on Lilos perilously close to danger or tried to paddle out until they were out of their depth. For me it was a real eye-opener about how important it was to teach Jackson to be aware of these natural signs and also why as parents we should never take our eye off the ball whenever we were with him on a beach.

At this point I became very concerned and shocked that there was only one lifeguard on duty covering all three sections. Almost every beach in Spain had been so heavily lifeguarded that I would at least have expected the same here. We witnessed two rescues in the space of half an hour. One involved the lifeguard swimming, with some degree of difficulty, against the current right across the river to rescue a woman on the other shore who had got out of her depth and was now being swept away. Luckily someone else got there before him, but it was terrifying to see the power the current had on a trained lifeguard let alone anyone else – and all the while he was in the water nobody was watching all the other idiots doing their damnedest to get into the same mess. Just watching this made me feel sick.

When we returned to our van we had been blocked in by a local and found a police notice on our window warning us not to park there again. Actually we were being watched because no sooner had we got there than a bloke came down from one of the houses to make a great point of telling us how we had ruined his day by taking his usual parking spot – which was in a public car park! We managed to stay polite and decided to get out of there and drive for an hour to some other Aire.

We'll never know whether our irate pal saved our bacon by holding us up or caused our delay. Whichever it was, we got no farther than the exit of the car park before coming to a standstill. After half an hour we had moved about ten cars' length and it soon became apparent that we were only actually moving forward into spaces created by cars turning round and leaving the scene. Police passed several times and it became clear that the road was closed in both directions. We knew from the previous day that if we turned round we would have to drive through hours of hairpins just to reach a main road to bypass this point, so we chose to sit it out. We knew that in a motorhome these situations were usually not as bad as they sounded, maybe a little frustrating, but with our engine turned off we could watch TV, prepare our food or have a cuppa. In fact we did all of those. A police car drove along making an announcement over a loud hailer, but our limited Spanish let us down and we were none the wiser. After an hour a kind passer-by noticed our number plate and let us in on the secret. Apparently a fish lorry had overturned on a hairpin and all the fish had to be picked up from the road. This explained why hundreds of people had been walking past holding their noses. Further elaboration revealed that the lorry was carrying sardines and the accident had happened on a sharp bend in a dip with a steep hill in both directions. They had cleared the fish up but then the first few vehicles to pass in each direction had spread the oil up both hills, turning the road surface into a skating rink, which in turn had caused the next few vehicles to get completely stuck. Specialist cleaning companies had been brought in to wash the road and coat it in a white powder to create grip.

It took another three hours before vehicles began to move, being waved on one at a time to ensure they made it up the other side before allowing one to enter in the opposite direction. As this was the only road, the tailback was miles long. It was now 10 p.m. and we had only covered two miles, so we parked up in the same picnic site as the previous night, hoping that it would all be cleared by the morning.

44. A FINAL FAREWELL TO SPAIN

IT WAS A day of mixed feelings. We would be bidding farewell to Spain and looking forward to the excitement of something new, but with that unavoidable realisation that we were entering the home straight and that, with only a matter of weeks before we would have to get Jackson back for the start of school, we were approaching the end at speed. I do realise that most people – including us, until now – feel at the start of a two-week holiday as if they have all the time in the world to look forward to, so my complaining that we only had a few weeks left may come across as exceptionally ungrateful. It's all relative, though, and whereas a day had felt like a week when we started out, seven months down the line a week felt like a day, and we were trying to hang on to every second we had.

We took what was supposed to be the coast road all the way out of Spain except that again the roads were winding and heavily wooded, blocking all the sea views. Every minute the sat nav took off its arrival time equated to four minutes spent on the road, making for a long and boring drive for Jackson, who made damn sure he made us extremely aware of it.

The towns we passed through were typically like those I've mentioned previously. The sheer volume of washing hanging outside the windows of high-rise buildings was enough to make you think you were driving through a giant laundrette. We stopped for a break at a small café bar with a neighbouring swing park and were served in total silence without so much as a smile. It's just my personal opinion but it was these tiny signals of indifference that often left me with a sense of unease about the Basque Country. I thought I saw a vast difference in the demeanour of the people who here seemed very down in the mouth and stern, while the towns generally lacked the soul we'd found in the rest of Spain. A perfect example was awaiting us when we left the cafe. We took Jackson to the swing park and when we walked back to the van the road was blocked by police, four of them in total. One was waving cars by, two were breathalysing any selected drivers and the fourth stood in the middle of the road with his machine gun out in the firing position. Jackson wanted to know what they were doing. I explained that you can't drive a car if you have had alcohol, to which he replied: *So if you have, will that man shoot you dead?* I had to laugh, but in fairness it really did look like it. That was the uneasy feeling that I've been talking about, as if we were always on the brink of something kicking off. Was there really any need for such heavy handedness?

Next stop was a wine stop – to take home, that is, not to drink right now. This was in the coastal city of San Sebastián, renowned for its upmarket food scene and nightlife. From what I had read it offered something for everyone, from beaches to culture, festivals and fine dining, and we would have stopped longer here except that its popularity and appeal meant we were in nose-to-tail traffic and struggling to find anywhere to park. Eventually we settled for a brief supermarket stop with me remaining in Dotty as a security measure while Geoff negotiated his way around the wine aisle.

I had been hoping to prove Geoff wrong in this instance as his opinion of San Sebastián had been tainted by a nasty break-in he'd experienced while travelling many years before. It had left him with a feeling that it would not have been possible to carry out the break-in without a great many local people witnessing it and that not one of them or the police were in the least bit interested in being helpful. This impression had stuck with him. Now, with all our worldly possessions in one vehicle, he was making it very clear that his preference was to bypass the city and get across the border. And yet so many more recent accounts from friends and fellow travellers had led me to believe this city deserved at least a second chance. I'm sure at an earlier stage in our trip we'd have persevered, left the motorhome in a secure Aire and used the transport links. But we couldn't risk just leaving it in a public car park when there was any doubt in our minds.

I must say our opinions of the Basque Country generally differ considerably from those of many of our friends and family, so I can't help wondering where we went wrong. It wasn't really like me to form such a negative opinion about a whole region and its people. Later we followed the Grey Gappers' blog (Karen and David, whom we met in Boiro) and their colourful accounts of the people, culture and culinary delights they sampled here, where we had turned up our noses. It felt like we were talking about two completely different places. Maybe the difference was about travelling with or without a young child. Unable to immerse ourselves in the nightlife or culture as Karen and David could makes me worry that I have unfairly judged the Basques. However, I can't pretend; I have to tell it as I felt it. In fact we encountered, quite often when we were travelling, two people's perceptions being complete opposites and some of our favourite places being someone else's idea of hell. So, who knows, when Jackson is older, maybe we'll come back here and wonder what we ever found to dislike about it.

The traffic got even heavier over the border into France. By 5 p.m. it seemed very unlikely that we would make it to our chosen Aire for the night. So I rang a campsite in Labenne, which was supposedly twenty minutes away, booked us in, and then it took us another whole hour to get there. We had promised, having endured an endless torrent of grief from our junior passenger throughout that last hour, highlighting the awful day he had been put through sitting in a boring van, that we would not drive the following day. On checking in at Camping Sylvamar, which boasted five stars and was priced at 25 euros per night had we been able to use our ACSI card, I explained that we would like an extra night. We had anticipated a minimal extra charge as we were now in a peak holiday period. I walked in and back out again pretty fast to break the news to Geoff that it was actually 60 euros per night – more than we'd spent in a month on camping. We were all so tired we had no choice but to accept it, for one night only. But now, not only tired and disgruntled ourselves at this rip-off, we had to confront an already grumpy Jackson with the news that our plans had just changed again and we would, after all, be driving again tomorrow, so he should make the most of this place while it lasted.

It turned out to be a lovely site, apart from there being only two spaces left out of 275 so that squeezing into position was difficult, to put it politely. The pool was fabulous. It had slides, a lazy river, a huge indoor splash pool for children with all sorts of fountains and games, and we managed to get an hour's worth for our 60 Euros before they closed. Later in the evening, entertainment was laid on in the form of a foam party. I can't imagine how I managed to escape one of these for over forty years, and my naivety showed: Jackson and I showered and dressed BEFORE we went. Such idiots! It was an assault on all our senses. There was enough foam pouring from the ceiling to drown us, smoke machines blinded us and the music was deafening. I spent the first ten minutes trying to stay clean like a woman with OCD, ordering my child not to put it on our clothes, to watch his skin, watch his eyes, etc. It didn't work, obviously! I eventually stood back, remembered this was supposed to be fun, I might never again get to share this with Jackson and I wanted him to remember it for all the best reasons. In we went, me with my new adventuring head on. We were nearly swimming in foam and I must have nearly cut off the blood supply to Jackson's arm, so tight was my grip so as not to lose him. To be sensible for a moment, it was pretty full on for little ones, all too easy for them to get trampled on, and with smoke, flashing lights and deep, deep bubbles I'm pretty sure they might have come to harm. But finally we managed to fight our way back out and emerged with nothing but our eyes showing, having never laughed so much in all our lives. Try to imagine the state in which we arrived back at the van, after standing in a shower fully dressed because we had no towels and squelching back in sodden shoes, getting completely lost among 275 white boxes on wheels in the dark. And found Geoff sat there watching a film... Jackson was unstoppable in his bid to relay all the fun to Daddy in every little detail, while I just giggled like a lunatic. My husband must have thought I'd lost my mind. Which indeed I had!

Due to the cost, we needed to move the next day. Following a tip-off from the ever obliging receptionist at the campsite, we ended up just twenty minutes up the road near Capbreton at another fabulous Aire right on the Océanides beach, which we would have used last night if we'd had time to gather our thoughts in between Jackson's complaining. It was a large and highly popular car park-style Aire with some spaces allocated for hook-up but most without, resulting in a constant reshuffling of its occupants to enable others to use the services. A bread van delivered daily, making its presence known by its unmistakable horn blowing and with a long queue confirming its value. Here it was again a case of anything goes. Our neighbours ranged from vintage VW camp-ervans to lorry-based off-roaders, with no one casting any judgments.

It was on this beach that Geoff broke his own record for the longest time spent/wasted studying the surf. The waves were perfect: well, either that or the other 300 people that were in were blind. Geoff opted to wait until the morning. We set an alarm but only I got up, checked out the scene and reported back: *It looks nice – no wind, a few in.* What I got in reply, without even opening his eyes, was: *Too early. Will get better with the tide.* I didn't bother to question why we'd needed to set the alarm. That was at 8.30 a.m. I think he actually went to the beach in person at 11.30 and decided that there was now wind on it – not good, apparently, though to me it still looked brilliant. He then stood there for two hours with his arms folded, looking intently at every wave. Nearly everyone slowly came out as the waves got steadily worse and worse, whereupon Geoff announced: *Right, now the holidaymakers and idiots are out of the way, I'm going in.* After all this effort he caught three waves.

Meanwhile Jackson and I had built a sandcastle on a mound and we were sat behind its walls waiting to see how long it could hold back the sea. The answer wasn't pretty! In one foul swoop a wave obliterated it, soaked both of us, knocked me backwards, thankfully still holding tightly to Jackson, and swept his tractor out to sea. I stood there with wet sand pouring out of my bikini and not a thing I could do about it, because under no circumstances was I going any closer to the water. Geoff's parting words as he'd entered the sea with his board came rushing back to me: *Be careful paddling today. It's rough!* Not for one second had I imagined the possibility of being swept off dry sand, though, and it now dawned on me that had we been on our feet, and had I not had a good hold of Jackson, exactly that could have happened.

We gave our bikes another airing here. Of late they had been neglected, partly due to the effort of moving all our junk around in the garage to get to them. But the network of tracks available here made this too good an opportunity to miss. We cycled into Capbreton, a lovely bright seaside town full of tourist shops, and then on to Hossegor, home of a great many surf shops. Between the two I felt in my element. We raced blackening skies all the way back and made it to the van about ten seconds ahead of a massive thunder storm. The change of weather got us moving the next morning when we awoke to grey skies and cool winds and decided we would have a driving day.

45. LAZY DAYS AROUND THE LAKE
AUGUST

V EXED BY THE weather not being quite on our side, we headed north towards Arcachon. Stopping at the local market in Léon to pick up some gifts, we managed to upset a local householder by parking on a grass verge outside her house and also to get our first official parking ticket of the trip. They were both completely unexpected as it was a really quiet road with no lines or any visible signs about parking, and we certainly weren't obstructing anyone.

Bearing in mind we had just spent more in the local market than the parking ticket was worth, and remembering some advice given to us before we left the UK, namely to ignore all parking tickets abroad as it is not cost-effective for them to chase up foreign number plates, added to the fact that we'd be out of France and back in Wales before the deadline for our ticket, we decided we'd put the theory to the test. We took the precaution of photographing the van as it was parked, just in case we ever needed to argue our case. But we never heard anything more about the matter. I wonder, though, if we'd have been so bold if we were still likely to be on French roads after the deadline. Mind you, we had also heard stories from people who had been given tickets while travelling and who had needed to drive right into the centre of towns in which they had struggled to find the correct office to settle up their account and had then been kept waiting for hours to get the matter dealt with. All of them said that after their experience they would never bother with any of it if it happened again.

On this occasion our intended destination was not Arcachon itself but some ten kilometres south of there to Lac de Cazaux, the second largest lake in France. Arriving at the lake at a town called Gastes, we found a beautiful grassy Aire partially under the trees, with lovely views of the water. Here for eight euros we had a security system, a large overnight plot where we could put the awning, tables and chairs out, toilets, dishwashing and laundry facilities, and service points for emptying and filling the van. All of these were cleaned twice daily and we had a prime view of the lake, its beach and all its activities. There were about a hundred vans here, about half of them British, all spending money in the local cafés and shops and feeding the coin machine on the security barrier system for the duration of their summer vacation.

A couple of them told us they came to France to escape the extortionate charges back home. Britain simply doesn't cater for motorhomes. Instead you are forced to use a campsite at considerably higher cost, and the concept of Aires, under any of its guises, simply doesn't exist. It's not just my opinion but that of countless other travellers of all nationalities with whom we conversed on this trip that we in Britain seem to be missing a trick here. Without getting into the politics of it, we seem to suffer from a national lack of insight as far as this kind of tourism is concerned. It was blatantly obvious in all the countries where we travelled that if you provide adequate facilities and attractions to draw people there, they will inevitably stay long enough to spend their money and boost the local economy. It is very evident that the income generated in the local areas outweighs the cost of providing these services. In which case, it's a double-edged sword, because by not sufficiently accommodating would-be travellers in Britain, we seem not only to put off foreigners visiting us, but we even drive the Brits out too.

The following morning we were miraculously up early for once and ready to go kayaking before the wind got up. We paddled a long way out into the middle of the still lake among rigs that we thought were for drilling for gas. Lakes of this kind in France are often very shallow and safe for children. Even so, lifeguards man the sandy shores and swimming areas are roped off. The water here was crystal clear and seaplanes were practising landing and taking off nearby. We rounded a rig to show them to Jackson, who was happily fishing with a piece of driftwood and declaring repeatedly that he was going to catch our tea for us.

We docked farther along the shore, pulling the boat up onto a lovely deserted beach where some wild ponies were sheltering under the shade of a tree. It was alive with dragonflies, butterflies and wildflowers, and luckily there were ripe blackberries to shut Jackson up because I had forgotten to bring food. We swam and Jackson learned to dive to the bottom to collect shells for me. My collection reached fifty before I finally convinced him we would sink the boat if I had to carry any more back. It was truly peaceful having this little slice of land all to ourselves for a couple of hours, although we paid for it when we left, for the wind was now up and our paddle back was a battle against choppy waves.

Having called on muscles we had forgotten we had, we pretty much collapsed on the beach when we got back. By way of contrast, Jackson, having had a lazy few hours as a passenger, trailing a stick and making our job harder, had energy to burn and ran around like a lunatic for a whole hour. There was plenty to occupy him between the sandy beach, a swing park and grassy ball areas. We met a lovely British couple with two boys around Jackson's age who were staying at the same Aire as us. They were the first English-speaking kids Jackson had properly played with in a long time. By now he was so accustomed to finding ways round the language barrier that there was no significant difference as far as he was concerned. We chatted over a bottle of wine while the kids ran riot.

Then something very out of the ordinary happened. Our four-year-old actually fell asleep before 9 p.m. for the first time in months, enabling us to put him to bed before heading back out of the van to enjoy a further sociable and now peaceful glass of wine with our other neighbours, a couple from Cardiff. They were taking a gap year, having worked for the same company for thirty years. They told us that this experience, much as with us, had changed everything and now they found themselves daring to reconsider their life choices. They were thinking about returning home but only to tie up loose ends before heading off again, and I could hardly blame them. Before embarking on an adventure like this I don't believe you ever consider the possibility that it might unlock something inside you which from then on simply cannot be contained. Suddenly your whole life lies ahead of you once again and you realise that choices are there to be taken. And certainly, while you are living the dream, anything seems possible and you begin to question why you ever waited this long. Over the past few months we had crossed paths with so many like-minded people and never once met anyone who regretted their decision. That evening I struggled to swallow my wine due to a persistent lump in my throat at the thought of all this coming to an end. I cemented over and over the promise to myself never to give up on the dream in future, never to talk myself out of it or allow other factors to crush me into thinking it could not be possible. I had already proved them all wrong and I intended to keep it that way ... and yet, for all my brave words, every time it left me questioning, *Why are we nearly home, then? Why am I worrying about school when I could just say: he's not going to school — simple as that?*

I was snapped out of this pensive sadness as soon as I stepped into the van. Luckily for the rest of the by now long-asleep campsite, that extra glass or two of wine had suppressed my nervous system and dulled my reactions when I clocked a flying creature out of the corner of my eye and then turned my gaze to discover easily more than a hundred moths on the ceiling. Clever thinking after the first bottle of wine had led me not only to leave a light on above the cooker for Jackson, but also to leave the door open so we could hear him if he woke. I had closed the mosquito net, but obviously not properly. Now the ceiling around the light was literally writhing with bugs, not flying but running around like a plague of beetles. I grabbed the fly swat but then thought better of it when I imagined the situation that would unfold after the first swipe. Instead we got wet flannels and grabbed as many moths as possible in one go straight off the ceiling. It took us an hour to get rid of them all, by which point my skin was crawling with the thought of them. Luckily Jackson had been in darkness at the back and they hadn't been attracted to him. He slept through the whole ordeal.

I went outside to regain my composure. The sky was crystal clear and gave us the best display of stars I have ever seen in my life. It was like being in space, completely spectacular and unforgettable. As far as Aires go this one rated as one of the best in our experience. Utter beauty and great company: what more did we need?

Studying the map that night we realised we were within easy reach of Sonia and Phillip, friends from Swansea with a holiday property in France, who just might be in the vicinity. A few drunken text messages later it was confirmed that this would be our next port of call. By now we were operating on a denial basis. If we refused even to think about our journey home, planning no routes, booking no crossings, making no decisions about specific dates no matter how many times members of our family repeated the same question, then somehow we might just get there without even realising it was happening, thereby eliminating some of the depression.

Tomorrow would take us near to Saint-Émilion, home to some of the best vineyards and châteaux in France. I had no doubt at all that our van would be considerably heavier leaving there than it was now.

No sooner had we left the Aire than we came across a very nasty accident involving two cars, both of them on their sides, roof to roof. It must have happened only moments earlier because the emergency services had just passed us. This inevitably caused a short hold-up and only fifteen minutes into what was to be a four-hour journey to Bordeaux we had already heard: *Are we nearly there yet?* from the back. *How long will it be until we get there?* was on repeat, and it was proof positive that a four-year-old has no concept of time whatsoever when my answer, say, was: *Three hours* and, five minutes later, he'd be asking again whether we were nearly there.

We took the motorway to Bordeaux and stopped for a coffee in a service station. Innocently seated at a picnic table in the sun about to enjoy a cake, I was approached by a man opening his fly. I had no time to react before he walked behind a wall right next to our table, at which point we all realised they were the urinals. Only the French would do this. It reminded me why I had dedicated an entire blog entry to toilets back in January, and now here we were again, one week into France and already having a picnic in full view of a stranger having a wee. How lovely! They may think us Brits are prudes but I can think of better places to encourage people to eat.

The rest of the drive was magnificent, surrounded by sunflower fields, vineyards and stunning châteaux. We passed Saint-Émilion and a little farther on reached Villefranche-de-Lonchat, a picturesque little village near Lake Gurson in the Dordogne region. We found a lovely spot to leave the van in pinewoods next to the lake and from there Phillip kindly drove us back to their place just up the hill. Suddenly feeling rather rude, we descended on an already full house where their daughter and four grandchildren were holidaying. Jackson, of course, was in his element with such an abundance of English-speaking children, a swimming pool and a garden full of toys – and the icing on the cake was his favourite lunch of fish fingers and chips. The conversation flowed as smoothly as the wine and afternoon merged into evening before any of us left the table, such was the amount of gossip from back home we had to catch up on.

By the time we returned to the lake we had been joined by five other vans. We were actually parked right alongside an official campsite and half expected to find a note on the windscreen asking us to pay and park inside the fence. But to our surprise no one bothered us at all.

We couldn't have asked for a nicer sight to wake up to when we opened the blinds to an uninterrupted view across a perfectly still lake. We noticed a really inviting beach on the far side and, as we breakfasted, a swan with all her cygnets paddled about right in front of our door. Such peace was short-lived as Logan, the youngest of the grandchildren, and his mum joined us again. He and Jackson played and fought, fought and swam, made sandcastles, stamped all over each other's and then fought some more. By lunchtime the thermometer hit 35 degrees, which did nothing to ease the disputes between two intensely competitive boys or the ability of their parents to negotiate and offer bribes for peace.

Parting company to follow up on last night's advice from Sonia and Phillip, we went on that wine search I'd been anticipating. Our perseverance paid off as we searched along unsigned single-track country lanes in the back of beyond, stopping to knock on three random doors and ask whether we were on the right track. Having envisaged a relatively big château with signs advertising its wares, we couldn't understand why these people couldn't give us directions instantly. We certainly doubted their knowledge when we finally pulled into a smelly farmyard full of tractors and manure in front of a partially collapsed farm building. After tooting the horn to arouse someone and then, with some embarrassment, enquiring whether we could purchase some raspberry champagne-style wine, we were led into a barn. At last the penny dropped. This was clearly where they sealed and labelled the bottles. Stood on an earth floor in front of a counter, surrounded by hay and cobwebs, our tasting session began. Because Geoff, of course, was driving, I had to graciously volunteer to sample two generous glasses of red in the space of ten minutes. Eventually we left with crates of raspberry champagne, rosé champagne, red and rosé wine, all at under four euros a bottle. For me the hidden part of the bill was a headache from drinking at lunchtime in 35-degree heat after a day in the sun.

From here a brief scan of the map tempted us inland towards the Dordogne river.

46. KAYAKING IN THE DORDOGNE

A RRIVING AT BEYNAC-ET-CAZENAC in mid-afternoon, we found it bustling with people and traffic. As we drove in alongside the Dordogne even the river seemed overcrowded. Not surprisingly the campsites were all full and there was no official Aire in this town. Perseverance paid off, though, because after enquiring at a few sites and then at tourist information we were pointed in the direction of our only hope, a campsite on the other side of the river, described as both basic and natural.

It turned out we stayed there for three nights and in all that time we never really worked the site out. On arrival I followed signs to reception where a woman was sat working on her laptop. Looking at me like I was stupid when I asked if I could book in, she pointed to the river below and said, in French, something that I assumed meant the owner was down there. In a field outside the campsite I found a man in a van selling what he called coffee, although if you had never tried coffee before you wouldn't want to try it again after sampling one of his. He said that for eight euros, we could camp under the tree down by the river. I assumed we weren't really to be part of the campsite at all, but when later it materialised that he was indeed the owner, I thought he had done us a favour because the proper site was officially full. However, when we walked around the site above, we could see other motorhomes up there and plenty of empty pitches with electricity. To this day we don't understand why we ended up like outcasts all on our own in a field, although as it happens it suited us just fine.

As for the proper campsite, though, why it hadn't been condemned I will never know. One toilet block had all the cubicles permanently locked because the floor had given way underneath them, except that you still had to walk across the unstable ground to reach a sink because the other toilet block had no sinks. To reach the toilets, once again you had to walk through the urinals and, with only two cubicles for the entire campsite, inevitably you were stuck in a queue while men just walked in and had a wee right next to you. To reach the showers you first had to wade across a muddy floor, meaning there was absolutely no clean way to make it back to your shoes after your shower, and we just resigned ourselves to putting dirty feet in them and scrubbing the whole lot when we left the site.

It was moments like this that made me wonder why we had spent so much money on a van with a shower; not just a shower, mark you, but a spa shower whose jets I was never allowed to test for fear of using too much water, or was it power? On this occasion I couldn't argue because refilling the water wasn't exactly an easy option when you're stuck in a distant field. However, I often heard people along the way during our trip questioning why we used public facilities when we had our own personally cleaned space on board. Whenever they asked me, my stern glance in Geoff's direction usually satisfied their curiosity.

Then there was the kids' playground where all health and safety went out of the window. They would probably have been safer playing in the fast-flowing river. And yet the whole place somehow had character and appealed to us in a funny way, which is why we stayed on. We even got electricity in the form of an extension cable running from the coffee shack to the van. They didn't stock milk so one morning we just took our own milk over to add to our coffee. The owner made us two coffees in egg cups, then handed me two plastic cups to transfer them into so I could add the milk. I nearly came away with third-degree burns when one plastic cup immediately melted in my hands. We could have easily made a much nicer coffee in the van but so often it was our daily visits to little cafés that had enriched my story.

We never seemed to find anyone official in the office, the only people in there being campers using the Wi-Fi. We were left to guess where the emptying facilities were. Geoff found a very broken plastic cover over a hole and emptied the toilet cassette down that, hopefully correctly. We then found a tap in our field and filled our clean water in the hope that it was in no way connected to that hole.

As for Beynac, you'd be hard pushed to find a more appealing village. The river wound its way alongside the road and under a bridge. The buildings were all made of stone and very old and crooked. They were built up a steep hill with narrow cobbled streets while up above them was the magnificent Château de Beynac, a beautiful castle built right on the edge of the cliff, which we would have explored if it hadn't been pouring with rain all day. The following morning, with the weather back on our side, we got up early to catch the bus. We arranged to pay a fee to have the local kayak centre transport us and our own kayak 22 kilometres upriver for us to paddle back down to the campsite. It took us five and a half hours to paddle down that river but we all thoroughly enjoyed it and there was far less of the: *Are we nearly there yet?* than we got in the van.

The scenery along the river was superlative. There were hundreds of kayaks on the river but it was completely unspoiled, with no buildings along its length, only a few campsites, little coffee shacks and burger huts. Otherwise we felt at one with nature, surrounded by greenery and birds. We started in a deep gorge, paddling between high cliffs and rocks with astounding views of châteaux high above us atop heavily wooded cliffs.

With more luck than skill, we negotiated some exciting rapids, even though we grounded ourselves in shallows once or twice. The farther down we went, the less dramatic it got as the steep sides gave way to a widening river. But there were still villages built into the rock face and wonderful splits in the river that had created islands with shingle beaches where people pulled their kayaks up for a picnic. We had three picnics en route, which is why it took us so long.

At the end we all jumped in for a celebratory swim, although Geoff got a little overenthusiastic in the moment and surfaced, mobile phone in hand, having completely submerged it in the Dordogne. That was the end of that, even after it sat in a tub of rice for the remainder of the trip in a futile effort to dry it out.

Back on dry land we found out the hard way that the effect of allowing a four-year-old to sit still for over five hours while you paddle constantly is that two opposing states of mind collide. As you hit the wall, so to speak, rendering you incapable of anything but total collapse, said four-year-old hits that wild, crazy, I've got to run and run and run stage. Solution, easy: take the stabilisers off his bike. That slowed him down a bit! It was a very proud moment watching him take his first ride completely on his own, and after that there was no stopping him.

We all wished we could have stayed there longer. There was more than enough to keep us occupied, but there was no way to avoid the fact that we now had weeks, not months, until Jackson would be rolling up at the school gates.

Suddenly it all felt very daunting again and I found myself wondering whether he was ready. Also, let's be honest, was I ready? (Definitely not, in my case.) How would I ever get him into the habit of going to bed at a reasonable time and getting up at stupid o'clock to get to school on time?

In that moment the thought struck home: what had he missed in nursery this year? What had his friends been taught that he might not know? (Nothing... surely...?) Had they really done anything other than play and socialise? (Because he was a pro at that by now...) They couldn't have learned to read or write – could they? Maybe I had better check, now that the doubt had struck me. And somehow I managed to convince myself that when I found the answer to that out from my friends the following day it would all be a breeze. I'd teach him to read in two weeks if I had to. And if I couldn't, he would just tell the teacher he had learned to swim and ski and ride a bike instead, and that would counterbalance the reading and the writing. (Yeh, sure, of course it would!)

47. BRANDY AND SEAFOOD

OUR DORDOGNE ADVENTURE over, we reversed our direction and made our way back towards the coast at La Rochelle. On the way we stopped for one night and a few brandies in Cognac. The town Aire was a small car park with a couple of designated motorhome bays, a service area and public toilets, nothing special but free nevertheless and adjacent to the river, and more than sufficient for us.

We missed our tour of a distillery after arriving slightly late, all thanks to me narrowly avoiding a toddler meltdown in a supermarket by caving in and allowing him to push the trolley completely unaided around the store. On the plus side this saved us 44 euros and they still generously offered us a free tasting. I desisted after one glass because I didn't like brandy before and what I'd just tried had done nothing to change my mind. Geoff, on the other hand, systematically worked his way through at least three more tasters, culminating in the most expensive and oldest blend. As our guide was pouring it out for him, she pointed out that it cost 300 euros per bottle and was usually reserved for those who had paid 44 euros for the guided tour, which blatantly we had not.

I wasn't clear about the protocol here and noticed many used, only half-finished glasses of brandy lying around on the counter. This made me wonder if the polite way for a tasting was to sip and then leave the rest in the glass, as opposed to Geoff's hearty approach of demolishing complete shots and practically licking the glass afterwards. If sip and leave *is* the right way, that does seem such a waste.

Then there was the shopping protocol to think about. Of course we felt duty-bound to buy something, but the cheapest option was over thirty euros… Once again Lady Luck came to our rescue when a whole party of French tourists descended on the shop after their tour, allowing us to sneak out.

I had some catching up to do, so we found a small bar with pavement seating where Geoff sampled maybe another two cognacs and I found something more to my taste. Enquiries dashed our hopes of stumbling upon a small local distillery like the one where we'd recently found the raspberry champagne. The set-up in Cognac seemed to be that all the distilleries were listed in a crammed booklet, all of them offering tastings for which you had to pre-book and pre-pay and all selling produce that was way beyond our price range. Studying the booklet, I got a distinct impression that dragging a four-year-old around would be frowned upon by these establishments. I'm still convinced there must be places selling local blends at bargain prices, but unearthing them would require either some advance research or a lot of determined exploring. The upshot was that Geoff had to settle for the freebies he had scammed that afternoon. When the morning came, his sore head sealed the decision to move on.

La Rochelle was a really pleasant surprise for me. For some reason I'd been expecting something like Monaco, but I soon realised it was very laid back and inviting. Again the Aire was free, located in a large car park by the marina. Aires of this type are fine if you are visiting a town or surrounding area and won't be spending much time in your van. The main drawback is that they lack shade so that, surrounded by concrete, the temperature inside the van can quickly become unbearable. They don't allow you to put your awning out or put chairs outside, and the best policy is to get out and about and return as late as possible.

Two minutes' walk away was the stop for the water bus to take us directly into the city's harbour, which we entered between the impressive watch towers that flank its entrance. We began with a lovely seafood lunch, a must in La Rochelle, the main challenge being how to choose between the hundreds of menus on offer at the waterfront. We then visited the very impressive aquarium. By mid-afternoon the streets were alive with entertainers. There were dance groups, painters, musicians and mime artists, all seeming to respect whatever was going on alongside them and waiting for one act to calm down before the other built up. We explored all the back streets, found a wonderful park, walked along the little town beach and the harbour and climbed a watch tower.

While we were waiting for the water bus to take us back to the Aire, I listened to a guitarist singing his own mix of *Somewhere Over the Rainbow* and *Wonderful World*. I was blown away, all goose bumps and a tear in my eye as I listened to the words. It felt like I was being uniquely sung to about all of the past eight months and as if his songs were a signature bringing our great adventure to its end.

As we sailed back towards Dotty I felt a reinforced determination to change my lifestyle. There had to be no going back. I needed to completely re-evaluate my home/work balance. My priorities were no longer based around making money, and I craved neither a larger house nor a better wardrobe. I had discovered the simple joy that living with your family by your side and making memories together can bring. What did it matter, I felt, if I was standing on a pavement having a cold shower instead of relaxing in a hot Jacuzzi? As long as we had our health and we were together, absolutely nothing else mattered in the here and now. One chance at life was all I had, so why waste it worrying about tomorrow?

These inspiring thoughts were balanced by more mundane concerns. I felt scared of how well I would adjust back to home life with all its necessary routines. Would I cope? Would each of us adjust differently and revert to seeing the cracks in our edifice? For the best part of one year, spontaneity was all we had known. It had been a new experience but it had worked out well for all of us, cementing us as a family. While we were on the road we were hardly ever anything but happy.

Trying to make sense of my thoughts and feelings, I succumbed yet again to that dreaded debate with Geoff. I wondered aloud why I had been stupid enough to reply to the head teacher all those months ago in the Algarve and tell him, yes, Jackson would be attending school this year. Now I felt that, while we were on this side of the Channel, we could still change our minds. What I was trying to do was regularly state my preference to do just that on the off-chance that somehow Geoff would change his mind. (He didn't!)

From La Rochelle we headed north through the salt marshes at Poitevin, where we visited the salt pans, and then enjoyed a luxury night in a campsite in Saint-Gilles-Croix-de-Vie. On the way to the site we passed a circus and I had to spend the next twenty minutes explaining to Jackson why it wasn't right to have ten camels in a small fenced area in the middle of a car park in the centre of a town, with two emus and then two zebras stood next to them, and posters showing six lionesses and a male lion sitting on chairs begging. I tried to find a gentle way to tell him that the animals didn't do this out of choice but from years of being forced to do so, otherwise they'd get told off, and that because they were scared of getting a row they always did as they were told. Back came the questions: *How do you tell a lion off? How do you make it scared of you? Wouldn't it just bite you?* It saddened and shocked me that this was still such a popular form of entertainment in a country so close to us and advanced as France.

Luckily for us there was a monster truck show next door to the circus. To some extent it turned out to be a bit of false advertising because for one hour and forty minutes all we got was cars being driven about on two wheels, which, although I have no doubt great skill was involved, equated to repetition and ultimately boredom. Finally there were twenty minutes of monster trucks at the end to remind us why we were all there in the first place, though I began to regret our choice of entertainment when the largest truck was driven directly at the crowd in the stand by a twelve-year-old. Jackson certainly enjoyed it, but even he said: *Next time I'd like just monster trucks.* One other small detail is that within the first five minutes he managed to fall through the stand seating and bang his head.

48. THE MORBIHAN ISLANDS

IN THE SOUTH of Brittany two peninsulas enclose what amounts to an inland sea, known as the Gulf of Morbihan. Open to the ocean only via a small passageway, it has a sheltered mild climate and attracts holidaymakers keen to sample its many water-based activities. It encloses some forty islands mostly owned by celebrities except for the two larger ones, which are easily accessible by boat and cry out to be explored. The bay is frequently listed among the best in the world. We'd imagined it would be perfect for kayaking but when we got there it was too windy, the water was quite choppy and we were warned about some particularly strong currents around the islands, which in those conditions only experienced paddlers should attempt.

We stayed at a council-owned Aire at very reasonable rates, which turned out to be one of the nicest we had found. It was all grass, as laid back as you could wish, you could park anywhere you liked, there were showers and washing machines, a playground and football pitch, and a free bus to the town or the port. As soon as we pulled in we felt at home and wished we could spend a few weeks right there.

There were a great many options, from sailing lessons to boat trips or windsurfing. Just about any type of boat you could think of could be hired and it seemed that after too brief a brief you'd be left to your own devices. We settled more modestly for the five-minute boat ride to one of the bigger islands, Île-aux-Moines. Reading up on it the night before, we decided to spend the whole day there. Very few cars are present on the island and our only available modes of transport would be cycling or walking. We ruled out our own bikes due to the state of our garage ever since we had started stocking up on wine while pulling kayaks in and out, but there was still the option to hire bikes either at the departure port or on the island itself. If we ever return there we will definitely choose bikes, for the fourteen kilometres of tracks are perfect for cycling. That said, though, we had a lovely walk.

The five-minute boat journey transported us to a place so different it felt as though we were in a different country, with a lifestyle you'd only find on a small island. It reminded us of a Greek island with its whitewashed fishermen's cottages dotted around the countryside, narrow winding lanes with hedgerows where wildflowers massed and cottage gardens with head-high blooms of colour. Everywhere we looked there was wildlife.

The footpath encircling the island was supposed to be a four- or five-hour walk. Certain that this would be too much for us we simply set off to discover where our noses might lead us. We turned it into a pirate adventure for Jackson in which we all had to imagine where they would hide their treasure. Overactively enthusiastic and talking non-stop about Captain Hook, he managed to give us both a headache by lunchtime. We couldn't pass a single tree without having to ascertain whether they could hide it under the tree, or up the tree, or in the frigging tree... At least it kept him walking if only to check out other potential hiding places.

There were thousands of sailing and fishing boats. It looked like you were a nobody if you didn't own a boat and a bike here. We must have walked about five miles and reached the north, east and west coasts. At every turn there were little beaches and coves waiting to be discovered. The main village with its mostly thatched cottages also offered a range of restaurants, bars and cafés. I thought I could quite happily have lived there.

Back at base camp Jackson and his new mate Tom, a French boy a little bit older than him, played until it was pitch dark with his train track and cars. The friendship ended in bitterness the next morning when Jackson did a knee skid across the gravel car park while playing football, leaving much skin behind and literally making the whole site aware of it with his screaming, only to be told by Tom: *That's not a real cut – this is!* He revealed one ten times worse from falling off his bike, which annoyed Jackson intensely because he now wanted a bigger cut.

We moved a little farther west along the coast to Carnac, famous for the largest numbers of aligned standing stones in the world and dating from 4500 BC. The stones have to be viewed from platforms or through a fence in an attempt to protect the grassland and vegetation around them in summer when visitor numbers are at their highest.

From there we drove out to Quiberon at the tip of another longer and very narrow peninsula. What a spectacular place it must be to live. Quiberon Bay lies between the outer coasts of the two strips of land enclosing the Gulf of Morbihan and this beautiful peninsula, so narrow in places that it becomes only a road laid over a strip of sand with a beach on either side. All told there must be some fifty beaches, some wild, rocky and rough and others like a mill pond. We hadn't really sussed that out when we chose to spend the day on an exposed windy beach, which was also thick with seaweed, although we did manage to get some sunbathing in. In the evening we drove to the main town where we walked all around the shops until we came to an ice cream shop with no less than five freezers standing in a line, each one ten ice creams in length and three rows deep. It took Jackson fifteen minutes to choose and then he picked out the same flavour he always has. I tried violet and Geoff the lychee, which were both stunning.

For the next two nights we found a free Aire near a surf beach, which knocked spots off the previous beach. The tide was in so it became a small cove surrounded by cliffs to begin with, with crystal-clear turquoise water. As the tide pulled out it gradually revealed a maze of routes waist-deep in water through all the rocks and around the cliffs, with more and more coves coming into view. With typically perverse timing the surf had been good here three days ago but now was flat again. But assuming this might be the last swim of our entire trip, we really could not have picked a nicer place.

We treated ourselves to a big seafood meal in a village on the opposite side of the peninsula, which was just twenty minutes' walk from one side to the other. Geoff chose crab, which came with various dissection tools, sparking off a whole range of questions from you know who, who then managed to steer this whole crab conversation round to his final statement, the cause of much amusement from the table next to us: *I pretty much think that boys don't have babies because they are scared of hospitals.* I'll leave it to you to imagine all the related topics he felt the need to discuss very loudly at the table.

After removing bits of crab shell that had landed in my bag courtesy of Geoff's unskilled hand with the hammer and nutcracker, we spent a few hours sitting with a delightful couple on our campsite. By now Jackson was in overdrive and they devised an ingenious game whereby you couldn't talk unless you were holding a designated pair of glasses. For a few minutes it worked a treat, allowing someone else to get a word in edgeways, except that he took the rule so seriously that he instantly shoved the glasses at anyone who dared to utter a word without them. Just as we were leaving, our friends revealed that both of them worked with children with behaviour issues. I felt relieved that they had seen the noisy Jackson but not the naughty one and that they had waited until the end to tell us so that I was saved from sitting there sweating. It was a great night, though, and were so sad that we had to leave this place.

49. SWIMMING WITH HORSES

MOSTLY BY ACCIDENT we ended up in Caen after spending eight hours in traffic jams and only covering half the distance we had planned. When we got there we were all a bit down in the mouth, Geoff fed up with driving, Jackson just bored, bored, bored and me exhausted by the constant demands from both husband and son somehow mistaking me for their servant. *Mummy, I'm hungry. / Couldn't get me a drink, could you? / How about a sandwich? / Are we nearly there yet?* I was up and down like a nonstop yoyo. To top it off the Aire was full but we parked along a hedge and bought a ticket hoping we would get away with it. We could almost have reached a hand out and touched the ferries coming in and out and we were treated to a live band and a humongous fireworks display somewhere nearby well into the early hours.

It crossed our minds to book our return ferry from here instead but enquiries revealed it was a seven-hour crossing and three times the price. So instead we decided to stay on here for one more day because there seemed to be so much on offer, even if it meant extending our trip by a day – what a damn shame that would be!

The next day we had a fun-packed day in the sun. We were just two minutes away from Sword Beach where the D-Day landings took place. In stark contrast it was now packed with families out enjoying the sun. It felt rather weird actually sitting on the historic sand among sunbathers and kids playing and screaming and, although monuments marked the history of the beach, I couldn't make up my mind whether it was right or wrong for people to be having so much fun here. There was every kids' activity you could dream of from go-karting to trampolining, fun fairs, Punch and Judy, swimming, pony riding, and much else. I could hardly have asked for more, as this was exactly how I had wanted it to end: somewhere where everyone was smiling.

Jackson had a pony ride. Slightly unexpectedly we were handed the lead rein and told to walk to the beach, round the memorial tree and back again, unaccompanied and weaving through dogs, bikes and kids on scooters. I sometimes wonder whether we go a little overboard with health and safety red tape back at home or whether the rest of Europe is behind the times. We spent some time in the sea sadly knowing that the very moment we came out of the water this time really would be the last one on this adventure. The shopping centre was perfect for all our last-minute gifts and after that we separated, Geoff heading for the war museum while I watched Jackson racing go-karts.

It's in places like this that are so geared towards information and education, should you seek it, that anyone travelling with older children can take full advantage. That was the approach adopted by the family in H. D. Jackson's book *Europe in a Motorhome*, thereby further educating their son throughout their journey. It had taken us all of an hour back in Paris in January to work out that we would have to adopt an entirely different approach with a young child, but I have to say I think we'd all benefitted from it. Jackson had opened our eyes to the little details that we would otherwise have walked straight past, from an icicle on a tree to the frost on a puddle. We might not have explored many art galleries but we had all expanded our minds all the same. One thing we had noticed though is that wherever you are it is relatively simple to turn it into an educational visit for older children. With a bit of imagination you can even tailor-make a trip to fit around a particular school curriculum.

The evening brought me one of the best highlights of my trip. I tried to book some horse riding but it was full so I was invited to go swimming with the horses when they got back from their ride. At least that was how we interpreted the French. I confess I had an unworthy feeling that I might just have paid to hose a sweaty horse down and clean its tack. Far from it, I was in for a surprise that turned into a really exhilarating experience. We rode down Sword Beach straight into the sea until the horses were up to their saddles in water. At first the feeling of water seeping into my trainers was slightly unpleasant but with plenty of spray and waves breaking up the horses' necks I was soon soaked from head to toe and couldn't have been happier. We were in and out of the water for about an hour. The walk back along the front to our van with water dripping from my clothes and squelching out of my shoes turned a few heads but who cared, I was on cloud nine.

That night, with a lump in my throat and a tear in my eye, I booked our return home. We decided to try the Channel Tunnel for the first time. No sooner had we done it than we met a really nice family at the Aire who were booked on the train departing before ours. They had a little girl and their elderly parents were travelling with them in their own motorhome. The two kids got along brilliantly so we planned to follow them for the last couple of days.

50. PREPARING FOR RE-ENTRY

M Y EMOTIONS WERE all over the place and the whole mood had changed to one of deep sadness, all of us counting every minute that we still had left. We couldn't even eat without mentioning it was our last lunch or our last breakfast. Although naturally we were all looking forward to seeing our family and friends again, right now we couldn't allow ourselves even a minute to think about home in case we wasted one precious minute of what was left of our dream. If someone had told me I could just go home for a month and then start all this all over again I would have hugged them.

We had lovely company for the last couple of nights as we followed our new friends and their little girl, Erin. We spent one night in Saint-Valery-en-Caux and of course consumed some wine with the excuse that it would make room on board for a fresh load to take home. There was an interesting medieval village within walking distance, which we visited the next day. It turned out to be the most expensive coffee stop on our tour. Since Spain we had noticed that prices had crept up from three euros for three drinks to eleven euros now for the same number of drinks.

Next stop was Cité Europe, a vast shopping centre right next to the Channel Tunnel. The supermarket was an eye-opening experience. I had never seen so much wine in my life, and so ridiculously cheap. Greed took over and I returned to the entrance for a second trolley, and by the time we checked out both trolleys were overflowing. It made me laugh to think about all that time we had wasted eight months ago, weighing and listing each item before packing it and removing every bit of packaging and unnecessary weight for fear of overloading the van. Now here we were lining up boxes of wine along the corridor, on the beds, in the wardrobes, any old where. There was an Aire here but the description in the book of Aires warned us that it wasn't very safe. The first signs of Europe's emerging migrant situation were already apparent

337

and, with some police activity visible nearby, we decided to move fifteen minutes out into the countryside to another Aire located on a farm. It was wonderful being surrounded by fields and wildlife for our last night, and from there suddenly we could see the English coast across the water. It did look cloudy over by there!

We had never used the Channel Tunnel before but I have to say it was very easy and quick. We arrived on British soil at 9 a.m. and were at Geoff's parents an hour later. It was brilliant to see them again although it only felt like yesterday that we were waving goodbye on their doorstep when we were about to head to Dover for our ferry. For fear of withdrawal symptoms we booked Dotty into a local campsite. It seemed simpler all round, for it had dawned on us that with all our belongings spread all over the van we couldn't very easily turn up with an overnight bag.

I'm not sure who had failed to tell the Brits that Christmas doesn't happen in August because walking across the field at night was like the Blackpool illuminations, with practically every tent draped in fairy lights. The weather was kind and allowed us to have one last outdoor breakfast where we met a few locals. It seemed that half the guests here lived within a five-mile radius of the campsite. It was perfect for Jackson and he revelled in the company of English-speaking friends. Sadly though there was some choice language being used by the older kids and yes, it has since come back to haunt me.

I cannot say our last journey was a pleasant one. A four-hour journey became a nine-hour one in solid traffic all the way. Instantly we found ourselves complaining about our road systems, not to mention the abominable weather. And, needless to say, it was both raining and dark when we arrived home. Jackson and I didn't even go into the house but shot off to collect a Chinese takeaway, which had been on my mind for the past six months. At a red light two boy racers sped past us and I commented: *That's so stupid – they could cause an accident.* To which the reply came: *They are fock and onions!* Yes, me too, it took a few seconds to work it out: for onions, read idiots. I laughed nervously, hoping it was a one-off bit of made-up language. But no, wishful thinking: he said it again. Oh dear, we'd all be doomed when school started.

Then we got back home and I finally opened our front door. My legs turned to jelly. The house seemed so overwhelmingly big and empty. I had to fight hard to hold back the tears, feeling a huge urge to run back out to the safety and comfort of the van. All I can remember thinking is: *I can't do this, I've changed now and I can't change back*, and it really frightened me.

THE END

TIME MARCHES ON...

ND I AM still asked, have I settled down now? And the answer remains, and I believe always will, a resounding NO! Whatever seed was planted inside me during this trip, it still thrives and simply refuses to be ignored. Fortunately, for those who have to put up with me on a regular basis, I have been able to indulge my craving for travel by reliving every moment in the writing of this, my first book. But with that milestone behind me I now feel the undeniable urge to plan the next adventure.

And Jackson? Well, he adapted the easiest of all of us, slotting immediately into school life and embracing it. But he never forgets his journey and regularly asks when we are going again. The idea of being homeschooled for a while excites him and he sees only the opportunity to make new friends.

It didn't take long for Geoff to question our choice to return, either. The surf was cold, the sky was grey, and the pressures of everyday life were thrust upon us in no time at all.

It took a five-year-old to put it all into perspective. I was in a supermarket car park when Jackson sprung a question upon me. *What have you done today to make you feel proud, mummy?* he asked. Met by silence, he added: ... *for yourself, I mean, something today that made you proud.* Ashamedly I honestly couldn't think of anything. I had taken him to football training, hoovered around the house and now, mid-afternoon, was busy loading the weekly food shop into the car. I felt tired, uninspired and frankly not proud of any aspect of my day.

The next question was: *What made you happy today, mummy?* And again I was stumped. My day, which was pretty average, consisted mainly of chores, and having this brought to my attention so innocently by my child did nothing at all for my self esteem. When we were travelling I could have answered both these questions with ease, enthusiasm and excitement every single day.

I'm not suggesting that motorhoming is for everyone, or even travelling in whatever mode happens to be your style. But if each night we all asked ourselves those two simple questions posed to me by my son, and if we aspired to be able to answer them with ease, it seems to me that all our lives would be much improved. It is all too easy to be swept along in the mundane daily grind. What is somewhat harder is to recognise that this is happening and to do something to change it.

Simply writing this book has proved to me that it is worth daring to dream. Years ago I would have come up with a thousand reasons for never undertaking a journey like ours, let alone writing a book about it. Today I ask myself: what was I so frightened of? What was the worst thing that could have happened?

And it is with these last two questions in mind that we find ourselves, as a family, juggling with thoughts of a year in New Zealand in a motorhome.

So, dear readers, watch this space...

ACKNOWLEDGMENTS

ABOVE ALL I owe a debt of gratitude to David Townsend Jones, a great friend and skilled editor, who was responsible for transforming my story into a book. And for all his words of encouragement, which have kept me going.

Thanks are due also to everyone we met along the way. So many times your advice and recommendations served to enhance our overall experience. And thank you for allowing me to include very small insights into your lives in my story. We made lasting friendships on our journey and still laugh at some of our memories today.

We wouldn't have been half as well equipped as we were had it not been for the invaluable printable packing list courtesy of Our Tours (www.ourtour.co.uk).

For the moments when we needed some reassurance or just a jolly good dose of laughter we turned to *Europe in a Motorhome* by H. D. Jackson. We read your story, laughed at your tales, all too regularly got ourselves into messes of equal proportion, crossed your documented path from time to time, and met people who had read your book, had your book on board, and in one case even claimed to be your relation. Your book made it into my 'must not leave home without' list.

Others in this list that were well referred to throughout our journey were:

All The Aires France, both South and North, by Vicarious Media;

Go Motorhoming and Campervanning by C. Doree and M. George;

CC Camping Card ACSI by ACSI Publishing BV (membership required);

The Wild Weather Book by F. Danks and J. Schofield;

As well as a range of road maps.

Lastly, but by no means least, a thank you to all our friends and family whom we left behind. A sincere apology too for continually bombarding you with idyllic photos of sunshine and fun just as you were about to set off to work.

And one last extra special thanks to Geoff and Jackson for making the whole experience so magical and unforgettable.